MOMENTS OF TRUTH

Moments of Truth

Robert R. Davila
The Story of a Deaf Leader

Harry G. Lang
Oscar P. Cohen
Joseph E. Fischgrund

RIT PRESS

ROCHESTER, NEW YORK

Moments of Truth: Robert R. Davila, the Story of a Deaf Leader
By Harry G. Lang, Oscar P. Cohen, and Joseph E. Fischgrund

Copyright © 2007, Rochester Institute of Technology,
RIT Press, and individual authors. All rights reserved.
No part of this book may be reproduced in any matter without written permission
of the copyright holders, except in the case of brief quotations.

Published and distributed by
RIT Press
90 Lomb Memorial Drive
Rochester, New York 14623
http://carypress.rit.edu

Cover photograph by John T. Consoli/Gallaudet University

Printed in the United States
ISBN 978-1-933360-26-3 (paperback)
ISBN 978-1-933360-30-0 (hardcover)

Library of Congress Cataloging in Publication Data

Lang, Harry G.
    Moments of truth : Robert R. Davila, the story of a deaf leader / Harry G.
Lang, Oscar P. Cohen, Joseph E. Fischgrund.
        p. cm.
    Includes bibliographical references and index.
    ISBN 978-1-933360-26-3 (pbk.) — ISBN 978-1-933360-30-0 (hardcover)
    1. Davila, Robert R., 1932- 2. Deaf--United States—Biography. 3.
Teachers of the deaf—United States—Biography. 4. Hispanic
Americans—United States—Biography. I. Cohen, Oscar P. II. Fischgrund,
Joseph E. III. Title.
    HV2534.D37L36 2007
    371.91'2092--dc22
    [B]
                                    2007029841

To deaf children and their families.

Contents

Foreword

I MET BOB DAVILA 12 YEARS AGO. As I came to know him and what I thought was his story, it became clear to me that it was one that should be shared with the world. The barriers he faced and overcame, as a son of poor Mexican immigrants to the United States who was deafened as a young boy, are uniquely remarkable.

Bob Davila's educational attainments and professional accomplishments included myriad "firsts"—such as being the first graduate of the California School for the Deaf to obtain a doctoral degree and the first Hispanic graduate of Gallaudet College (renamed Gallaudet University in 1986). Subsequently, he was the first Gallaudet College graduate to serve as vice president of that university, the first deaf person to hold the top elected position of the three professional organizations for deaf educators in the United States—the Conference of Educational Administrators of Schools and Programs for the Deaf (CEASD), the Convention of American Instructors of the Deaf (CAID), and the Council on Education of the Deaf (CED)—and he served as an assistant secretary in the U.S. Department of Education, the highest government post ever held by a deaf person. I was proud to offer Bob the post as the first deaf director for the National Technical Institute for the Deaf (NTID) and vice president for Rochester Institute of Technology (RIT) in 1996.

I asked a colleague, Harry Lang, who is renowned for his scholarship, especially his proven record of producing biographies of outstanding deaf individuals, to write an authorized biography commissioned by RIT to honor Bob. Harry sought out two co-authors also familiar with Bob and his accomplishments. Oscar Cohen and Joe Fischgrund agreed to work with Harry—as long as Harry would drive the project.

Little did I know that Bob's story would be even more extraordinary than I realized. Moreover, the ability of these authors to dig for facts—personal, professional, humorous, and sad—is superb, reaching a standard I did not know existed.

Harry, Oscar, and Joe tell the story of young Bob working in the fields with his parents and siblings—absorbing lessons such as a relentless work ethic, responsibility, and perseverance that would carry him through his life. Bob remembers seeing his father die unceremoniously in those fields.

As Bob's story unfolds, we observe a wiseacre little kid growing up in the Mexican barrio speaking only Spanish; growing up in poverty but not realizing it; growing up with discrimination but, initially, not knowing it. We see how he turned the tragedy of sudden deafness into a rewarding career and life.

The authors talk about Bob as a precocious teenager, discovering the wonders of learning, and daring to go where no poor Hispanic deaf person had ever dreamed of venturing.

The authors write of Bob's professional prime—the challenges, the wins and losses, the triumphs and disappointments.

The authors tell of Bob and the courtship of his devoted wife, Donna, and the raising of their two children: how hard Bob worked, how often he was away, and the lessons of life he taught his boys.

We learn of Bob's challenges and, especially, his contributions as a teacher, change agent, academic administrator, and ambassador, and his quest to become the highest ranking deaf person in the federal government. Many dimensions of the history of the education of deaf and hard-of-hearing children in the United States and around the world are shared and we see Bob's influence on it.

I did not have to read, of course, about Bob's outstanding contributions as a leader and first vice president of NTID. He was one of my most trusted, experienced, and influential advisors, a loyal colleague, confidant, and partner, as we worked closely together for eight years. I remember telling the search committee for his position at its first meeting that I wanted it to recommend the best person, hearing or deaf, for this important position. Without question, that person was Bob Davila. He happened to be deaf.

And then Harry, Oscar, and Joe talk about Bob's "retirement." We discover—not surprisingly—that "retirement" is not part of Bob's lexicon or mindset as we see from his recent appointment as not only Gallaudet University's ninth president, but its first minority president. As this implies, the Bob Davila story—happily—has no ending. Bob, while certainly doing different things, still works hard (he does not know how not to work). He continues to contribute to both the hearing and deaf communities and to both the Hispanic and non-Hispanic communities.

The authors go back and forth in time as they weave a fabric, which shows, in the brightest colors, the different stages and important events in Bob's life to date. We see how Bob dealt with the administrative, personnel, public policy, political, and institution-building challenges he faced. We are privy to his thought processes, principles, convictions, and leadership style. We see the adversaries, the allies, the controversies, and the compromises.

We hear how Bob drew so much from his Hispanic culture—epitomized by his hard-working mother with whom he remained in close contact until her death—and from the deaf culture, which he has helped to shape over the years. From these two cultures he learned to dream, to take risks, to never say "cannot."

The authors tell Bob's story in a captivating, cohesive, and, especially, integrative fashion. Where it is important to talk about family, upbringing, ancestry, and deafness, they do so, always with professional and policy contributions in the background. Then there are times when the policy and professional achievements are in the foreground, with Bob the person very much part of the story but in the background. All in all, an insightful balance is achieved.

I believe all readers, especially those who are deaf, have disabilities, or are members of an ethnic minority, will find the Bob Davila story both inspirational and motivational. In telling this story, the authors create a rich tapestry of the life of a talented individual who showed what courage, hope, and vision could achieve, in this way blazing a path for others to follow.

Albert J. Simone, Ph.D.
President Emeritus
Rochester Institute of Technology

Acknowledgments

As EDUCATORS WITH A LONGSTANDING INTEREST in bettering the lives of all children, especially those who are deaf and members of ethnic minorities, we know that children learn resilience from models in their lives, whether they are fictional heroes in books, tales of ancestors, teachers, parents, or classmates. Thus, when Rochester Institute of Technology president Albert J. Simone invited us to summarize Bob Davila's life and work, we saw the potential of a biography to inform educators and parents through a case study of a deaf Hispanic person who reached the pinnacle of his profession after having begun life in a migrant worker camp in California. As a story of a child's self-discovery of previously unrecognized strengths in the face of profound deafness, we also saw the story as holding promise to inspire children to become self-directed learners. It is hoped that this story will serve as a resource to help families and schools provide opportunities to nourish resilience in deaf children.

This book could not have been completed without the help of many people who provided support and assisted us with the research and editing. We thank Al Simone for providing the financial support and James J. DeCaro, former dean and director of NTID, for managing the project's funds and providing feedback on drafts. We are grateful to the cadre of interviewers, graduate students, and other professionals who edited the drafts, made important suggestions, and encouraged us along the way, particularly Kathleen Sullivan Smith, Susan Stevenson Coil, Patricia Mudgett-DeCaro, Bob Finnerty, Julie Ann Mountain, and Bonnie Meath-Lang. We owe much to David Pankow, Amelia Hugill-Fontanel, and Marnie Soom at RIT Press, as well as their editorial colleagues Patricia Cost, David Prout, and Diane Forbes. We are grateful to Mary Lamb for her logistical support and Paul Scherer for supporting our meetings in New York City. RIT librarians Joan Naturale and Linda Coppola, and Ulf Hedberg and Michael Olsen at Gallaudet University Merrill Learning Center were instrumental in helping with our searches for information. Mark Benjamin's superb photographic work is much appreciated. Jill Welks deserves special appreciation for the many hours she contributed as a research assistant in gathering materials and information, and providing thorough critiques.

Many others provided comments, stories, and information that enriched the book. We especially acknowledge Fran Parrotta, Susan Murray, Jeanne Glidden Prickett, Ramón Rodriguez, Taras Denis, Gil Delgado, Robert F. Panara, George Propp, Arlene Rice, Frank Turk, Phil Bravin, Bob Lennan, Bernard Bragg, Victor Medina, Fina Perez, Gus Thompson, Cheri McKee, and Catherine Ford.

We also extend special thanks to Bob's wife Donna Davila and sons Brian and Brent for sharing their personal lives and their reflections on family life.

Finally, we thank Bob Davila for the many hours he spent, sometimes awkwardly, reminiscing with us about the politics of education and the impact of his contributions. May this book summarizing your life's work fighting for equal opportunity in education help a new generation of deaf children believe that they can indeed make a positive difference in their own lives and in the lives of others.

Introduction

"THAT WAS A MOMENTO DE VERDAD FOR ME," Bob recalled when discussing the January afternoon in 1989 when he met with Secretary of Education Dr. Lauro F. Cavazos in the U.S. Department of Education building in the Nation's capitol. It was a "moment of truth."

Despite having experienced an already-impressive career, including the accomplishment of being the first deaf Hispanic vice president of Gallaudet University, Bob was nevertheless daunted by the imminent meeting with Secretary Cavazos. It was certainly a long way from his humble boyhood roots in a family of migrant farm workers. Fran Parrotta, his administrative assistant at Gallaudet, was serving as interpreter. In a short time the conversation with Cavazos became rather informal and pleasant. Because his ethnic and cultural background was much like Bob's own, Cavazos took great interest in asking Bob about his parents, their home in Mexico, and their early years in the barrio in California. Cavazos even tried a little Spanish with Bob for good measure. The secretary of education also expressed interest in how Bob related to people who were *not* deaf and how he had managed to complete graduate school against staggering odds.

Cavazos looked squarely at Bob. "Have you given thought to any particular position for which you might wish to be considered in President George H. W. Bush's Department of Education?"

In that short moment, Bob's life quickly flashed through his thoughts. The recent "Deaf President Now!" protest of the spring of 1988 was now history and Gallaudet University was back in business. During that tumultuous time, Bob had applied for the Gallaudet presidency, but he failed to even be selected as a finalist. He had already served as president of the three major organizations in his field. There seemed to be little opportunity to advance further in the field of deaf education.

1

Bob sat there a bit nervously. His throat had become dry and his speech a bit slurred as he stammered his reply to Cavazos. With all the confidence he could muster, he answered, "I believe that I am qualified to be the assistant secretary for the Office of Special Education and Rehabilitation Services. That position is more in line with my interests and qualifications."

Cavazos smiled and told him that was exactly what he was thinking. He then offered Bob one of the finest accolades he has ever received, "Actually, you are qualified to be assistant secretary in *three* of the divisions in the Department of Education."

An anonymous Spanish writer once wrote, "*No conquistarás el océano si no tienes el valor para perder de vista la playa.*" ("One cannot conquer the ocean without being brave enough to lose sight of the beach.") These words reflect well this significant event in the life of Robert Refugio Davila. Indeed, as a young boy in Southern California, Bob loved the beach, and spent much time walking along the shore. After spinal meningitis left him profoundly deaf at the age of 11, he found a way to figuratively sail away from his native barrio, thus enabling himself to further his education in a school for deaf children. From there, his career took off as he gained control of his own destiny.

Bob's life story is not so much a "rags to riches" saga as it is a portrait of hard work and, as the title of this book implies, many "moments of truth" as he learned to believe in himself and his abilities. The challenges Bob remembers facing as a Mexican-American boy were not only those of the discrimination and racism faced by many migrant families, but also those of profound deafness, which sometimes engulfed him.

In understanding Bob's success, one doesn't have to wonder long whether it was the educational system that served him well or his unusual abilities that allowed him to access opportunities created primarily to serve children of the dominant culture. The schools he attended provided him with opportunities to learn early that he could set higher expectations for himself.

Bob is not in any way a product of his time. His achievements were not obtained without the struggles that Hispanic and other deaf children of color still face today. "To be both Hispanic and deaf," Bob said in 1986, "is to be blessed, as well as tormented." For him, it is not easy to determine which factor has had a greater impact on his life. As he put it, "I am inextricably a product of dual heritage." Being Hispanic, he explained, means more than having a Spanish surname. Similarly, being deaf implies more than an inability to hear. "Hispanics share a common culture and language," he pointed out. "Deaf people, too, know the influence of indigenous social standards and a unique mode of communication." In the United States, Hispanic and deaf people are both minorities with a strong tradition of community and a language apart from the dominant Anglo and hearing cultures.

While Bob's leadership in national organizations and at the U.S. Department of Education led to his actively addressing Hispanic and deaf issues, his political empowerment was generally of a broader nature, encompassing the rights of all marginalized children and adults. He traveled along this career path of social equality, and the Hispanic community welcomed his achievements and held him up as a hero of sorts. Over time and on an increasing basis, he accepted the challenge to become a spokesperson for and champion of the Hispanic community. He knew that his success story was critical to the Hispanic Deaf world and could also provide an opportunity for him to serve as a role model for many deaf students who were not Hispanic.

There is a strong need for educational leaders who can bridge cultures and affirm ethnicities. Children with disabilities need to see adults who have succeeded despite these challenges. As a teenager, Bob developed the belief that he could fulfill his dreams. Such positive feelings about oneself go hand in hand with academic achievement and motivation. Later, after becoming a champion of all deaf children, but especially those who were disenfranchised, Bob argued for decades that the system that enabled him to succeed often failed to help other deaf children of color. Then as now, these children struggle to gain quality education, despite decades of civil rights legislation and educational reform. Social reformer and political theorist John W. Gardner, author of the book *Excellence*, wrote, "For every talent that poverty has stimulated it has blighted a hundred."

The story of Bob Davila rising from poverty to become one of the foremost leaders in special education is of particular interest in light of the austere statistics of his fellow deaf Hispanics. Thousands of deaf children in the United States are from Spanish-speaking homes. These children frequently score well below their deaf Caucasian peers on standardized tests. They are also more likely to drop out of school or be placed in vocational programs.

Paralleling the trend in general education, there has been a disproportionately small number of deaf Hispanic students enrolled in or graduating from postsecondary education programs. Likewise, there are far too few deaf or hearing Hispanic professionals in the field of deaf education. Bob cannot recall ever having been taught by an Hispanic teacher, something that discouraged him at times. When Bob was a faculty member at Gallaudet College, he pointed out to an interviewer that fewer than one percent of Hispanic professionals (deaf or hearing) were in deaf education. "That must mean me and someone else," he said.

The Spanish pioneers who lead the way more than 400 years ago in the education of deaf students gave Bob an interesting talking point. Educators of deaf students are well aware of that history, which dates back to Pedro Ponce de León in the sixteenth century, who established the world's first school for deaf children in the San Salvador de Oña Benedictine Monastery near Burgos. Less than a century later, de León's fellow countryman Juan Pablo Bonet published the first book on the education of deaf children. With the passage of time, educators in other countries throughout Europe opened schools for deaf children.

The story of the development of schools for deaf children in the New World is well known, beginning with the efforts of Thomas Hopkins Gallaudet and the deaf Frenchman Laurent Clerc to establish the first state-sponsored program, American Asylum for the Deaf (now the American School for the Deaf) in West Hartford, Connecticut in 1817. As the country expanded westward, so did schools for deaf children, with at least one being created in nearly every state. This included Bob's alma mater, the California School for the Deaf in Berkeley, which was founded in 1860.

However, the lack of progress in the education of Hispanic deaf children since the time of Ponce de León was indeed disheartening to Bob. He wanted to reduce the achievement gap between Hispanic deaf children and their Caucasian peers, but he needed others to join him in that effort.

While Bob ultimately surpassed hearing and non-minority candidates to become the assistant secretary for Special Education and Rehabilitation Services (OSERS) under President George H.W. Bush from 1989 to 1992, his path to such an esteemed position was long and diverse. Coming from a migrant farm camp in Gilroy, California, he worked as a mail sorter, assembly line worker, teacher, Linotype operator, college professor, headmaster at a state-supported private school for deaf children, president and leader of numerous national and international professional organizations, vice president at Gallaudet University, and vice president for the Rochester Institute of Technology and director of RIT's National Technical Institute for the Deaf. Over the years, in addition to learning Spanish, English, and American Sign Language, Bob developed a reading knowledge of Italian and Portuguese. Through his interactions with many other professionals, he promoted programs for the deaf in many foreign countries, but especially in the United States.

The lesson parents, teachers, and students may learn from Bob's story is that such a confluence of challenges as Bob Davila experienced can either empower or weaken students, depending on their personal attributes and the support which the community, family, and school can provide.

Terms and Abbreviations

ADA	Americans with Disabilities Act
ASA	Autism Society of America
ASL	American Sign Language
CAID	Council of American Instructors of the Deaf (Formerly "Convention of American Instructors of the Deaf")
CEASD	Conference of Educational Administrators of Schools and Programs for the Deaf
CED	Council on Education of the Deaf
COED	Commission on the Education of the Deaf
CSD	California School for the Deaf
FAPE	Free and Appropriate Public Education
ICED	International Council on the Education of the Deaf
IDEA	Individuals with Disabilities Education Act
IEP	individualized educational program
ITP	individualized transition plan
JNAD	Junior National Association of the Deaf
KDES	Kendall Demonstration Elementary School
LRE	least restrictive environment
MSSD	Model Secondary School for the Deaf
NAD	National Association of the Deaf
NASDSE	National Association of State Directors of Special Education
NCI	National Captioning Institute
NCLR	National Council of La Raza
NETAC	Northeast Technical Assistance Center
NLTP	National Leadership Training Program in the Area of the Deaf
NTID	National Technical Institute for the Deaf

NYSD   New York School for the Deaf at White Plains
OBELMA   Office of Bilingual Education and Minority Language Affairs
OSEP   Office of Special Education Programs
OSERS   Office of Special Education and Rehabilitative Services
PEN Intl.   Post-secondary Education Network---International
RIT   Rochester Institute of Technology
RSA   Rehabilitative Services Administration
SAFE   Schools Are For Everyone
TASH   The Association of the Severely Handicapped

CHAPTER 1
A Sense of Loss

IN 1940, WHEN ROSALIO AND SOLEDAD DAVILA worked in the fields with their children, more than three-quarters of California's 200,000 farm workers were Mexican or Mexican-American. Their existence was a transitory one. They followed the potato, cotton, lemon, plum, orange, and pea harvests that together formed the majority of the state's agricultural output. Recruited by farm owners who exploited their desperate poverty, these Mexican workers were paid significantly less than white American laborers. They lived in shacks roughly patched together from different crude materials such as burlap and canvas—even palm branches—and they clustered in camps strung alongside irrigation ditches, which created poor sanitary conditions and health issues.

It was customary for Mexican migrant workers in the region to leave their homes for months at a time, families in tow, and make an annual trek to various points in the San Joaquin Valley to harvest the fruit and vegetable crops. Many of these families maintained year-round homes in southern California and then spent springs and summers tending and harvesting the crops up north. They usually returned to the same farms and orchards each season, where families would work as units. It was not uncommon for children of migrant workers to skip school during these treks north, as did Roberto, their fifth son. He knew that his father did not enjoy this kind of labor. Near the end of the summer the family preferred working in the orchards because the fruit trees offered welcome shade from the harsh California sun, and there was less need to work bent over in the heat.

Roberto knew his mother was also unhappy. She disliked leaving Carlsbad for Gilroy. Living in labor camps involved confinement in box-like quarters, sometimes without roofs. Usually cooking and washing were done

*Bob's mother, Soledad Trejo Davila,
in 1932. After Bob's father died in 1940,
she held part-time jobs to support the family.*

outside, and there was little privacy. Meals often were prepared using make-shift stoves fashioned from overturned metal drums. In the evenings, Roberto would sit and watch his mother baking tortillas on an oil drum with the smoke wafting into her face. As he recalls, "I never again experienced anything so desolate as the view of my mother preparing dinner in this crude fashion after a full, hard day of work in the orchards."[1]

As for Rosalio, a heart condition occasionally kept him at home under a doctor's care. Sometimes he took on construction jobs, ignoring the doctor's advice and working on roads or building houses. Soledad worried about the strain that fruit picking placed on her husband, but she knew that the harvesting was "family work" and everyone had to pitch in. This was the early 1940s and, like countless other Mexican-Americans, Roberto's parents believed in the concept of "growing" a large family. The income earned, they hoped, would eventually bring a harvest of prosperity to all of them.

While watching his sisters play comfortably in the shade away from the family workers, Roberto would sometimes be given a pail and a couple of boxes to fill with stray fruit from the trees in the immediate area as he waited. The day's quota was six tons of fruit, at roughly 35 boxes per ton, or about 200 boxes per family. The pay was something like $6 per ton, before the employer deducted charges for use of the camp facilities and water. As meager as these earnings sound, while working over a period of about four months, a family the size of the Davilas working an average of six days per week could earn about $1,500 after their employers took nearly 60 percent of their earnings for expenses. It was usually enough to tide them over until the following spring. Since it was not easy to meet such a high quota, hard and consistent work was required. And there was always a lot of worry about whether the section of the orchard assigned to the family was a good one in terms of meeting the quota. To speed up the harvesting, the family would spread a sheet of canvas under a tree and Rosalio or one of Roberto's brothers would climb the tree and shake it vigorously, while the other family members filled boxes with the falling bounty. Children were not spared from such demanding responsibility and, therefore, Roberto and his siblings grew up accepting hard work as a basic requirement of anything they did to earn money. As Roberto reflected later:

> At times, I would join the family to work alongside them for part of the day and different members would take turns caring for the girls. This became pretty much the routine whether we harvested fruit or vegetables. I recall that on several occasions, my father would carve a switch from a tree branch and tell me to use it as a weapon to ward off snakes when my sisters were sleeping under a tree. I would sit there and imagine all kinds of heroic deeds as I slaughtered slithering reptiles, but the truth is that I cannot recall ever encountering one of the critters.[2]

In this sense, Roberto's father empowered him and made sure he knew that even seemingly little things in life came with great responsibility and deserved full attention. Sitting there and caring for his sisters each day gave Roberto a lot of time to think. The heroic stories that he imagined did not come from books. He had grown up in a house without books. Rather, his imaginary stories sprang from the ideas of the Mexican-American storytellers who spun tales in Spanish around campfires after dinner during the harvesting.

On those rare evenings when Soledad had the energy, she would enthrall and charm the children in Spanish with stories of their heritage. In her soft, sad voice, she would take them back to 1910, the year Mexico erupted in revolution. Over the next few years, as Soledad remembered, armies fought for control of territories. Guerilla units destroyed *haciendas* and *ranchos* as both the rich and the poor suffered. During the first decade of the revolution, more than a million people died as this violent chapter in Mexico's history unfolded. Pancho Villa's Northern army, Emiliano Zapata's Indian peasants in the South, and local bands of revolutionaries all held grievances against the dictatorship of President Porfirio Díaz, and resented how national wealth

*Bob Davila, age 6, with his sister Rose
Marie, age 3, in Southern California
in 1938.*

and power had fallen into the hands of so few. It was during this tumultuous revolution that the paths of Rosalio Davila's and Soledad Trejo's families
crossed, by chance or destiny.

Through these stories, Roberto and his brothers and sisters learned
about their paternal grandparents, Abraham Davila and Brigida Rodríguez,
who had married and raised a family in Ocampo, Guanajuato, located in central Mexico. Founded by the Spaniards in 1557, Guanajuato later flourished
as a silver mining center. Abraham and Brigida's son—Roberto's father, Rosalio—was born in Guanajuato on September 4, 1892.

Soledad told them about how she had been born ten years later, on
April 25, 1902 in Jerez, Zacatecas, in the heart of Mexico. Her parents, José
Pablo Trejo and Josefa Vanegas, had lived in the same town for most of their
lives. Members of both Rosalio and Soledad's families, like many of their
countrymen, escaped the famine and desolate conditions caused by the Mexican Revolution. Soledad's father was the first to leave, bound for California in
1911. Three years later, Josefa and her two daughters, including Soledad, then
12, traveled by train to El Paso, Texas. Shortly afterwards, the family was once
again united in San Diego.

Rosalio Davila did not immigrate to California until 1916, when he
was in his early 20s. He found work with the Santa Fe Railroad in Los Angeles.
Shortly after relocating, he traveled south to San Diego with a work crew to

repair bridges that had been damaged by a fierce rainstorm. The devastation by floods in January of that year, compounded by the collapse of Lower Otay Dam, had washed out most of the freshly laid tracks along Campo Creek. Due to the efficiency of Rosalio and his crew, train service was restored by February, albeit running on temporary tracks.

Soledad would also reminisce with her children about the day she met Rosalio. When her own father fled his country in 1911, he had also found employment with the Santa Fe Railroad Depot in San Diego. It was there that he encountered young Rosalio at work. Soledad's father remembered Rosalio and his family from nearby Guanajuato, Mexico, and invited him to the Trejo family home in Encinitas.

Soledad and Rosalio soon fell in love and were married December 26, 1918, at Mission San Luis Rey in Oceanside, California. He was 26 years old and she was 16. Since she was not of legal age for marriage, her father granted his consent in writing.

Shortly after the wedding, the young Davila couple joined Rosalio's godparents in moving to Jerome, Arizona. At the time, it was a thriving copper mining center. Located between Prescott and Flagstaff, Jerome was once the fourth largest city in the Arizona Territory, peaking at 15,000 in the 1920s. Men and women from all over the world made their way to Jerome to find work and maybe a new way of life. At its height, Jerome produced an astonishing three million pounds of copper per month. Later it would become well known as a "ghost town" for tourists when the once-vast deposits ran dry.

Rosalio found employment in Jerome's mines as a drilling machine operator. The United States had recently declared war on Germany in what would come to be called the First World War. Since copper was desperately needed by the military, the unprecedented demand sent prices soaring. Within a short time, unrest between copper companies and fledgling unions led to labor strikes. Fires also erupted in the underground tunnels, creating hazardous conditions and many mines were forced to close, including the one in Jerome.

Like many other men who had worked in the mines, Rosalio sought jobs wherever he could find them. In 1920, Soledad gave birth to a son, Antonio (Anthony). Three years later, a daughter, San Juanita, was born. When Soledad's grandfather, who had also immigrated to the United States, became ill, Soledad and Rosalio and their children visited him in California. While there, San Juanita, just six months old, became ill and died. The family was devastated. After burying their child, they decided to remain in California. Rosalio saw his friends involved in migrant farm work and, despite the hard labor, he knew it was an opportunity to earn at least *some* money to support his family. He also realized that there was little promise of finding employment again in the Jerome mines.

Born July 19, 1932, Roberto Refugio Davila was the last of the Davila boys. He had followed Gabriel (Gabe), born in 1927, Alejandro (Alex) in 1928, and Rosalio Reymundo (Ray) in 1931. Two girls, Rosa María (Rose Marie) and María Helena (Mary Helen), were born in 1935 and 1938, respectively.

The loss of a child and years of working for the railroad, in copper mines, and in the orchards placed extra stress on Rosalio's heart. Both his doctor and his wife warned him continuously to be careful, but he ignored them.

ₔ₰ ₔ₰ ₔ₰

The first "moment of truth" in Roberto's life occurred when he was eight years old. He was watching over his baby sisters. Mary Helen was in her crib and Rose Marie, about five years old, was playing next to him. Their parents and older brothers moved methodically between the rows of prune trees that formed the orchard in Gilroy, California. The backbreaking work caused the sweat to glisten on his father's face. Rosalio Davila occasionally glanced down to make sure his youngest son was keeping an eye on Rose Marie and the baby. Not yet old enough to help harvest the prunes, Roberto felt a sense of responsibility as he carried the baby's crib to each new row, following in his father's wake. He never questioned this role.

Everyone in the family worked hard. As he had done throughout the endless days of the sweltering heat of the summer, Roberto watched his father shake each tree vigorously while his mother, Soledad, harvested the fallen fruit from the ground. He could hear the voices of his older brothers Gabe, Alex, and Ray bantering in Spanish as they collected fruit from nearby trees. His oldest brother, Anthony, was back home in Carlsbad working at his first independent job for a construction company. Anthony had finished high school a year before. He was a bright, bilingual and capable young man. However, the country was still climbing out of the Depression and good jobs were hard to find.

On Monday afternoon, August 19, 1940, Rosalio had once again ignored his poor health in order to support his family. The stress of climbing the trees to harvest the fruit placed too heavy a burden on his heart. As Roberto was caring for his sisters, he looked up just in time to see with horror his father suddenly fall from the prune tree and remain motionless on the ground. It was a memory he would never forget, and one that he could still vividly recount decades later:

My father was following his usual practice of remaining ahead of the tree the family was working. He would climb the tree to shake the higher branches, thus allowing difficult-to-reach fruit to fall to the ground to be picked and placed in pails and later into boxes. When he suffered a heart attack and fell to the ground, there was no warning. I only heard my mother screaming. Friends from another Carlsbad family, the Cantabranas, also heard my mother's screams and rushed over to offer assistance. My father was placed sitting up against the base of a tree and Mr. Cantabrana asked one of his sons, Cecilio, about 15 years old, to run for help. This was well before cell phones and when even land-line telephones were still a luxury item, so there was no place nearby to call for an ambulance. We were in the middle of a fruit orchard and away from roads or buildings. I do not know where Cecilio ran for help, but I recall it took forever. When help finally came in the form of an ambulance moving slowly over rough terrain between rows of prune trees, it was too late. By the time the ambulance reached the hospital, my father was dead.[3]

A few days later, Rosalio Davila was buried at a cemetery in Gilroy. He was only a couple of weeks shy of his 48th birthday.

Roberto had never sat in his father's lap or had a one-on-one conversation with him. Still, he would later remark in recounting this moment of truth in his life, "The loss of my father was the most significant happening in my very young life and one which remained unsurpassed in terms of impact, anguish and trauma until my mother died 54 years later."[4]

Early the next morning, Soledad discovered that an article of clothing had been left at the base of the tree where Rosalio had fallen. Cecilio and Roberto went to retrieve it. Thus, Roberto had the experience of returning to the spot and standing there for a while thinking about his father. Memories flashed quickly through his head. He saw in his mind's eye his father's face during those fleeting, final moments, and his mother's fearful expression as she cried for help. He recalled, "I shall never forget that moment as long as I live."[5]

CHAPTER 2

Waking Up in Silence

T HINGS CHANGED DRASTICALLY FOR THE DAVILA FAMILY after
Rosalio's death. "When the burden of raising a large family befell my
mother," he remembered, "I almost never saw her afterwards, especially during the important development years. She was gone day and night. She would
come in after dark, often when I was already asleep, and she would be gone
before I got up."[1] Now 38 years old, Soledad worked in the vegetable fields
around the small towns near Carlsbad. She also cleaned other people's homes
on weekends and babysat in the evenings. Often exhausted, she would arrive home to prepare food for the next day. By 5 a.m., she would be gone
to pick more vegetables. None of the children resented her for not being
home for them. Rather, they all grew up independent because they had to do
many things for themselves. Rosalio's untimely death did not trigger change
in the family's world outlook—hard work was a Davila trait. As Roberto
still remembers:

> The pleasures and security that comes from living as a group and spending
> quality time with each other and helping each other was always missing. But
> all of us understood why conditions in our family were the way they were and
> there was never any anger or fault-finding. It was a way of life.[2]

As the children grew up in Carlsbad, California, where Roberto's ma-
ternal grandfather and his aunt and uncle lived, attendance at school was
sporadic. Children of migrant workers were enrolled in public schools, but
the monitoring of their presence was lax, especially in the spring of each year
when the farm harvests were heavy in the San Joaquin and Imperial Valleys
and throughout San Diego County. Such was the case with the Davila chil-

dren. Roberto did not go to kindergarten and he was never enrolled in grammar school after fifth grade, except for occasionally accompanying his brothers for a few weeks at a time.

Roberto's oldest brother and two sisters managed to graduate from high school, but circumstances forced the others to drop out. It was difficult for Soledad to keep her children in school, especially after being widowed. She accepted that whatever her children could do to help the family make ends meet financially was the highest priority. Still, she knew that education was important for her children, and she did everything she could to support their attendance.

Soledad was fatalistic, believing that hardship was God's will and thus unavoidable. Her youngest son saw things differently, however. Even as a young boy, Roberto argued with her that a person could have more control of his or her own destiny. There must be a way out of this kind of life, he told her.

Roberto seldom saw his brothers, who were often away at work, and so he had no one to look up to as a role model. When he was not working to help support the family, he joined the countless kids roaming the barrio. He followed his friends to the beach, walked the streets, and even had his wrist tattooed with his name. In the barrio he would bet on anything, most often staking a dime a bet. One of Roberto's techniques involved wagering with other kids on who could eat a lemon the quickest. In one slurp, his lemon would be gone and he would win. That was how he picked up loose change— and his taste for lemons.

Roberto tried his best to support his mother in raising their family during what were painfully meager times. One morning, she handed him a $5 bill and asked him to go purchase paint at a local hardware store. He knew just how much $5 meant to his family and he felt exceedingly honored that his mother would trust him with such a significant sum. He left home for the long trek into town with a sense of pride in being able to help in this way.

When he arrived at the store, he realized, to his horror, that he had somehow lost the money en route. Terrified at what his family would think of him, he spent the night alone on the beach in utter disgrace. He hoped that when he finally returned home, his mother would be so relieved that he was safe, she might forget about the precious money with which he had been entrusted.

Naturally, Roberto's mother forgave him. Yet, he knew that $5 meant a whole day of labor in the hot sun and he anguished over his inadvertent transgression.

That event, too, was a moment of truth. It was to be one of the last memories young Roberto would recall of his days in the migrant farm camp.

In 1943, at the age of 11, possibly as a result of the unsanitary conditions in the camp, Roberto Davila contracted spinal meningitis. His mother thought he had the flu and so he was treated at home with bed rest and soup, but his condition didn't improve for weeks. When Soledad finally contacted a doctor who came to the house, the young boy was sent to the hospital.

ҙ&   ҙ&   ҙ&

"No te dolió mucho, ¿verdad?" ("It didn't hurt that much, did it?"), a Spanish-speaking nurse asked Roberto in the operating room after he received a spinal tap.[3] He had been in the hospital for several weeks and his only memory of the ordeal was being taken into that room, screaming and resisting as the nurses held him down. These were the last words he ever heard.

When the spinal tap was over, he was exhausted and he drifted into a long sleep. He recalls:

> The next morning I woke up to silence. When they brought my breakfast tray, I could see the aide's lips moving and I thought she was playing a game. She looked at me and went out of the room to call a nurse, who came in to check me out. That's when their examination indicated that I could no longer hear.[4]

When Roberto woke up again a few days later, he thought it was Sunday. It was quiet and the streetcars did not seem to be running. On this morning, his older brother, Alex, was sitting next to him. Alex had arrived home from the Marines and came to the hospital as soon as he learned of Roberto's illness. Drowsy and having forgotten about the examination results, Roberto looked at Alex talking to him and thought his older brother was also playing a game. "He was moving his lips but I could not hear anything," he remembered.[5]

After a trying period of adjustment, Roberto continued going out with his friends in the barrio, but he immediately felt left out, and was sometimes teased. They called him *el sordo* ("the deaf one"), which bothered him. His brother Ray would hear the teasing and get into fights over it, telling Roberto later what had happened. At first, Roberto did not understand what deafness was all about. He still had a strong memory of sound and speech and would often blurt something out and disrupt the communication of those around him. "The guys in my group didn't hesitate to bawl me out and tell me to shut up."[6] Mostly he did a lot of the talking and would ask his friends to scrawl a word or phrase in the sand or dirt or, if he had a pencil and paper, he would hand it over. But, Roberto rarely did this in open places where people could see him. "I didn't want people to know I was deaf because their pity embarrassed or enraged me."[7]

At first, Roberto was embarrassed when others would resort to gestures to communicate with him. Soledad developed the habit of volunteering to friends and strangers alike: "*Este es mi sordito.*" ("This is my little deaf one.") Roberto would get angry with her for telling people that. He eventually withdrew from his once-close friends, and dreamed of one day waking up hearing again. As he remembers, "That is what eased my adjustment. I considered deafness temporary. Well, obviously, it was not."[8]

He escaped into reading, borrowing books where he could find them. There was no television at home. The family would listen to a radio, but Roberto, naturally, was unable to hear it. When his mother could afford to give him a quarter, he would go buy a sports magazine. At times, he would rather see a movie, and so would stop along the way to glance at a magazine so as not to disobey his mother, who had specifically encouraged him to read.

Roberto grew up without religion. Soledad was Catholic, but she attended church only occasionally. She sometimes took one of her daughters to church, but there was little time for fostering spiritual life in her children while holding several jobs.

Roberto's spiritual lessons sometimes came through personal tragedies. His father's death had presented him with a moment of truth that challenged him personally. Three years later his family was suddenly again forced to cope with a staggering loss. Cecilio, the neighbor's son who had run for help the day Rosalio died, was killed fighting in the Philippines at the age of 19. The young soldier had been very close to the Davilas and they shared in the grief of Cecilio's family.

ॐ   ॐ   ॐ

Over the months following Roberto's illness, Soledad Davila, a sensible, no-nonsense woman, was forced to think about what to do about her deaf son. She knew that education was the ticket out of the migrant fields for her children, but she had no idea what to do about Roberto's schooling. She had done her best for her children while living in poverty, but how could she have Roberto properly educated at the local school?

Roberto reminisced that despite the initial shock, being rendered deaf was not as devastating as it might have been for a child in better circumstances. "In a family where there is no money and no food, hearing isn't so much," he would recall decades later.[9]

I grew up poor. There was no privilege connected with being disabled in a large single-parent family. Competition in the family for the food on the table, the better clothes to wear (We seemed to all wear practically the same size!), our mother's attention, the care one requires when one is sick, etc., taught me that I was just a player in the family group like everyone else. I never thought of myself as special. No one else thought I was special either. From infancy I had a strong work ethic. It was instilled in my mind early that I would have to work hard to get anything I desired. So I grew up without the mistaken notion that being deaf entitled me to anything different.[10]

Within a short time, a friend recommended to Soledad that she consult a social worker. Through this professional she received information about a well-respected school for deaf students in northern California. Until this time, Roberto's schooling had been sporadic. When he did attend school in Carlsbad, or when he occasionally learned from adults in the migrant farm camps, the communication was predominantly in Spanish. Soledad did encourage her children to learn English. Anthony had learned especially well. But Roberto had learned very little, and Soledad had no idea if his background would be acceptable to officials at the California School for the Deaf (CSD) at Berkeley. There, she knew, he could learn more English and perhaps pursue an education beyond what most of his siblings had thus far been able to enjoy. Moreover, she learned that CSD was a state school and deaf children were admitted at no cost to the family. Despite the attractiveness of this opportunity, it was a difficult decision for her. As he explained:

> The decision to send me to the California School for the Deaf was painful to my mother. She told me so. Since CSD was a "residential" school, I would have to live there ten months out of the year. She said it was for my own good and not because she did not love me. She asked me to be good and to respect my teachers. That was it…This send-off admonition became a permanent memory and I was always mindful of her parting words.[11]

It was late summer 1944 when Roberto, then 12 years old, stood on a train platform, trying to mentally and emotionally gird himself to live 500 miles away for most of the year. As he remembers, "I was scared. Homesick. Determined. My mother…had instilled in me…a strong sense of purpose. I knew, as did she, that it was necessary for me to leave home if I wanted to better myself through education."[12]

This moment of truth, however, was short-lived. With a hand-lettered sign pinned to his shirt bearing his name, home address and final destination—the California School for the Deaf in Berkeley—he boarded a train, waved goodbye to his family, and silently departed his Spanish-speaking world. Although it would not be fully recognized until years later, Soledad's choice would irrevocably and permanently alter her son's life experience, expanding it beyond anything his family could ever imagine.

Much to the dismay of the already-nervous Roberto, that first trip to Berkeley would ultimately include an overnight stay in a train station waiting room. In those days, traveling to Berkeley from Carlsbad was difficult. All trains for the northern areas of California originated in Los Angeles. Thus, travelers coming from the south had to change trains in the city. People arriving on the last evening train to Los Angeles were required to wait overnight for the morning trip to Berkeley.

For this first trip, Roberto's mother accompanied him to Oceanside, several miles away, in order to show him where he would board the train to Los Angeles. She kissed him goodbye in Oceanside and left to return home. Roberto then took the last passenger train for Los Angeles and arrived at Union Station around 8 p.m. He knew ahead of time that he would have to spend the night in the waiting room. It was 1944—wartime—and the young deaf boy was lost amid a beehive of activity as he waited for his morning train connection to Berkeley. At this time, there was only one school for the deaf in California, and a large number of deaf students from southern California attended the Berkeley school. Although the school wisely sent several staff mentors to escort the southern California contingent of students north in reserved cars, Roberto was the only child who arrived the evening before.

Exhausted and bewildered that evening, he fell asleep in a chair. Bob later remembered this as a traumatic experience. Within a short time, a policeman woke him up. Roberto assumed that he was inquiring why a young boy was alone so late at night. He pointed at the sign attached to his shirt indicating he was going to the school for the deaf in Berkeley. Communication was a nightmare. Fortunately, a Spanish-speaking officer came to the rescue. After some struggle attempting to speak to him by voice, the officer resorted to a pad and pencil. Struggling with his rather poor Spanish reading skills, Roberto was nevertheless able to explain by voice that he needed to catch the morning train to Berkeley to attend the school for the deaf. "My mother could not be called because she had no phone," Bob recalled.

But it had a happy ending. The police officers decided to allow me to sleep on a cot in an open jail cell and in the morning they escorted me to the train station, where I met the people holding CSD placards at the gathering point for the students going north.[13]

CHAPTER 3
Out of the Barrio

B EING SENT AWAY TO LIVE AT SUCH A SCHOOL was not at all unusual for pupils within the deaf education system of that era. Federal legislation had not yet been passed to provide more choices to parents. Approximately 80 percent of the deaf children in the U.S. were enrolled in residential schools, with some returning home on weekends, but most living on the school campuses for months at a time. Today, those statistics have been virtually reversed, with the majority of deaf students enrolled in mainstream schools and living at home. A deaf child in Carlsbad today would likely attend a local public school or the California School for the Deaf (CSD) Riverside, a little over an hour's drive from Carlsbad.

CSD traces its roots back to 1860, a mere decade after California's statehood. That year, a group of progressive minded women in San Francisco organized a Society for the Instruction and Maintenance of the Indigent Deaf, Dumb, and Blind. As the fledgling state's first school for deaf students, it began with three pupils and within six months its enrollment had quadrupled. Undaunted by the Civil War, the school relocated to new buildings in nearby Berkeley in the 1870s. Over the next few decades, additional buildings were erected and eventually the California school grounds evolved into an attractive campus. From the front windows of the Educational Building, a magnificent view of the San Francisco Bay created a stunning vista.[1] From his dorm room, Roberto enjoyed the same view.

Throughout the early part of the twentieth century, CSD established a solid academic reputation, with pupils' test scores consistently high. Because of its critical mass of deaf students, the school was able to graduate a number of students well prepared for college work. The students were assigned to academic and vocational classes based on their abilities in each area. The

Bob with his new friends at the California School for the Deaf at Berkeley, 1945.

Vocational and Industrial Arts program offered shop courses in such areas as baking, art, printing, sewing, shoe-making/repairing, and domestic science. It was in this program that many minority children were placed. At CSD Berkeley "Roberto" quickly became "Bob." By the time he entered, there was also one class reserved for hard-of-hearing pupils under the assumption that their special needs could be more effectively met by teaching them separately. To accommodate these and other changes, CSD had recently added to the faculty several teachers with specialized knowledge.

While there were generally lower expectations for the children of Mexican descent in CSD, Bob's instinct for survival helped him to "read" his teachers and their attitudes and thoughts. He discovered that some teachers, entrenched by the misconceptions of the times, simply didn't expect to find success in a boy from a Spanish-speaking home. In particular, most of the other students with Hispanic surnames attending CSD were enrolled in vocational education.

This was the moment in his life when he realized that *the rest of his life would be different.* CSD presented Bob with a tremendous culture shock, totally unlike anything he had known before. Schools for the deaf at this time were largely monocultural. It was generally assumed that somehow deafness ameliorated ethnic, racial and cultural differences. These were, after all, institutions founded to deal with children's deafness, and the overcoming of this "handicap" was their focus. The schools no doubt also reflected the melting pot assumptions that were dominant in American culture at that time, so it was no surprise that CSD, or any other residential school for the deaf, was not particularly sensitive to individual or cultural diversity during that era. The school was, in short, a very Anglo institution. There were several dozen children with Spanish surnames but Bob was different from most of them as well. None of them spoke Spanish and he could not communicate in sign language well enough to converse with *any* student in the school.

Previously appearing precocious to adults in his Spanish-speaking migrant camp, Bob was now perceived as a truly bright kid by his teachers at CSD. Despite his need to learn both English and sign language in order to catch up with his peers, school officials placed him in the advanced academic program.

Bob was up to the challenge. He worked hard to do well. He spent an extraordinary amount of time looking up words in dictionaries and reading everything he could get his hands on. The teachers nurtured his intellectual curiosity and he thrived on their encouragement and the challenging curriculum. As he recalls, "I was highly motivated on finding that the rewards went to those who were brightest, ran faster, jumped higher and scored best on tests."[2]

Bob loved the attention he received at the school. It was unlike anything he had experienced in the barrio. He also loved the comforts the school had to offer—his own bed, good food, healthy surroundings, and eventually peers with whom he could communicate.

Used to life in a migrant farm family, Bob was shocked at CSD when he learned that he had to go to bed at 8:30. Back in the barrio, he often did not arrive at his house until that time. Returning from wherever he had been all day, it was often in the late evening when he would look for something to eat.

During the months at CSD, Bob weathered various reactions by teachers and students as he adapted to a whole new lifestyle. Although he was from the barrio, he had not been born deaf. Although his prior schooling was irregular and incomplete, he was extremely bright and conscientious. And although he was initially awkward with sign language, his sense of humor quickly won him friendships. The street-smart kid found ways to take advantage of every situation. His confidence developed in leaps and bounds. Yet all the while there were constantly moments of truth when he was reminded that he would have hurdles to jump in the future as well. In one class discussion about future goals, he told his instructor that he would like to be a teacher and naively asked her if Mexicans could be teachers. "I'm not really sure," she told him bluntly. "I haven't seen one."[3]

Bob reflected further about the first few months at CSD, "I wanted so much to find acceptance that I rolled with the punches."[4] He quickly overcame the struggle to communicate, learning sign language rapidly. By his first Christmas at CSD, only four months after arriving at the school, he could communicate with reasonable fluency in signs. This was not easy. His mental processes were still articulated in Spanish even while signing in American

Sign Language (ASL). His world had, in effect, rapidly evolved into a trilingual one (Spanish/English/ASL). He nevertheless succeeded in keeping one foot grounded in the language and culture of his boyhood.

After Bob's father died his mother had encouraged her family to become bilingual, and Bob's brothers and sisters all began to concentrate on learning English. Bob's deafness interfered with this development for a while. But now his bright mind enabled him to adapt to two new languages simultaneously. As at essentially every school for the deaf in the country, spoken English was the established language of learning at CSD. Raised in a primarily Spanish-speaking family in an insular environment and having rarely heard English spoken, Bob credited the fluency he developed in English to his deafness. This was in stark contrast to what happens to most deaf children. "With perseverance, dedicated instruction and good fortune," Bob recalled, "I learned the complexities of English along with American Sign Language which came so naturally to me after I could no longer rely on my ears."[5]

Bob did not know of any other person who had the same kind of upbringing or experiences. He learned to read and write Spanish independently. He had a knack for languages.

Bob's first Christmas away from home was especially difficult. One night he sat in his dormitory room and thought about the only Christmas he remembered having with his family prior to enrolling at CSD. It was the year before he became deaf, a Christmas when the family had actually put up a tree and exchanged gifts. How his mother got the money for this celebration remains a mystery to him. There never was an absence of love or caring in his family. Now at Christmas in 1944, he sensed that his mother and siblings knew that he was being taken care of at Christmas.

And they were right. There was plenty of support for him at CSD. His deaf friends were his family. He could communicate with them. There were enough children who did not go home for the holidays to provide him with the companionship he needed. They spent half days cleaning bathrooms, polishing brass door hardware and sweeping floors. They helped the grounds people set up auditorium seating for the first day of the students' return after Christmas. Bob also went with his friends to see a few movies in Oakland. He watched the boats on the bay, and visited a museum. He was so busy having fun that he did not think much about being away from home at Christmas.

Still, the sudden thrust into a very different world occasionally became emotionally troubling for him. One night he remembered the farewell at the train station and how his mother had admonished him not to cry. "Every time I felt like crying, I remembered my mother's words. I steeled myself not to shed tears." Years later, Bob reminisced, "That was a mistake. It is okay to be afraid, to miss family, to feel lonely. Little kids *should* cry."[6]

The stiff upper lip that he developed lasted a lifetime.

– – –

CSD was definitely not a full substitute as a replacement family. With Soledad having to support her family with multiple part-time jobs, and still raising two young daughters, there was little time for her to write to Bob. At mail calls, a dorm supervisor stood in the dining room and fingerspelled the names of boys and girls who had received letters. The students would then excitedly go up to the supervisor to retrieve their mail. This was generally a gleeful and exciting part of the day's lunch hour. With a degree of sorrow, Bob would recall, "For me, it was mostly a time when I wished I wasn't there."[7]

One day, the supervisor called his name. "Davila!" Or so he thought. "I couldn't believe it—FINALLY I had mail!"[8] He walked up slowly and took the letter, only to realize it was not addressed to him. The letter was for a young schoolmate, Richard Avila. Nevertheless, he clutched the letter to his chest and basked in the moment. When the students were dismissed, Bob made a beeline for the bathroom, where he opened the letter. In it was a one-dollar bill. He was sorely tempted to keep the dollar since he never had any money. A moment of truth—he gave the letter and its contents back to the supervisor.

While he was growing up, his family never had time to attend church together. Keeping a roof over the Davila household and food on the table were his parents' primary concerns. Many migrant families were traditionally very religious, but comfort in their lives was generally not forthcoming. Now, CSD offered opportunities and services Bob had never experienced in the barrio. The school, as a home away from home, did everything that the family was supposed to do, including providing religious education. It was not unusual for even state schools for the deaf to offer religious education in that era. The doctrine of separation of church and state was not widely recognized at that time, and even public schools held religiously oriented celebrations.

Even when the doctrine of separation of church and state took on greater significance, "release time" for religious education remained an accepted practice in schools. Children were released for an hour a week to attend religious instruction at neighborhood houses of worship. Since most houses of worship were unable to provide adequate communication in educating deaf children, the practice of "release time" being permitted within schools for the deaf became the norm, with experienced lay teachers providing the religious instruction. Deaf education itself had a strongly religious bent since many schools were founded by religious orders or church-related groups. In fact, Reverend Thomas Hopkins Gallaudet's interest in sign language and his subsequent involvement in establishing schools for the deaf in America came from his desire to "save the souls" of deaf people and his concern that unless clergy learned the language of signs, they would not be able to convey their religious belief system to deaf people. CSD sent Soledad a request for permission to include Bob in religious instruction classes and asked which religion she preferred for him. His mother was delighted that someone was willing to instruct Bob in Catholicism, and he subsequently received the sacraments of First Communion and Confirmation.

Over the next three years at CSD the development of Bob's identity as a deaf person went hand-in-hand with the development of the work ethic he had originally adopted after his father's death. He established increasingly high expectations for himself as he mastered English and thought about his future. "I was influenced by two thoughts," he summarized later. "I needed to succeed and didn't want to fail."[9] During school breaks, most CSD students went home. Since Bob's family could not always afford the train ticket for a visit home, he sometimes stayed with his cousin, Mike Acuña, in nearby Richmond, California. Mike and his wife worked all day, so Bob stayed in their house and waited until they returned for the evening.

Bob learned much from his twice-a-year traveling experiences. Advised by his older brother to spend time in the safe harbor of the restroom, during future commutes he would disembark from the Oceanside train at Union Station in Los Angeles and make a beeline for the men's restroom, where he would lock himself in one of the stalls and sit there all night to wait for the morning train. "The only diversion I had was the graffiti on the walls," he recalls, "I memorized a number of choice words and terms which shocked my teachers when I arrived at CSD and asked them for the meanings."[10]

Bob soon learned another interesting fact about his itinerary for the trip to CSD. The train stopped at San Quentin, one of the toughest penitentiaries in the country. Some of the guards who accompanied the convicts waiting for his train would recognize Bob and occasionally they would let the young deaf boy walk up and down the aisles, giving water to the convicts, who were chained to their seats. In return, some of the men gave him dimes from their pockets.

Bob spent the first summers at home, most of the time on the beach, which was only three blocks away. His sister Mary Helen remembers how he used to read to her and give her nickels to buy candy at the neighborhood store.[11] Never a loner, he would hang out with his hearing friends, soaking in the sun, and playing games for hours. Communication with his friends in the barrio remained tenuous; they didn't know sign language. They nevertheless got along, engaging in typical mischief. During one foolish occasion, Bob and his friends threw a box of bullets into a bonfire. One of the exploding bullets struck Bob's leg. The scar is the size of a quarter and still brings back memories of how close he came to a more serious injury.

During these summers Bob would also take the bus to San Diego, walk to Lane Field and stand with other fans on top of railroad cars to watch the then minor league Padres baseball games—at least until the police officers commanded them to get off the cars.

Bob's quick adaptation to the new routines at CSD sometimes introduced awkward moments back home in the barrio. He sometimes felt he was an annoyance, bringing with him the rules that he had learned in school. "I think that my family got tired of me correcting their way of eating meals," he recalled.[12]

In the fall of 1945, Bob cherished being back in the classroom—with all deaf students. Sometimes he felt quite different there, since few of his deaf friends understood his barrio-home life. After each summer at home, he required a short period of readjustment. Even surrounded by deaf friends, he was sometimes alone with his thoughts. Nevertheless, Bob knew that CSD was a path he had to continue on. The alternative was life in the barrio. His deafness, ironically, had shown him that there was a better life elsewhere.

Indeed, Bob gave much thought to this "better life" while taking solo walks on the beach in the summer or in his dorm room at CSD. Quiet thinking times helped him shape his ambitions and sort out his thoughts about living in such different worlds.

Bob was also always looking for work or other ways of raising money. He made every effort to disguise his poverty: not many of his friends ever realized how poor he was. He would decline participation in an event or activity for all sorts of reasons but never because he could not afford it.

Fortunately, for the most part, traditional residential schools for the deaf generally functioned much like classless societies. Theoretically, in the eyes of the staff and faculty, no student was entitled to—or received—special privileges. The children all slept in dormitory rooms, awakened together, showered and dressed, marched single file to the dining room, to the school building, to the playground, to study hall and then went to bed all at the same time. Furthermore, everything required for daily living such as food, medical care, and school supplies, was provided by the school. Within such an environment, Bob was able to achieve parity in a reasonable amount of time. As he remembered:

> Having a strong work ethic, great curiosity and plenty of "street smarts" actually made me superior in many aspects of growing up at that age. It's really no wonder that I sopped up learning and language in search of a "pat on the head" and a taste of the better life.[13]

Even with his success in assimilating into the school, Bob occasionally encountered discrimination. Some of his teachers and peers accepted him and his ethnicity unequivocally, others a bit tentatively. One incident occurred during a spring when the school had a problem with ants infesting the kitchen. None of the students were willing to squeeze into the crawl space under the porch to spray the area with poison. A staff member responsible for supervising the task decided that this was the type of job that Mexican boys were better suited to handle, so he selected Bob, the only Mexican student in the group at the time, to complete the unpleasant assignment. Thinking that he was being honored, Bob performed the task with enthusiasm. It was not until years later that Bob realized this might have been racially-biased.

Bob looked back on such experiences with a certain degree of amazement. While gone for the school year, he had a lot of time for himself and he wondered as an adult just how he could have grown up as a generally good kid. He was never in trouble and was steered in the right direction even if he wasn't given a lot of help in reaching his destinations.

Bob was a gregarious boy. One of the close life-long friends he met at CSD was Terry O'Rourke, who would years later leave his mark on history and the deaf community by promoting interpreting as a profession and educating the nation about the need to learn sign language. Terry, or "T.J." as he was called, also later founded T.J. Press, the first deaf-owned, deaf-run publishing company in the United States.

Bob and Terry enjoyed escaping from the school at times to watch the Oakland Oaks baseball team in nearby Oakland. Terry was extremely bright and his English was superior to Bob's. With a debt of gratitude he owed his close friend, Bob reflected: "I befriended him and I think I probably learned more English from him than from anyone else when I was growing up."[14] Bob would ask Terry to give him the English for a sign whenever he knew only the Spanish meaning. Terry literally helped Bob translate a lot of vocabulary into English. The two remained close friends until T.J.'s death in 1991.

Terry O'Rourke's mother was a wonderful woman, who served as Bob's "mother away from home." Bob would visit Terry for the weekend at his family's home in nearby Richmond. At times, these visits could be quite adventurous. If Terry did something unacceptable and was about to be berated or disciplined by his mother, he would instantly blame the misdeed on a flabbergasted Bob. It remains a wonder to Bob today that he was never thrown out of the house as a result of these shenanigans. On the contrary, Mrs. O'Rourke sewed his Boy Scout badges onto his uniform and did many things his own mother would have done.

Bob's resilience clearly emerged during these years at CSD. Along with a developing curiosity, he built an even stronger work ethic than he had brought with him from his childhood. "Street smarts" were slowly replaced by knowledge, and a desire for his mother's approval gave way to an internal motivation to be the best in everything he did. This caring about his own education was a somewhat unusual trait for an adolescent. Determined to join his deaf peers who made the honor roll and thus were treated to dinners and movies, he became a diligent pupil. This motivation worked for him. Again and again, his name was among those who earned the best grades in the school.

There were few opportunities in those days for the boys and girls at the school to socialize. Bob was thus surprised one day when he received a handwritten note that said, "I like you." The 13-year old had no idea who had sent it to him. Then he got a second note explaining that he should go to the library. There, he met Wanda Long, a classmate, who confessed to having written the notes. Since dates were not permitted, they simply enjoyed each other's friendship.[15]

When the romantic attachment between Bob and Wanda grew, the dean of girls, Ruth Birck, concerned about this liaison, wrote a letter to Wanda's parents, apprising them of the unfolding situation: "Wanda has become very close friends with a young boy named Robert Davila. I feel that I should also tell you that Robert is a Mexican."[16] When Wanda showed Bob the letter, the young and innocent-minded boy interpreted the words literally. *Yes,* they had become attached. *Yes,* he was a Mexican. He completely missed the underlying message of discrimination. Wanda, too, was clueless.

Several years later, Bob developed a crush on an attractive teacher at CSD. Valuing her praise, he sought to earn it, constantly offering to clean the blackboards, sweep the classroom, and carry things for her. Naturally, Bob was upset to discover one day that another student, a popular football player, had been going to this teacher's well-to-do suburban home to do garden work. One day, Bob approached her after class, gathered his nerve, and told her that he would be happy to help her at home and wondered why his classmate had been chosen, rather than him. She looked at Bob and told him that she knew he could do that work excellently and that she knew he needed the money more than Howard, but she wondered how she would explain him to her neighbors.

Bob was bewildered. Bright as he was, he did not grasp the implications of her words. These were not "moments of truth" at the time. He remembered these events decades later—with more nostalgia than bitterness—and it was the process of reflecting on these experiences that made him realize the extent of the challenge he had faced as a young boy. It suddenly seemed to him, in adulthood, that being Hispanic and deaf as a child had been a double disadvantage.

ॐ   ॐ   ॐ

A moment of truth that *did* change Bob's thoughts about his identity occurred one weekend when he was invited to spend a few days at his friend and classmate Leonard Marshall's house. Leonard's parents were both deaf and lived near the school. Bob was completely awed by the surroundings as he and his friend rode the bus to the suburban neighborhood and then walked to Leonard's home. He couldn't believe that a deaf family had such a luxurious house. This experience galvanized within him the full realization that deaf people *could* succeed, and this epiphany drove him to immerse himself in his studies with renewed vigor. He had quickly discovered within a few short years that he was a good student; he developed and nurtured a fierce love of learning. He learned that education was the key to his success. Whether he was in the classroom, on the athletic field, or picking crops during summer "vacation," he worked hard—something that was expected by his family.

CSD was the gateway to a life Bob had never expected. He was so bright that he skipped several grades. By his senior year, 1947–48, he had not only excelled academically, but was also involved in a wide range of extracurricular activities. He enjoyed boxing and won in his weight class in an inter-dorm boxing tournament. Boxing was not a varsity sport, however, and although he had sought out an athletic niche, he was too short and too light to excel in the major sports. He nevertheless went out for the football team and invariably ended up on the bench, although he played enough football his senior year to letter in the sport. He did much better on the basketball and track teams.

His high school yearbook included a "Class Prophecy" about a visit to the White House to attend a ball. In the fantasized story written by Wanda Long, the future president of the United States was classmate Pat Kitchen. In

*Bob and classmates
at the California
School for the Deaf,
Berkeley, 1946.*

the story, Wanda the reporter learned that a famous boxer was also attending the presidential event and had recently knocked out the indomitable Joe Louis. The story continued:

> We crowded through to another group. All in the group were men, so this must be the boxer. Sure enough, it was, but Pat and I stood staring at him. We looked at each other—each knowing what the other was thinking—and both grabbed him by the arms. He was so shocked he didn't know what to do. "Ladies," he said, "I've had girls after me before but never this bad." As if we could help it, for this was Robert Davila, another classmate.[17]

Bob looked up to the deaf teachers at CSD. His concept of a role model had metamorphosed as he adjusted to a new culture and acquired languages. In the barrio, his models had been the characters he had learned about during the storytelling around the campfires—fictional heroes. Now, as a young man, he needed both deaf and Hispanic role models. But he could not find a deaf Hispanic to emulate in any way. He admired the Hispanic professional tennis player Pancho Gonzalez, and collected his photographs from newspapers.

Nagged with doubts about his future, he looked to his real-life heroes, his deaf teachers, who advised him on directions to take in his life. "I always had wondered what happened to deaf kids after high school," he recalled. "Then a deaf teacher told me about Gallaudet College in Washington, D.C. [the only college for deaf students in the U.S. at the time]. It became an obsession with me to go there."[18]

His primary alternative, working as a printer, was not very attractive to him. Many deaf men were employed in this occupation and this was the trade Bob had learned at CSD in the two-track vocational/academic system then in place. In particular, deaf men were trained to be Linotype operators. The Linotype had been invented in 1886 by Ottmar Merganthaler, a German immigrant who had settled in Baltimore. It allowed typesetters to complete a full line of type rather than set type by hand, letter by letter. A Linotype operator worked on a ninety-character keyboard, not with individual pieces of type. Not only was the Linotype process much faster than setting type by hand, but it also helped publishing companies weaken the unions that dominated the older composing rooms.

Ironically, those unions had provided a safe-haven for the deaf men entering the field by ensuring high wages and excellent working conditions. Deaf men were often trained and hired as Linotype operators because of the perception that they could more easily concentrate on the task in a noisy, busy print shop. The Linotype machines themselves were large and incredibly loud, and it was thought that deaf workers would be immune to the noise and thus be perfect for the job. Typically, deaf men would move to a community with a small local newspaper for experience and entry into the union, often leaving their families behind. Once possessing a union card, their safety net, they would return to their own cities to work at large urban newspapers, reuniting with their friends and family and earning a very decent living.

But with the spread of computer technology in the 1970s, reporters typed their own stories on computer terminals and submitted them electronically to editors, who then sent the revised copy to phototypesetting machines. Linotype operators were laid off. By the late 1980s, most newspapers had closed their composing rooms and literally thousands of deaf men lost their jobs.

Had Bob not taken the path that prepared him for college, he would have ended up as a Linotype operator in a local composing room. But he wanted something more. With the support of the school staff, he envisioned his future with clarity—a future that included going to college and becoming a teacher.

In his senior high school yearbook entry, Bob identified his favorite subject as literature. His pet aversion was "long lectures." His weakness was "sports." His classmates remembered how "he kept us in stitches most of the time!"[19] "Collecting clippings" was recorded as his hobby. Most of his newspaper clippings were of Pancho Gonzalez, the tennis professional. Gonzalez was the eldest of seven children, whose parents had migrated from Mexico to the U.S. in the early 1900s. He had a troubled adolescence during which he taught himself to play tennis, surprising many at the age of 20 when he won the U.S. amateur championship at Forest Hills in 1948.

Bob emulated Gonzalez by surprising others with his ambition. He had been erroneously identified as an aspiring Linotype operator, but actually wanted a more academic profession. "I, Robert Davila," he declared in the "Last Will and Testament" that the senior class collectively issued, "do hereby bequeath and bestow my position as sports editor [of the school newspaper] to Jerry Cunningham, and my ambition to be a Linotype operator to anyone who wants it."[20]

Bob graduated in the spring of 1948 at the precocious age of 15. Because of the associated travel costs, no one from his family attended his high school graduation. Although lonely that day, he had grown used to being on his own.

He bravely took the next step in his upward journey—the once far-fetched dream of attending college.

CHAPTER 4

A Rough Start

T HE IRONY OF BOB'S DEAFNESS opening the doors to a bright future was not lost on him as he looked back, decades later. "My deafness was actually a blessing in disguise....I had opportunities that my brothers and sisters didn't."[1] His mother so fully appreciated the capabilities of the CSD teachers that she later told Bob that she had wished CSD would accept his hearing brother, Ray, so that he would be blessed with the same quality schooling. Bob thought of this all his life. "It is a sad commentary that the plight of minority children sometimes can be addressed only in the event of a catastrophe or extreme happening."[2] Thus, in terms of his education, Bob was actually fortunate to have become deaf since he was provided this singular opportunity in his family to receive an excellent education. His brother Ray, although he was hearing, never had the opportunity to complete his schooling since he needed to work to support the family.

The perception of deafness as a blessing in disguise is indeed enigmatic, yet it is one shared by many deaf people in different contexts. While the onset of deafness has made life difficult for most deaf children, in some cases it has opened doors of opportunity and enabled children to escape a life of poverty.

When Bob enrolled at Gallaudet in the fall of 1948, there were 250 students attending the college, including hearing graduate students who were in the teacher preparation program. The Gallaudet faculty was so small that the same professor taught such diverse subjects as Latin, American history, psychology, and methods of teaching reading. Bob's family did not need to pay tuition, a lucky break considering that they certainly could not have afforded his college education.

Gallaudet was a government-sponsored institution where individuals with disabilities such as deafness could receive funds to further their education through the Vocational Rehabilitation program, at no cost to their families. The federally-funded Vocational Rehabilitation system in the U.S. was established in 1920 by an Act of Congress primarily to assist in the rehabilitation of individuals with physical disabilities, especially those injured in World War I. In the 1940s the system was expanded to include individuals with developmental delays, emotional problems, and other disabilities. One focus was to support training programs; thus deaf students who were eligible for vocational rehabilitation services could also receive tuition assistance to enable them to attend Gallaudet College.

Gallaudet then was a very different college from the Gallaudet University we are familiar with today. At the time Bob entered, members of the faculty were not required to sign. The groundbreaking work of William Stokoe recognizing American Sign Language (ASL) as a language was not published until the 1960s. So spoken English was the primary language of instruction, and Gallaudet in 1948 had few deaf faculty and administrators.

Bob was the first Hispanic student at Gallaudet. During the next two years, several other Hispanic students enrolled, including Ramón Rodriguez from Kansas City, Dolores Ramirez from Arizona, and Art Montoya from New Mexico. Bob's ethnic background didn't seem to matter to his classmates. If anything, Bob felt different because of his poverty.

Though he doesn't recall encountering any overt discrimination, Bob constantly was reminded of his family situation simply because many of his peers came from more affluent families. He often would go on long walks off-campus, sometimes even trekking into neighboring Maryland, to collect bottles along the roadside. He would carry them back to campus, take them to the dormitory basement, wash them, and then deliver them to a grocery store for small change refunds. As he explains:

> My pop bottle business was known only to myself and to a few guys who just happened to walk in when I was washing the bottles in the basement. And that was for essentials, not spending money per se. Not entertainment, but basics like paper, pencils, etc. School supplies were not provided.[3]

ॐ ॐ ॐ

Like most of the incoming students, Bob was placed in the "Preparatory Year" program to give him an extra year to prepare for the more rigorous work that occurred at the baccalaureate level. To prepare for advanced study

Bob taking a Spanish grammar class at Gallaudet College, 1951.

on the college level, Bob took geometry, algebra, social studies, art, and physical education. He was also taught how to use library resources.

While at CSD, Bob had taught himself to read and write Spanish well enough so that when at home during visits, he could help his mother translate something from Spanish to English. His older brothers were away in the service during wartime and Soledad became dependent on him to interpret. He recalls, "It was also a cultural thing to communicate to my mother exclusively in Spanish."[4] Now at Gallaudet he was able to formally study Spanish. Since he had grown up hearing and speaking it as his first and dominant language, he knew the words and syntax, but had never learned to read or write it fluently.

Bernard Bragg, a freshman and Bob's roommate during his prep year, was already an extraordinarily talented student actor and immersed in theater activities. Bernard got to know Bob quickly and was impressed with his curious mind and keen interest in anything that came his way—whether it was sports, education, or politics. As Bernard would recall decades later, his roommate "talked incessantly and still does, only a bit more economically. Perhaps he says the same thing about me. He is unafraid of sharing his viewpoints on a lot of things, but always straightforwardly."[5]

The pair shared many trials, tribulations, and joys during their college years. In a strange coincidence not devoid of irony, Bernard would go on to teach at Bob's alma mater (California School for the Deaf, Berkeley) after graduating, while Bob's first teaching job after college was to be at Bernard's alma mater (New York School for the Deaf, White Plains). Bob and Bernard's successive career paths were very different. While Bob pursued administrative positions in schools and the government, Bernard went on to a successful career in theatre and show business.[6] One was destined for public service, the other for the arts.

Despite having different interests, the friendship between Bob and Bernard remained strong long after both men had graduated from Gallaudet. "We have argued, joked, teased, and laughed at each other's expense—but always with respect and support for each other in the pursuit of our respective careers," Bragg would later say in describing the special bond the two shared.[7]

ॐ ॐ ॐ

Bob officially became a college freshman at age 17 in the fall of 1949. In those days, students did not choose a specific major. He hardly gave a second thought to being so young and already in college. By now he knew how to be a self-directed learner and was ready for almost any challenge that came his way. Despite a busy academic schedule, he once again immersed himself in activities, clubs, and athletic teams. He was a good three years younger than most of his peers, but he had learned at CSD how to deal with others. He knew that older students, in particular, were sensitive to age differences and could feel less capable intellectually, thus resenting younger students joining their classes. He had learned to cope as a late-deafened boy thrust into environments where the majority of his friends were born deaf. He was street-wise and knew how to earn peer respect.

Bob mastered English so well that he became a feature writer for the Gallaudet monthly student newspaper, *The Buff and Blue*. Bragg also was a *Buff and Blue* reporter, writing columns with Frank Turk, a spirited young man who also later became a leader in the deaf community. "Oh Yeah!," a column Bob co-authored with his classmate and good friend Bettie Dunn, offered an informal and often humorous view of campus life, displaying a side of Bob usually reserved for only his closest friends. He and Bettie thought collaborating on the column was great fun. Bob had volunteered for the column because he wanted to improve his writing ability. At the same time, he enjoyed the prestige of being among the elite group of more capable writers associated with *The Buff and Blue*. Through the newspaper work, his fraternity, and involvement in organizations, he developed leadership and interpersonal skills and thus passed through the college social scene without difficulty.

The cocky freshman with a ducktail haircut often walked around campus with a pack of cigarettes tucked in his rolled-up shirtsleeve. One day, he was scrutinizing the newly arrived students during the line-up where the preparatory students ("preps") were chosen by the undergrads as "Little Brothers" as part of the mentoring program. There he saw an Hispanic prep—Ramón Rodriguez—who had come to Gallaudet directly from the Missouri School for the Deaf. Ramón was older than Bob. His first impression of Bob was that he was still a kid and he was surprised to see him in a college environment:

> This was my first encounter with Bob Davila, dressed in a bright-colored outfit that no one would dare wear unless he were on a golf course. We actually met nose to nose! After a close examination of each other, we exchanged information about ourselves. He couldn't understand how I ever came from Kansas City, Missouri. I recall him saying, "We Mexicans are either from California, Arizona, New Mexico or, heaven forbid, Texas. That is where you are supposed to be from!" After that, we became good friends.[8]

Bob and Ramón learned that they had many things in common, especially their Hispanic heritage and work ethic. They both had begun working at a very young age to help support their families. Ramón recalls, "Bob told me that he had learned about the seasons and geography by traveling up and down the coast and by the fruit the family was harvesting."[9] Like many Hispanic deaf students who attended schools for the deaf, Ramón had never learned Spanish fluently, even though his parents were fluent. Like Bob, Ramón was interested in reading and sports.

One afternoon, Bob and Ramón were strolling down H Street in Washington, D.C. and came upon a pawnshop. The proprietor was hanging a nifty-looking navy blue blazer in the window. They asked him to bring it down for inspection, and they both tried it on for size. It fit them both as if it were tailor-made for them. The college boys haggled the price down from $22 to $16, but when they emptied their pockets of bills and coins, all they had was a little over $14. The proprietor complained that it was "robbery," but let the boys "steal" it for the money they had piled on the counter. As Ramón recalled:

> The issue then was who was going to wear it first. We flipped a coin and Bob won. He looked very Ivy League as he walked back to Kendall Green. We didn't know it, but it was the beginning of a three-year battle over who would wear (and dry-clean) that blazer. When Bob graduated from Gallaudet it was well-worn, and he left it to me.[10]

℥   ℥   ℥

Bob's most significant "moment of truth" in his freshman year occurred when his need for more spending money led him to a foolish prank that almost got him expelled from Gallaudet. One evening, in a move of uncharacteristic poor judgment, hoping to collect some easy change instead of walking miles picking up bottles, Bob and a classmate broke into a candy machine on the first floor of their dormitory. Afraid of getting caught in the hallway, they lugged the machine to the men's bathroom, where the glass front of the machine shattered. A senior classmate came in and caught them in the act of filling their pockets with the candy and planning to retrieve the change. Bob begged the upperclassman not to report their transgression. He feared getting expelled since the college was very strict about such behavior. To their dismay, the senior appeared to have no sympathy for Bob and his friend, and explained that it was his duty as a good student to report the incident.

All weekend, Bob agonized and fretted about being expelled for the prank, especially given how senseless it had been. Finally, he sat down and wrote a letter, fabricating some of the narrative to lessen the severity of the crime and delivered it Monday morning to the Gallaudet College business manager. The letter read:

> While trying to fix the frame [which the students had broken], most of the glass broke from the hammer blows. They decided to leave it alone, and to report it first thing in the morning so that nobody would think somebody had damaged the machine on purpose....Their mistake, they realize, was that they should have left well enough alone without having made things worse by trying to fix the machine.[11]

The manager read the letter, written by Bob and signed by both boys. He looked at Bob, nodded with understanding, and signed, "Those things happen."[12] Bob learned later that the upper classman had never reported him. He (and his friend who later became an ordained Episcopal priest) had learned a valuable lesson in life about taking such risks.

ã¢ ã¢ ã¢

Bob's sophomore year passed quickly. He continued to study, build friendships, and participate in athletics. During his junior year (1951–52), war was raging in Korea as he studied. Robert F. Panara was Bob's English teacher. One piece of fiction Bob wrote during that year was selected as the "Short Story of the Month" by his peers in the editing room at *The Buff and Blue*. In the story, "The Fix," Bob writes of a star college basketball player named Johnny Norris, who has no spending money. Down and out, Johnny meets an unsavory character who offers him $2,500 to throw an important game against a rival team. The chemistry major desperately struggles with the temptation until he sees the sheer spirit of his teammates the night before the big game. Overwhelmed and resolute, Johnny runs two and a half miles to his coach's house that night and reports the attempted "fix."

Bob's story reflected the headlines appearing across America at the time, when probes into illegal betting on sports occurred regularly. In Bob's story, the surprise ending perhaps reflected some wishful thinking on the part of its author. Not only did Johnny's hard work and honesty pay off with a game win and with the arrests of the syndicated gamblers, but he was also awarded tuition assistance for the remainder of his education, relieving him of any financial burdens.

Bob and Ramón never went home for school breaks during their years together at Gallaudet. One Christmas break they learned, to their dismay, that the Gallaudet dining room was closed. Wondering where their next meal would come from, Ramón suddenly recalled how one of his old friends used to work for the U.S. Post Office during the holidays. Ramón and Bob made the chilly trek from campus to the city's main post office near Union Station and sought out a supervisor. Ramón remembered:

> We had never seen someone so happy. Before we could explain that we were looking for work, he ushered us into his office and instructed us to go down the street and pay $5 for a bond in order to work in the Post Office. Of course, neither of us had any money. So, we hit up Ed Scouten, a hearing man who had recently graduated from Gallaudet and who was the well-regarded prep English teacher, one of our favorites. After losing a coin toss, I was chosen to knock on Professor Scouten's door. The only time anyone would do this is when he or she was in serious trouble. We explained that any money he would loan us was simply an "investment" to be returned in several weeks.
>
> Scouten asked us how we planned to eat, and we had not thought that far down the road yet. Good fortune smiled down on us as he loaned us each $20. We started sorting mail that same day.[13]

After a few days, Bob and Ramón noticed that the post office was still short on staff and asked the boss if the office wanted to employ more deaf college students. They were promptly sent back to Gallaudet to recruit their classmates. By the end of the week, they had about 35 young men from the college working with them. The income not only kept them going until the end of the school year, it began a tradition. Each holiday season for years afterwards, a good number of deaf students found temporary employment at the Union Station Post Office.

The following summer Bob and Terry "T.J." O'Rourke, his old friend from the California School for the Deaf who had also come to Gallaudet, shared a small room. They worked together at an ice cream factory, cleaning out the vats coated with residue. They had to get into their bathing suits and crawl into the vats with water hoses and brushes. The temperature in the vats, however, offered a welcome respite from the heat typical of Washington, D.C. summers.

Dorm room selections were made according to student grade point averages. Because of his academic standing, Bob could pick one of the best dormitory rooms. He and Ramón roomed together for the next three years. Ramón always felt privileged that Bob wanted him as a roommate, but found the amount of Bob's smoking at times unbelievable. Bob would also bet on anything and everything. Like so many friends from Bob's childhood and youth, Ramón was also stunned by his roommate's ability to slurp a lemon or lime faster than anyone around. "It was amazing," Ramón still recalls. "He would just suck it down and it was gone."[14]

For several years, Bob dated Wanda Long, his CSD classmate, who was also attending Gallaudet. Although she was several years older than Bob, the girls could not stay out past 10 p.m. on Fridays and Saturdays and, besides that, no one had any money. Social life was thus largely limited to college-sponsored dances. Despite these restrictions, Bob found his college years a revealing learning period that shaped him in many ways. Gradually, as he began to spend more time with his buddies and discover that he needed more space, he and Wanda parted ways.

While at Gallaudet, Bob served as manager and scorekeeper for the basketball team under D. Robert Frisina, a hearing graduate student studying for his master's degree in deaf education who was earning his tuition and room and board by coaching the team. Although Bob had played basketball and football in California, he was too small to play on the college level and so instead focused on track and cross-country.

Bob was an outstanding track and cross-country runner, once described as "stepping away from everybody in the distance departments, namely 880, mile, and two mile."[15] He had become a member of the varsity track team during his prep year, earning a description in the *Buff and Blue* as "The speedy California youngster."[16] At this time, the students had to prepare the actual running track and care for the equipment. They rode to track meets in rickety buses. The prestige was in the fact that athletes attracted the attention of the college's women. In addition to this limelight was the

Bob excelled as a long-distance runner on Gallaudet College's track and cross-country teams as shown here in 1950.

qualification to get second servings in the cafeteria in what appeared to be Gallaudet's definition of a training table.

Despite always having a pack of cigarettes, the street-smart kid competed for Gallaudet as part of the Mason-Dixon Conference with such schools as Catholic University, Towson, Roanoke, Bridgewater, Randolph Macon, and Lynchburg. The other runners all knew Bob—he usually led the pack, losing only a few races in his college career.

ॐ ॐ ॐ

At Gallaudet Bob also discovered how professors and administrators can leave positive impressions in the minds of young people. At the time, a young man named Bob Lennan was one of Gallaudet's nine "Normals," a nickname derived from the "Normal School" program, which prepared teachers of the deaf. Lennan was a hearing student like all Normals. He remembered Bob as being a protégé of Dr. Powrie Vaux Doctor, a distinguished Gallaudet professor and editor of the *American Annals of the Deaf.* "It was quite obvious that Dr. Doctor thought very highly of Bob and viewed him as a student of great promise."[17] Lennan recalls. "Doc" especially encouraged Bob to become involved in a variety of activities. This paved the way for Bob to develop leadership skills.

Leonard M. Elstad, the president of Gallaudet College from 1945–69, was another individual who influenced Bob. Elstad was loved by colleagues

Bob began developing leadership skills while a Gallaudet College student, serving as a writer and sports editor for the student newspaper and as "Head Senior" in 1952–53.

and alumni and by deaf persons from all walks of life. He had a kind word for everyone. Bob recalled the days when grade cards would be distributed outside the mailroom and Dr. Elstad could be found mingling among the students offering a word of praise for good results and a word of encouragement for those who needed it. The president believed firmly in the purpose of the college and worked diligently to promote its needs and develop its future. Elstad traveled extensively to spread the good word about educational opportunities for young deaf persons at the college.

But Bob's own first attempts at political leadership at Gallaudet were quickly dashed. He ran for student body president in his junior year but lost to David Halberg by just two votes. He was disappointed. Halberg, a classmate from Connecticut, had been the standing vice president and appeared to be a shoo-in; Bob had only decided to run at the last minute but had gotten a good amount of support.

Halberg was a pleasant young man, extremely quiet, and rarely took sides on any issue. This gave him an aura of maturity, wisdom and objectivity. On the other hand, Bob was more outspoken about positions on issues he cared about, and brash on definite positions he thought the student body should take. This was especially the case regarding the paternalistic and overprotective attitude of the administration regarding student independence. Most of the students were over 21 years of age, but were required to observe weekend curfew hours. Women had to sign in as early as 10 p.m. Bob ran at the urging of some close friends, but he did not mount a campaign sufficient to get the votes to win. "Losing by two votes was a moral victory of sorts and put me on the path to leadership in my future associations,"[18] Bob said.

Bob's political aspirations did not cease with this defeat. On the contrary, he was eventually selected by his classmates to serve as "Head Senior," a position indicative of the respect he commanded both from his fellow students and the administration of the college. Elwood A. Stevenson, superintendent of the California School for the Deaf where Bob had graduated, wrote to him that spring: "Little birdie tells me that you are Head Senior. Quite an honor!" Stevenson, however, admonished Bob for not writing a single letter to him in the five years he had been attending college. "You owe something to us in California, but we are proud of you."[19]

CHAPTER 5
Bedazzled

THE SUMMER FOLLOWING BOB'S JUNIOR YEAR was spent at home in California. His brother Gabe, now a World War II veteran, was working in construction and attending college with support from the GI Bill, which was available to all World War II veterans. Bob, now 20 years old, found work at North American Aircraft, assembling fighter jets.

While socializing with his CSD friends one evening, Bob met an 18-year-old deaf woman named Donna Lou Ekstrom. Donna and her sister Betty, both from Seattle and students at the Washington School for the Deaf, were in Los Angeles visiting their sister, Ruth, who had married young, divorced, and had recently remarried. Bob immediately developed a crush on Donna.

Bob was the first deaf man whom Donna had ever dated. "He was gentle and a gentleman," she recalls. "I was very impressed. He was so nice that I had the feeling that he thought he was on earth for me alone."[1]

Bob, in turn, was enthralled by Donna's natural beauty. "She was very pleasant, had a dazzling and beautiful smile, and always seemed upbeat. She was great company and we enjoyed our times together."[2]

Since Bob was a college student, he couldn't afford to spend much during their dates. They took long walks, went to the beach, sat and talked, and went to the movies. "In short, we really enjoyed each other's company."[3] Bob recalls that Donna had an immediate positive influence on him. He learned to temper his desire for many things he liked to do so that he could spend more time with her. Until then he had liked to spend much of his time at the beach and go out on the town. He learned to put that in his past and started spending all his available time with Donna.

Bob and Donna depended on Ruth and her husband Bill to drive them around on dates. Bob didn't know how to drive. Whether it was a trip to the beach, a party at someone's house, or visits to the Los Angeles Club for the Deaf, they always had to be chauffeured. Because of this Bob would sometimes end up staying at Ruth and Bill's home, sleeping on the sofa in the living room.

About five months later, Donna moved to Washington, D.C. Bob had returned to Gallaudet in the fall for his senior year. Donna's mother had found a sponsor to take her in. The sponsor, Irja Konno, a deaf Gallaudet graduate, was working in a library and had an apartment of her own near the Gallaudet campus. Donna's sister Betty was also planning to go to D.C. to join her own boyfriend, Dick Amundsen. One of two brothers born deaf to hearing parents, Dick was a stocky 6′ 2″ and a terrific athlete. He and Betty knew each other from their years in the Washington School for the Deaf and started going together before she graduated.

Donna and Betty were now only a few blocks from Gallaudet College. Donna had done clerical work in California for a while and in Washington, D.C. she found a job as a file clerk in a drugstore chain headquarters. She saw Bob on weekends when she was off from work and he was free from class. Although her apartment was not far from the Gallaudet campus, this was long before the development of the TTY modem and so there was no easy way for them to communicate with each other during the week.

Who was this bright young woman with whom Bob was spending so much time? Donna Lou Ekstrom had been born in Balta, North Dakota, on July 11, 1934. Much of her family was congenitally deaf or hard of hearing. Her father, Rudolph, who was of Swedish descent and hard-of-hearing, spent most of his life serving as an interpreter for his family. He had two children with his first wife, a hearing son and a hard-of-hearing daughter. After his first wife died, Rudolph married Donna's mother, Inga, a deaf woman who had been born in North Dakota, the daughter of Norwegian immigrants. Together they had three daughters, all of whom were deaf. Ruth, Betty, and Donna attended the North Dakota School for the Deaf before the family relocated to Seattle, where they then transferred to the Washington School for the Deaf. Donna's parents had always wanted her to go to college, but she could not imagine being apart from Betty, from whom she was inseparable. In 1952 in Washington, D.C., Betty wanted to work rather than attend college until she and Dick Amundsen could marry, and Donna had decided to work as well. Years after her own marriage, Donna realized that separation from her sister had been inevitable, and regretted not having taken advantage of the option to go to college, a choice that remained rare for women of her generation.

That summer of 1952, Bob experienced several "moments of truth." He realized his need to abandon his adolescent ways and take more responsibility as his relationship with Donna developed. In July, he received a letter from the Gallaudet College dean, Irving S. Fusfeld, which gave him additional food for thought about his future. It was not the first time that Bob had made the Honor Roll at Gallaudet, even though only 17 students (8 men and 9 women) had attained that distinction among the 209 students throughout the four classes and Preparatory Class. "In a sense," wrote Fusfeld in 1952, "such results are the mark of outstanding accomplishment, and we like to feel they mean more than academic achievement. To us they imply also that you have the power to assume a position of leadership, and we trust it will be a power that grows with the passing of time, regardless of the nature of the work you are called upon to do."[4]

A more personal "moment of truth" in this chapter of Bob's life occurred when Donna first met Bob's family in California. It was a very uncomfortable moment. No one knew sign language. They just sat and stared at the beautiful Scandinavian woman. She had little experience with hearing people and the Davilas had never encountered a congenitally deaf person before. The lines of communication were not established that day. Sadly, the Davilas and Donna never found a comfortable way to talk to each other.

This is, of course, a very common experience for deaf couples with hearing families. But it was made more difficult by the fact that even though the family was now largely bi-lingual, Bob respected his cultural heritage and would often speak to his family in Spanish. The family, in turn, would either speak back or write down what they wished to communicate in Spanish. The mix of Spanish, English, and American Sign Language that came into play during family visits never seemed to work well.

By the spring of 1953, after almost a year of courtship, Bob and Donna felt they could not wait any longer to be together permanently. They announced plans for a wedding after Bob's graduation. But Betty, still dating her high school sweetheart, Dick Amundsen, and financially better off than the struggling Bob, was horrified that so far there was no engagement ring for her sister.

Bob had saved all the money he earned that year during his traditional Christmas post office job. Additionally in March he had also held a part-time job at a printing company near campus, stacking *National Geographic* magazine bundles as they came off the press. He was earning about $30 per week while studying full time. Finally he used his hard-earned wages to buy an engagement ring, explaining, "I just knew she was it. She was intelligent, had a wonderful personality, and was the best-looking girl I had even seen or met or known."[5]

One night Bob took Donna out to dinner and surprised her with a ring that he had hidden in a napkin. When she opened the napkin and discovered it, she cried. She had never expected it.

After the unpleasant experience of divorce, Ruth, in California, had been understandably wary of how quickly her baby sister was falling for Bob. Yet Donna and Bob's daily letters showed a serious relationship blossoming. Ruth nevertheless encouraged Donna to exercise caution and not to rush into anything. But as soon as Ruth learned about the engagement, she endorsed the relationship strongly—a relief to Donna.

With his engagement to Donna happily settled, Bob set about finishing college so they could marry. Bob edited a column, "This Side of Sports," reporting on the college's sporting events and meetings of the Athletic Association. Even in this role he developed leadership skills.

In April 1953, for example, he evaluated a proposal to build two asphalt tennis courts opposite the gymnasium for the purpose of establishing an intercollegiate team. He attempted to remain neutral in his reporting of the proposal's support and opposition. "I shall not attempt to find fault in this because there is nothing wrong with playing tennis," he wrote. "In fact, I would play a set or two myself if I had a racquet."[6] But Gallaudet had a small enrollment, and Bob did not see the wisdom in the plan. Demonstrating his developing analytical skills, he asked his readership whether the college was ready to plunge into intercollegiate tennis competition.[7] This experience was good practice for a young man who would one day make decisions about proposals and the costs involved.

Throughout his senior year at Gallaudet Bob thought a great deal about what was next for him. At this time, employment for deaf adults was very limited. Not much had changed since he was a senior at CSD. Everybody he knew had become a teacher or a printer, and he was thinking of both (and he did work in both professions either full-time or part-time over the next 15 years).

A door opened for Bob in the spring of 1953. Bob Lennan interviewed for a position at the New York School for the Deaf at White Plains. While meeting with the superintendent, Daniel Cloud, an icon in the field of Deaf education, Lennan had put in a good word for Bob. Cloud's hearing daughter, Ann, was also in the Normal School with Lennan and knew Bob. During a subsequent visit to Gallaudet, Cloud asked to see Bob. He told Bob he was looking for a deaf teacher for a group of students who were not responding well to ordinary instruction.

Talking with Bob must have left a positive impression with Cloud because within a few weeks, Bob received a job offer. He was the first deaf student

Bob and Donna Davila were married on August 8, 1953. Theirs was a double wedding with Donna's sister, Betty, also getting married at the ceremony.

at Gallaudet to be offered a teaching position that year, especially significant in light of the open discrimination against deaf teachers in those days that had resulted from the longstanding preference for instructors who could teach speech to deaf children. Since the latter half of the 19th century, "oralism," the emphasis on teaching speech and speechreading (lipreading) had gained a strong foothold in the education of deaf students in the United States.

Bob earned his bachelor's degree from Gallaudet that spring. Due to the high cost of traveling and also to their not being comfortable in the deaf world, especially one where sign language predominated, Bob's family members did not join him on his long-awaited graduation day. Donna was there, of course. Bob graduated with many friends who continued to be part of his life.

Bob and Donna were married on August 8, 1953. It was a double wedding ceremony in Seattle celebrated with Betty and Dick. Bob's mother, now remarried, more out of convenience than of love, had begun managing a small restaurant. José María Romero, her new husband, was not in good health, but he was an excellent handyman. As a migrant farm worker from Mexico, he hadn't had much of an opportunity to get to know Bob, having joined the family after Bob had already left for school.

Certainly, Bob shared Donna's disappointment on their wedding day that none of his own family was able to attend. He had no answer for anyone who asked why his family was not at the happy occasion. He knew the reason was economic, but out of respect for his family, he shied away from discussing their absence. Bob didn't realize until much later that Donna's family had bought wedding gifts and put his family's name on them, to spare him the disappointment of not even receiving a token remembrance of this special day.

CHAPTER 6
Breaking Down Barriers

IN SEPTEMBER 1953, Bob began his career as a teacher at the second old-est school for the deaf in the United States—the New York School for the Deaf (NYSD) at White Plains. It opened its doors in 1818, about one year after the American School for the Deaf in Hartford was established. Of the campuses on which the NYSD has resided, perhaps the most beautiful and memorable campus was the 37-acre property in the Fort Washington section of Manhattan. Surrounded by the scenic "Fanny's Woods," NYSD acquired its nickname, "Fanwood School" to which it is still often referred, even though "Fanwood" is now located in White Plains. Enrollment consisted of both boys and girls through elementary school, but only boys stayed through the secondary school years. The Lexington School for the Deaf in Manhattan also consisted of both boys and girls through elementary school, but all older students were girls. Fanwood sent its older girls to Lexington, and Lexington sent its older boys to Fanwood. Bob was assigned at first to teach the younger boys, and ultimately taught mathematics and social studies in the high school for 14 years.

Before Bob arrived, friends at Gallaudet who had attended Fanwood—Bernard Bragg, Allen Sussman, and Sulemein Bushnaq—warned him that the kids there were a rowdy bunch. This was almost certainly compounded by the fact that the boys no longer had to wear military uniforms. Some had visited the Gallaudet campus during Bob's years there and he remembered how they would often get into disputes with the college students. The Fanwood kids had established a reputation in Bob's mind as rabble-rousers.

Thus, Bob was apprehensive when he entered his first class in the high school program and saw before him a group of 19-, 20-, and 21-year olds who were considered academically delayed. He himself was barely 21 and, in

55

fact, months younger than several students in his class. But he certainly wasn't about to tell them that. Bob had learned at CSD to hide his age, and this strategy served him well at Fanwood.

A classroom incident helped to enhance Bob's stature among the rabble-rousers. One day, while Bob was handing out papers one of the boys noticed the old tattoo on Bob's wrist. The kid imagined that it was a gang symbol. He had learned that Bob grew up near San Diego. He told his friends and all of a sudden, the other kids sat forward and paid attention when Bob began class.[1]

But this was also a moment of truth for Bob. The tattoo on his wrist was a vestige of his days in the barrio, something he had tried to hide by wearing long sleeves for a while. Although it helped him connect to the students at Fanwood in this way, Bob realized that it was unacceptable in an academic environment. It was time to have it surgically removed. It no longer represented the man he had become.

Over time, Bob had a profound impact on some of his students. One of the so-called "rowdy students" was Dominick Bonura. Dom was a child of deaf parents, a fluent signer, an outstanding athlete and a class leader, and at times, a self-admitted class cut up. He was, however, not overly interested in academics, and fully expected to be, like his deaf father, a Linotype operator at the *New York Times*. But Bob sensed immediately that Dom was a bright student and a potential leader, and thus challenged him to improve his English skills so that he could go to Gallaudet College and further his education. Dom did go on to Gallaudet College and earned his degree. He later earned a master's degree in educational administration from California State University at Northridge (CSUN), and became a nationally recognized leader in deaf education and the Deaf community. To this day, Dom gives Bob, one of *his* first deaf teachers, credit for inspiring him to become an educator and community leader.

Bob had moved to the Fanwood campus in August, three weeks after his wedding. Without any money, the young couple decided it was best for Donna to stay with her parents in Seattle and work for several more months until Bob could find appropriate housing in White Plains. Superintendent Cloud generously offered to let Bob and Bob Lennan live at the school until they could find housing in the community. Both young men apparently overstayed their welcome, however, because one evening, about a month after their arrival, Cloud recommended that they expedite their search for housing. By Thanksgiving, Bob had borrowed money, found a place to live, and sent train fare to Donna so that she could join him.

Throughout his years at CSD and Gallaudet, Bob had developed keen observation skills and learned from everyone around him. This continued at Fanwood. During his first year of teaching, he learned that Gallaudet College President Leonard M. Elstad was scheduled to come speak to a group of parents and students at the school. However, a violent hurricane on the Eastern seaboard closed down most public transportation in the area, and everyone assumed Elstad, despite driving by car, would not be able to make it. Just in case he did, Bob, along with a few friends, showed up at the scheduled time and location. Despite the storm, Dr. Elstad arrived completely unruffled at the appointed hour, set up his equipment, delivered his presentation, courteously answered questions, then got in his car to drive back to Washington, D.C. that same evening because he did not wish to miss an important meeting on campus the next morning. That dedication impressed Bob and strengthened his own sense of commitment as a professional.

Keen observation skills did not lead immediately to self-confidence, however. Bob, like most of the teachers at Fanwood, was utterly intimidated by Superintendent Dan Cloud. The stern superintendent was so feared that when teachers saw him coming down the hall, they would try their best to disappear into the first available open doorway. One time, to avoid the approaching Cloud, Bob entered a broom closet by mistake. Much to his embarrassment, Cloud opened the door and admonished, "What are you doing in there?"[2]

The other first-year teachers, including Bob Lennan, who taught across the hall from Bob, and Lou Fant, the son of deaf parents, were also wary of Cloud's authoritative style as they sought to find their way as fledgling educators. Fant, fluent in sign language, was destined to be known for his work with the National Theatre of the Deaf and his masterful sign language skills. Along with veteran teachers Taras Denis and Des Philips, they had lots of good times together.

During one weekend camping trip, Bob and Lennan, as scout leaders, took a group of students up to Lake George, rented canoes at Bolton Landing, and set off for Big Turtle Island, which was to be their campsite. It was a windy day and the surface of the lake was rough. Bob had no experience with canoes and became concerned about their safety, but they made it to the island after a long, hard paddle into the wind. The feeling of safety, however, did not last long. On their way back to school, the transmission in Bob's car became stuck in second gear, making the trip home a nightmare.

≈ ≈ ≈

Dan Cloud had brought the three-tier academic system from the Illinois School for the Deaf to White Plains. This meant that oral, signing, and hard-of-hearing students were taught separately. Bob taught the signing students a mix of subjects for four years and when Cloud saw his ability to teach mathematics, he assigned Bob to teach both English and mathematics in the high school program. He taught those subjects for five years.

He held a second job while teaching at Fanwood, working as a Linotype operator at the *New York Times* to earn a few extra dollars and offset the high cost of living in Westchester County, one of the nation's wealthiest counties at the time. After a full day of teaching, he would drive down to the city to work the night shift along with his fellow teacher, Taras Denis, whom he knew from his days at Gallaudet. As Lennan reflected, "I was absolutely amazed by his stamina and his determination to better his financial situation. Teachers certainly were not well paid at the time."[3]

In 1957, Lennan was offered a position at the California School for the Deaf in Riverside, which had opened only a few years earlier. Bob had hoped to land a position there, too, so he and Donna could return to his home state. However, he predicted that, as a deaf person, his chances of getting a teaching post were rather slim compared to those of Lennan, who was hearing. As Lennan, who relocated to California, recalled, "His prediction proved to be right and we parted company."[4]

After teaching at Fanwood for four years, Bob realized that the field of educating deaf students was in transition. Only recently had deaf professionals begun to take more control of their own destinies and demonstrate their need to level the playing field through higher degrees and upward mobility. It would be years before other deaf men and women would pursue such educational opportunities, and even longer before teaching posts would be filled by deaf people in significant numbers.

Donna and Bob settled into the community of Elmsford, New York in Westchester County. Located a few miles from school, the one-mile square village is midway between White Plains and Tarrytown. Its name had been inspired by a mammoth elm tree, nearly 30 feet in circumference, which had been a landmark since Revolutionary War days. Donna became one of the first deaf persons ever hired by the *Reader's Digest*, and worked in Pleasantville, about 15 miles from where they lived. She worked for almost three years until their first son, Brian, was born in December 1956.

Soon after Brian's birth, they found a babysitter and Donna returned to work. However, the experience was a valuable lesson in economics. Babysitters in the area were very expensive and Bob and Donna discovered that the arrangement was not only inconvenient, but also a losing proposition because the babysitter cost almost as much as Donna was bringing home after payroll deductions. So they decided that she would be a full-time mother and home-maker. Donna stayed home for several years. Later, she learned to use the new automated technology that replaced hot metal typesetting in newspaper composing rooms. She worked part-time for a few years for the *Patent Trader*, northern Westchester County's leading newspaper located in Mt. Kisco, until it was agreed that she was needed more at home than at work.

Brent, their second son, was born in April 1960. Both he and Brian were hearing. Throughout the White Plains years, they were "regular" boys, participating in various activities, such as sports and Boy Scouts. During this period, Bob, Donna and the boys also made a few trips to the West Coast to see relatives. After their wedding, Donna's sister Betty and her husband Dick had settled in Eugene, Oregon, and he worked at first in the lumber mills where his father was an official. Later Dick turned to printing, an occupa-tion he continued after a move to the Bay area in California. They had three children, one deaf, one hard of hearing, and one hearing, and had settled in Fremont before Bob's former school, CSD, moved to that city from Berkeley. During the time their deaf and hard-of-hearing children were in school, they commuted to Berkeley.

Visiting family remained difficult for Bob and Donna for financial rea-sons, too. They had to scrimp and save so they could travel to the West Coast. Yet, as Bob remembers, it was worth it despite the communication challenges: "Whenever I have been there to visit, I have been showered with love and at-tention. My reunions at home, especially in adult life, have been wonderful family gatherings."[5]

When their two sons reached adolescence, Bob and Donna decided that the family's economic needs and saving for the future were more important than spending every hoarded dollar to visit family. It was difficult to be away from their close-knit families for long periods at a time, especially for Donna. As for Bob, since he had experienced separation while at CSD and at Gallau-det, and although he missed his family the need to see them was not as urgent.

Bob never did return as a full-time resident to his home state, even though he was offered a position at Riverside after he had begun his graduate studies in 1960. At this time in history, a master's degree in deaf education was a status symbol. Relatively few teachers earned master's degrees, and only a handful of deaf teachers had done so. At the time, most deaf teachers taught in vocational departments, since the general feeling among almost all superin-tendents and principals, predominantly hearing, was that deaf persons could not successfully teach academic subjects. In addition, since the field was still primarily one of oral education, "good speech" was seen as a prerequisite for a classroom teacher in most schools.

Bob began studying for his master's degree at Hunter College in New York City in 1960. Founded in 1870, Hunter is one of the oldest public colleges in the country. Bob and Taras Denis, Brian's godfather, both began studying there with no interpreters or other support services, as Bob explains:

> It was very difficult. I had to beg my classmates for permission to put carbon paper under their notes so I could get a copy. In return, Donna would type up their notes and I would give them copies of their own notes neatly typed at the next class. One time I got an A and my notetaker got a B. Next semester, I asked him again for the same arrangement and he told me to go to hell. Well, that was OK. I grew up knowing you win some and lose some. The idea has always been not to lose them all![6]

One day, when one of Bob's classes at Hunter was dismissed, he saw José Santana, a blind man, walk quickly to the door and turn around and fingerspell, "There is a deaf man in this class and I would like to meet him!" Bob introduced himself and learned that José worked at the New York Institute for the Blind in the Bronx. "Believe it or not," Bob reminisced later, "the thought that went through my mind when I saw him was 'I've found my interpreter!'"[7] And in a way he did. Bob sat next to José and watched his blind friend fingerspell salient information presented in the lectures. In turn, Bob would tell José what he saw on the board at times. The two of them became very close friends. Bob remarks, "To this day, he calls me his brother." When José's daughter, Janet, got married, Bob was asked to be the best man, but he was able to beg off as "too old." José went on to earn a doctorate at Columbia and later enjoyed a distinguished career at the University of Puerto Rico.

Most people were supportive and enthusiastic about the educational aspirations of Bob and his friend Taras Denis, which were not typical for deaf persons at the time. The two of them enjoyed taking classes together and sharing many experiences. One evening while driving home together from Hunter, "Chico," as Taras called Bob, exceeded the speed limit. Taras recounted:

> All of a sudden we saw a police car coming from behind with flashing lights. Bob pulled over and told me not to say a word and just show that we were deaf. We had used that excuse successfully several times in the past. The cop came up to the driver's window and Bob pointed to his ears, and the cop said,

"Oh, you can't hear?" He then started signing! His family was deaf. We got the ticket anyway.[8]

Studying hard at Hunter, Bob completed his master's degree in Special Education in January 1963. He did not see a reason to participate in his graduation ceremony the following spring. His family was not there. "I didn't want to go through the anguish of experiencing that alone, even though Donna would have been there for me, of course," he rationalized.[9]

In the spring, Bob joined the typographical union, finished the school year, and spent the summer working for the *New York Times*. He started the new school year in September 1963 with a feeling of relief that his studies would not compete for his time anymore—for the time being.

Bob's experience during the tragic assassination of President John F. Kennedy in November 1963 demonstrated his ingenuity. It was not easy for a deaf person to understand television in those days. There was no access through interpreters or captioning. Nor were there any telephone relay services or other federally-mandated services available. The whole nation, hearing and deaf, remained riveted to the television set during the chaotic weekend following the assassination. Bob and Donna, like most other deaf parents, had to depend on their children to interpret as much as possible. In the Davila home, the children were too young to fully appreciate the historical implications of the weekend's events. Bob remembered:

> Donna and I stayed glued to the set and as events unfolded, such as the police station shooting of the alleged assassin by Jack Ruby, we were not able to follow events with full clarity in every situation. Our sons were not able to help much because they were too young to grasp the meaning of every announcement being made, so we set up a relay message system that sent one of our sons to a neighbor's home with a note asking for an explanation here and a clarification there, etc. We decided that we would try not to excessively impose on any particular neighbor so we rotated inquiries among five or six neighbors and would remind the boys not to go back to the same house with another note until all the others on our list had been queried. We just assumed correctly that everyone was glued to the set, too.[10]

Even communication *within* Bob's family was sometimes tedious. During their early years the boys only spoke English. They didn't even learn fingerspelling. According to Brent, his father never pressured them to learn sign language. It wasn't until he was six years old, during a family trip to Maine, that Bob presented the boys alphabet cards and challenged them to learn fin-gerspelling. "If you do, I'll give you fifty cents," he said.[11]

Donna wore hearing aids and used them as well as possible to com-municate with her sons. The boys eventually used sign language with her, but she knew their voices and it was very easy for her to understand them. Even though the family had little money, every Christmas there were gifts and there were nice birthday parties as well. "I'll say this," Brent reflected, "my mother was always there for us. It didn't make a difference if she was deaf because she could drive; and she would always take me and my friends places if we wanted a ride."[12]

Bob's absence, however, sometimes put a strain on the family. Brent, who played a lot of basketball, baseball, and football, remembered, "When he could, my father would always try and make time to go to the games. I know it was difficult for him because there were a lot of games he had to miss."[13] Brian, too, sensed his father's absence during these early years. He grew close to his mother and he "kind of became the man of the house."[14]

Teletype-telephones (TTYs) had still not come out and deaf people had yet to realize independence in terms of telecommunications. During the 1960s Bob and Donna had a regular voice telephone in their house and their older son Brian, like many hearing children of deaf parents in those days, felt the burden of having to make many phone calls for his parents. "I can remem-ber not even understanding what I was talking about," Brian recalled.[15] Brian also would sometimes accompany them to the doctor in order to interpret. When his brother was not around, Brent would take on the responsibilities. Brian remembered:

> It was difficult at times. In Elmsford, which was just down the street from Fanwood, I was about seven years old and had to get directions by telephone to help my parents get to New York City. So then I had to give mother the di-rections and when the person on the phone said take the third left, to me every curve in the road was a left turn! We never got there. The phone calls were the only time that I realized; this is something my friends don't do.[16]

Brent rarely thought about his Hispanic heritage. Nor did he consid-er his parents as having any disability. "I didn't know any other way so to me that was perfectly normal."[17] Because the boys rarely saw relatives, they consequently heard few stories about their parents. As Brent recalled, "Over the years before I got married, I would have girlfriends, and I was really sur-prised to see how much people would cherish the family gatherings and get-

Bob and Donna with their sons Brent, and Brian, 1962.

togethers and so forth. We never had that."[18] In fact, while living in Maryland, Ramón Rodriguez spent enough holidays with the Davilas that Brent "thought Ramón Rodriguez was my uncle for the longest time!"[19]

Brent remembered a trip to Carlsbad, California in 1970. By that time Soledad, Bob's mother, owned a pool hall and the boys loved hanging out there during the visit. The boys' great grandmother was also still alive, although very frail. But such contact with Bob's family was very rare.

Up until 1963, Bob had viewed his studies at Hunter as a task that had to be accomplished. There was not much else to it. It was not an exciting challenge or a dream of his—just a necessity. However, once his master's degree was completed he soon began viewing his future from another perspective. He dreamed of launching a career journey unparalleled in the field of deaf education.

This dream intensified when a very important byproduct of a federal study affecting the education of deaf children was released in 1965—the "Babbidge Report." A Congressional commission, headed by Homer Babbidge, then president of the University of Connecticut, had been brought together to study educational services for deaf children. The commission's report stated that the American people "have no reason to be satisfied with their limited success in educating deaf children."[20] There was the challenge candidly stated—and some educators, including Bob, set out to effect changes in the field.

At Fanwood, Bob saw several opportunities to take leadership roles. In 1967, he made an impassioned pitch to be considered for a vacant supervisor's post in the elementary department of the Fanwood School. Dr. Roy Stelle, from the Illinois School for the Deaf in Jacksonville, had taken over as headmaster of the New York School. Stelle, a gentle giant of a man, recognized Bob's potential as an educational leader and appointed him to the post. He was likely just as impressed by Bob's assertiveness as he was with the younger man's initiative in getting his master's degree at Hunter College at his own expense and without interpreting services.

With this appointment Bob became one of a very small group of deaf supervisors in the country. He held that position for three years and was responsible for the performance of 20 instructors and 125 students, developing curricula, coordinating staff training, and overseeing the development of program strategies to respond to individual needs. In 1968, his work as a teacher and supervisor was rewarded when he was honored by the Fanwood School with the "Teacher of the Year" award.

Then in 1969, Bob helped establish the New York School for the Deaf chapter of the Junior National Association of the Deaf (JNAD). Founded in 1961 to develop interest and leadership among young deaf students in state associations and/or deaf organizations, JNAD provides deaf and hard-of-hearing students in grades 7 through 12 with opportunities to develop leadership skills and demonstrate citizenship. Bob organized and conducted a workshop on "Student Apathy." He saw JNAD as "the brightest star on the horizon" in terms of its potential impact on young deaf students and its ability to become a driving force for bettering the status of deaf people.[21]

ॐ ॐ ॐ

Bob began to dream of pursuing a Ph.D. Since his graduation from Hunter College, a doctorate had remained on his mind as the next logical step in his career. But his sons were young and he had a prestigious position at Fanwood and a nice, though small, home in Elmsford, so Bob held back for awhile. He had been at White Plains since graduating from Gallaudet. Going for a doctorate would require a lot of time and money. He had neither, and with a wife and two small sons, he could not make any rash decisions. The pay at Fanwood was meager and Bob had sought other means of income over the years, holding part-time jobs at the *New York Herald Tribune* and the *New York Times* as a Linotype operator. After receiving his master's degree and serving as supervisor, he knew he was capable to move up in administration, but the principal at Fanwood was about the same age as Bob so his chances for promotion there seemed slim. Donna also knew that Bob would never be happy if he gave up his dream for a doctorate and she understood its importance.

This was also the beginning of a new era for deaf educators in general. Previously, only a handful had worked in administrative and supervisory positions. Consequently, national conferences of educators had so few deaf participants that they were not concerned about interpreting services. When the first Symposium on Research and Utilization of Educational Media for Teaching the Deaf was held in 1965 in Lincoln, Nebraska, no more than three or four deaf educational leaders attended. This dearth was not just due to a lack of deaf people in senior administrative positions; only those who had travel funds available were able to participate. Within 15 years of that first symposium, however, several dozen deaf educators were attending the annual conference, reflecting the increased opportunities that had resulted from self-advocacy and activism.

Both during and after his studies at Hunter, Bob earned extra academic credits. These included graduate level summer courses at the Institute for Teachers of Mathematics funded by the Media Services and Captioned Films Branch of the Department of Education in 1964 and 1965. The following year, he studied curriculum development at Ball State University. In 1968, he spent the summer focusing on instructional graphics at the University of Tennessee's Southern Regional Media Center for the Deaf, and in 1970, he researched programmed instruction at New Mexico State's Southwest Regional Media Center for the Deaf.

In New Mexico Bob was mugged one night while walking on campus to mail a letter to Donna. Donna, Brent, and Brian were in California visiting Donna's sister Ruth and her family at the time. Bob gave up his watch and wallet to the robbers, losing his license and credit cards. Donna was very upset by the incident, but thankfully Bob was not harmed. Donna wondered how Bob, without a license, could drive West to pick them up after his studies were finished. Shortly afterwards, however, the wallet was found with the license intact. But his money was gone and a photo of Donna was also missing. Bob tried to make light of it, telling her that the thieves "had good taste" in taking her photo, but she was not amused.

ᡝᡃ ᡝᡃ ᡝᡃ

At this time, interest in the application of media and technology to K–12 programs for deaf children was expanding rapidly. Gil Delgado, who had joined Gallaudet College's teacher education faculty shortly after Bob graduated, was also of Hispanic descent. Delgado had made rapid progress as a leader in the field of educating deaf students. Bob first met him during visits to see his friend Ramón Rodriguez at Gallaudet. Bob and Ramón looked to Delgado as *un padrino*—a godfather. Gil already had many Hispanic connections, especially in Sante Fe. After working as a teacher and principal at several schools for the deaf in California, Delgado worked in Washington, D.C. with John Gough, who had been the director of the Department of Education's Media Services and Captioned Films Branch since 1959, and Mac Norwood, a deaf man who was destined to become in the director of this branch in the years to follow. Delgado was always on the lookout for promising deaf Hispanics. He had met Bob numerous times at professional meetings and had taken an interest in his career aspirations as they became friends. He encouraged Bob to try for promotions, to take more courses, anything that would help him get ahead.[22] Whenever the Media Services and Captioned Films Branch sponsored workshops or meetings or initiated new projects, Delgado made sure Bob was among the participants.

The Media Services and Captioned Films Branch spent years negotiating a fellowship program to train specialists in deafness and educational technology at the doctoral level. During the summer that Bob was in New Mexico the announcement of the new program at Syracuse University came out. After consulting by mail with Donna, Bob made the decision to apply.

Up until July, when Syracuse was chosen for the doctoral program, Bob had only taken Gil Delgado's suggestion that he consider studying there half seriously. Few deaf persons had pursued doctoral degrees in the past, and this became Bob's primary motivation. As he remembers, "The idea of a [Hispanic] deaf person earning a doctorate [also] enthralled me. I wanted to be that person."[23] Yet, "People laughed at the idea," he recalls. Bob's wife Donna was a major supporter of his resilience. She encouraged Bob to not give up the idea of pursuing a doctorate, telling him, "I know you will never be satisfied if you don't do this." When Bob learned that Gallaudet Dean Richard Phillips, who was also deaf, had earned a doctorate, he was inspired.

It was a frantic task for him to obtain the long-distance references he needed and take the tests required for admission to the doctoral program. When his summer program in New Mexico ended in early August, Bob traveled to California to meet Donna and their sons. After Bob's arrival, he and Donna stole away for a weekend in Las Vegas to celebrate their wedding anniversary. It was nearly 100 degrees and, with no air conditioning in those days, they decided to wait until the early evening to start the drive back. Still in Las Vegas, they both felt sleepy. Donna moved to the back seat to take a nap so that she could help drive later. On their way, Bob fell asleep at the wheel. He woke up as the car rolled over several times, plunging down a ravine, and finally coming to rest upside down.

Bob is convinced the move to the back seat saved Donna's life. There were no seat belts in those days. He first felt his limbs to see if he could move out of the car. Turning off the ignition as he felt something dripping on his face, he realized he was unable to move his body. His back was badly injured. Donna then kicked out the window, climbed out of the car and staggered through the brush to the highway, attempting to flag down a passing car. After several cars went by, finally a couple from Connecticut stopped to help her. The woman was a nurse and returned with Donna as the husband drove to find an ambulance.

Bob was in and out of consciousness several times while waiting for the ambulance. When they finally took him to the hospital, the staff would not accept him because he had no paperwork showing insurance or medical coverage. By the time he woke up again in a second hospital several days later, Donna had found someone to call Bob's brother Gabe in California, who had come immediately. The car that Donna had worked so hard to purchase with her own money was completely demolished. Gabe was amazed that Bob survived the accident.

Brian and Brent were staying with Donna's sister in California. Brent was only eight years old at the time, but he remembered the phone call informing the boys that there had been an accident. The boys remained with their aunt and uncle for about a week. When they finally went to the hospital out in the desert "in the middle of nowhere" (Barstow, California) the hospital officials would not allow the boys in the room. They were not yet 16 and could not see their parents. They stood outside the hospital window to see their father.

ຂ∙   ຂ∙   ຂ∙

One evening back in White Plains a few weeks later, young Brian approached his father in tears. He had to tell the truth. He had taken a can of coins given to him by his friends so that he could purchase some firecrackers in California. Brian had hid about $35 worth of coins under the car seat and he needed to repay his friends. Those coins were still in the demolished car on the West Coast. He looked to his dad for support.

This was another moment of truth for Bob. Listening to his son's story, he was reminded of his own mistake as a young student when he broke into the snack machine at Gallaudet. Now it was his time to make a quick decision and teach his son a lesson in life. He told Brian that he would pay off the debt, but "You will owe me the money."[24]

The story didn't end with that agreement. Bob paused a while longer and then said to Brian, "Son, I want you to try something. Write a letter to the police and tell them your story."[25]

Brian did just that—and within a few weeks the police responded. They had found the can of coins in the wrecked car, subtracted the cost for postage, and sent the boy a money order.

CHAPTER 7
Syracuse

THE MOVE TO SYRACUSE IN THE FALL OF 1970 was a positive experience for the Davila family. Though Bob, Donna and the boys knew that the primary reason they were there was for Bob to complete his doctoral studies, they nevertheless found their increasing time together a joy. Prior to the move, Bob had always been engaged in earning extra income, which, not unlike his own father, often kept him away from home and the family. Now in Syracuse, he was more confined, away from familiar surroundings and friends. Despite the demands of his studies, Bob spent much more time with Donna and the boys. Even though they missed their friends, the family fused together in a way they had not done previously. Bob rediscovered his family and became much closer to his sons.

Bob had always gone above and beyond what was expected of him professionally, sometimes to the detriment of other aspects of his life. By the time he arrived at Syracuse University, he had already accumulated 42 credits above those required to earn his master's degree. This he had done by taking optional courses at a variety of schools, including New York University and New Mexico State University. Now, as he walked across the Syracuse campus, he certainly did not look his best. Bob remembered his arrival shortly after the automobile accident: "I stuck to my plans and appeared at Syracuse in a green jump suit over my cast, looking like a maintenance man without a broom. That was my inauspicious beginning to doctoral studies."[1]

During the first semester, Bob struggled to follow what was being discussed in his classes and to interact with professors who did not have any prior experience working with deaf students. There were several classmates who knew sign language, but since doctoral programs are very competitive, Bob knew he could not expect his classmates to interpret for him and still be able to follow their own studies. During the second semester of this first year, Bob struck up a conversation with Professor Donald Ely and asked him whether there was any money in the Department of Education grant for interpreter support. Ely looked into it and shortly afterwards told Bob the good news that he had found money for part-time assistance. But because the funds were very limited, Bob had to be selective, requesting an interpreter only for significant speeches by prominent visitors, special classes such as course reviews, and for study groups before exams. After the first year, Ely was able to acquire funds from the Department of Education for ongoing, but not full-time, interpreter support. However, Bob still had to be selective. He never had a full-time interpreter to work with him. Desiring to maximize his communication access, he also taught fingerspelling to some of his professors, including Ely.

The Davilas found a comfortable apartment complex in Liverpool, New York, a suburb of Syracuse, near Onondaga Lake. During the winters there, Bob and his sons discovered ice fishing and other winter sports. Brian, the older son, developed an especially great love for the outdoors, including hunting.

One morning, about a month after the family had finally settled in their new apartment, Brian and Brent came running into their parents' bedroom. A blizzard-like snowstorm had struck and Bob, Donna and the boys got into a festive mood, knowing that the family would be stuck at home together. They sat down at the kitchen table and began debating the plans for the day. The boys wanted to go sledding. Donna wanted to go to the lake. Bob was more than willing to take a day off from his studies. In the middle of the discussion the boys heard the doorbell ring. Bob answered the door and saw a man bundled up in winter clothes. It was the school bus driver. "Are your boys coming to school today or not?" He knew the Davilas were new to the neighborhood—and not aware that school was rarely closed for weather conditions. The boys were crestfallen. It was the family's introduction to Upstate New York winters.

For extra income, Bob brought with him a "travel card" from the typographical union of the *New York Times* and took on part-time employment as a Linotype operator at the *Syracuse Herald Statesmen*. Because he quickly found that he needed weekends to do library research for his courses, he gave up that work after a few weeks. Donna got a job as a typesetter operator and took a midnight shift so Bob could be home with the boys while she worked. With all the snowy weather in Syracuse, Bob worried so much about her that after about a year, they decided to just supplement their modest income from the fellowship with drawings from their savings. By the time his studies were over, two years later, the savings were gone. Bob and Donna thus had the nervous experience of starting all over again financially.

ə❧ ə❧ ə❧

In 1970 Alvin Toffler published *Future Shock,* describing ways people could cope with the unprecedented rate of change initiated by new technologies. At the time, educators of deaf students were just beginning to meaningfully explore instructional television, captioned films, and multimedia approaches. Educational technology had taken root as a field of study involving the development, utilization, and evaluation of processes and resources for learning. Among the pioneers in the theory and practice of educational technology design was Professor Ely, chairman of the Department of Instructional Technology at Syracuse. When Bob began his studies there at the age of 38, Ely was working on his book *Teaching and Media: A Systematic Approach,* which was published in 1971. Ely also took an interest in the applications of media in classrooms for deaf learners.

Syracuse required a semester-long internship experience and Bob decided on an opportunity at the University of Nebraska at Lincoln. George Propp, a deaf friend who had earned his Ph.D. at the University of Nebraska, was for quite some time the only other deaf person in the nation who could carry on a worthwhile discussion about educational technology with Bob. George had become the coordinator of in-service training in the Media Development Program for the Hearing Impaired. George admired Bob and considered him one of the best interns the program had ever accepted. Through this internship, Bob and George solidified their friendship, which had been born of their parallel experiences.

Bob also had chosen Nebraska over a number of other attractive internship sites because of Bob Stepp, a professor of education who had a reputation as a pioneer in the use of technology in teaching and learning. Stepp, the father of a deaf boy, was the director of the Barkley Media Center at the University of Nebraska and director of the Midwest Regional Media Center for the Deaf, one of four federally funded media and technology centers serving deaf education programs around the country. Stepp had also been conducting the annual symposium on the Research and Utilization of Educational Media for Teaching the Deaf since 1965.

The Media Development Program, for its part, appreciated the interns. They were needed not only to assist with a six-week program to train educators, but also to help prepare myriad training materials that were given to those taking the course. Although University faculty had typically only met once with previous interns to schedule specific tasks, Bob immediately set up a workspace of his own. Stepp saw Bob as a young man with an agenda. He had arrived from Syracuse with a list of things he wanted to do, and he quickly started to address them upon his arrival. This was a characteristic that Bob soon became known for—he rarely arrived at a meeting or workshop without adding something to the agenda.[2] For some, this was a sign of his motivation; for others, it was an annoyance.

Stepp's annual symposium was attended by educators from around the country. Through these meetings, the many papers and demonstrations enabled schools for deaf students to remain current in their knowledge of the most recent educational developments. The technology explosion was just about to begin in deaf education, and Bob was convinced that the visual nature of technology could be effectively utilized to teach deaf students. Even something as simple as the overhead projector was superior to writing on a blackboard, which required the teacher to turn his or her back on the students. By sitting around the overhead projector in a horseshoe arrangement—a seating arrangement that became the norm in classrooms for deaf students—the students could both look at the teacher and the sentences that were written on the overhead and projected on a screen or wall. The use of videotapes and captioning was still in its infancy, but Bob and a few others recognized the potential of these visual means and advocated for the greater use of media and technology in classrooms in schools for the deaf.

During his summer 1971 internship at Nebraska, Bob participated in the annual symposium, the summer school, administrative workshops, and other projects. When George Propp picked him up at the airport, Bob was extremely upset because the airline had lost his briefcase, which contained a draft of a project document he was working on with three Syracuse classmates. He had planned to use any free time he could find during the summer to finalize the paper. It was a catastrophic loss for him and although the airline staff assured him it would be delivered the next day, the briefcase failed to materialize. Ever responsible, Bob sent an apology to his classmates and proceeded to rewrite the entire paper so the group could meet its deadline.

The next spring, after the fall term and winter in Syracuse, Bob returned to Lincoln, Nebraska for a symposium. George Propp picked him up again and took him to the downtown hotel where Bob customarily stayed. The clerk who checked Bob in held up his finger, indicating that he should wait a few minutes. When he returned he had the briefcase, missing for a good nine months. "Is this yours?" the clerk asked. While the conscientious doctoral student had completed the project paper on time, he did learn a lesson about making sure his name and permanent address were on his briefcase![3]

After this internship, Bob served on the advisory board for the Media Development Program for the Hearing Impaired in Nebraska for many years and was extensively involved in its annual symposia. Through his training in educational technology, he developed a passion for curriculum innovation. Consequently, be became attached to the Barkley Center at the University of Nebraska. Propp often involved Bob in projects, meetings, and groups investigating or reviewing mediated technologies. The center became very involved in training teachers in the use of technologies and Bob frequently participated as a presenter.

In Rochester, New York, a little more than an hour's drive from Syracuse, Dr. D. Robert Frisina had since 1967 led the establishment of a new college for deaf students, the National Technical Institute for the Deaf (NTID) at Rochester Institute of Technology (RIT). Not surprisingly, NTID also sponsored various meetings and colloquia on instructional technologies and the use of audio and visual media in the education of deaf children. During several visits to NTID, Bob had the opportunity to renew his friendship with Frisina, for whom he had served as manager when Frisina coached the Gallaudet basketball team back in their collegiate days. When Frisina learned that Bob was studying for his doctoral degree he was impressed but not surprised.

ẻ❦   ẻ❦   ẻ❦

The "moment of truth" for Bob during his Syracuse years related to how his studies had forced him to spend more time at home. It certainly brought him closer to his sons. It was at Onondaga Lake that Bob, Brian, and Brent learned about the harsh winters of the region. Taking up ice fishing during the first winter, they were oblivious to the dangers of exposure to the cold air. One winter day, Onondaga Lake had been declared sufficiently frozen to permit ice fishing. When Bob and his sons arrived, they saw cars and small planes with pontoons scattered on the lake's frozen surface. Anxious to reach the center of the lake, Bob pulled nine-year-old Brent on a sled to a good fishing spot far from the shore. Brian and Bob nearly ran to the spot where they wanted to drill a hole in the ice. As Bob began to drill with the awl, he looked down at Brent who was bundled up on the sled. As he recalls:

> My heart skipped a beat! Brent's face was blue and his lips were purple. I realized he was freezing and it was because I had pulled him across the ice in a wind for almost half a mile. I became very frightened and yelled to Brian to start running for the shore. There was a restaurant near where we had parked

the car. I picked up Brent and started blowing warm breath on his face and ran for the shore as fast as I could on the slippery ice with the boy in my arms. I finally made it to the restaurant where the waitress poured some hot chocolate and we gave it to Brent sip by sip, until his face became pink again.

The experience did not discourage 13 year-old Brian who took up hunting, fishing, trapping, and camping with great enthusiasm. His love for the outdoors included spending many weekends on camping excursions. Since he had Outdoor Survival training and years of experience as a Boy Scout, Bob and Donna were confident that he knew how to keep himself safe while enjoying winter sports. In December that same year, Bob arranged with a farm owner to allow Brian to go ice fishing by himself for his birthday. They negotiated a price for any trout the young boy would catch, levied by the pound. Prior to their arrival the farmer had drilled several holes, and while Brian was fishing Bob and Donna went to get some coffee for an hour.

Upon returning to the pond, Bob noticed a black mound next to Brian. To his horror, he found that his son was pulling up the fish almost as fast as he could re-bait the lines. Brian looked at his father with the happiest look on his face and signed, "This is my best birthday gift ever!"

Recalling his days in the math classes at the New York School for the Deaf (Fanwood), Bob estimated that there were about 30 or 40 dollars worth of trout in the pile. He wasn't sure he had enough money to pay for it and he had no credit card at the time. He and Donna silently communicated about what to do. Fortunately, they had barely enough cash to cover the bill after pooling every cent they had. Brian of course had no idea what was happening. The family rode home in a festive mood. Bob recalls, "Although the fish was expensive, the look on my son's face was priceless!"[4]

Brian remembered how his father realized at this time that over the first 15 years he had been missing out on his son's growing up. "He and I would go fishing because he knew I liked to go fishing so much," Brian recalled. But Bob also liked going out with his buddies. On the night before opening day of trout season, April 1, Bob had gone out to play poker and had stayed up all night long. Donna was angry with him because he had promised to go fishing with Brian. As his son recalled:

> He took me fishing and ended up sleeping in the car the whole time I was fishing. And it just so happens I was lucky that day and got my limit of fish where all the other old fisherman were getting stumped. I was only 14. When my father woke up, he was so proud that I had caught all these fish![5]

Bob and Brian also went on deer hunting trips together. They would either go for one long weekend or an entire week. Brian reflected:

> I guess because my father had had spinal meningitis he would lose his sense of balance. I didn't like using a flashlight in the dark and because he had no sense of balance he would make so much noise while walking through the woods because he couldn't hear. I would have to find a place for him to hunt and put him in his spot first so I could walk far away and find a spot for me where everything would be quiet![6]

Reuniting with his sons over this two-year period, despite the pressures from his doctoral studies, meant much to Bob. When he first began at Syracuse, he had no idea what he would do with a Ph.D. Bob just thought it was another level to reach. Donna was his "rock." She helped him tremendously, typing papers for his courses when he collapsed in bed from exhaustion. She would also often take the boys out so he would have quiet time to study. As he continued to foster his dream of taking a leadership role in the field of educating deaf students, he grabbed every chance he could to develop administrative and networking skills that would help him in his professional life. He also established many lifelong friendships and a fierce loyalty to Syracuse University athletic teams that has never faded.

Paul Peterson, a hearing Syracuse student who was studying with Bob while taking a short leave-of-absence from teaching mathematics to deaf students at the National Technical Institute for the Deaf in Rochester, recalled Bob as a "deceptively low-key chum with an iron will."[7] Bob was determined to finish his doctoral work in two years. Peterson remembers, "He was the most down-to-earth individual I ever ran into. He never talked much about his background, never put on a show for anybody."[8]

Bob's dissertation, completed in 1972, was titled, "Effect of Changes in Visual Information Patterns on Student Achievement Using a Captioned Film and Specially Adapted Still Picture." In this study, Bob conducted one of the earliest research projects on the effectiveness of captions on learning. His pioneering study would often be cited in later years when colleagues wrote proposals to the government requesting funding. Along with other studies, Bob's dissertation research fueled interest within the U.S. Department of Education to increase funding to provide more captioned educational materials for deaf children. Today, deaf people see captioning not only as a vital tool for learning and access, but as a right recognized by federal law. However, many of those who know Bob are not aware of his groundbreaking work in this area.

Bob didn't request an interpreter for his graduation. He figured that he would be lost in Syracuse's expansive Manley Field House. So, yet again he chose not to attend his own commencement ceremonies. "Looking back, I regret that I didn't go," he confessed later. "I did not attend either of my graduate school commencements and I realized years later that they represented significant milestones in my life that I should have attended and enjoyed."[9]

CHAPTER 8
Giving Back to the Profession

I N THE SUMMER OF 1972, with his Ph.D. completed, Bob felt it was now time to begin contributing to the field of deaf education. His marriage to Donna, two children, graduate studies, and part-time jobs kept him so busy that he seldom looked back. His family life in the barrio had become a distant memory. With a degree in educational technology under his belt, he was indeed excited about the transformation taking place in schools. The Nebraska symposia had brought him into contact with many educators who were similarly enthusiastic about the potential of technology in deaf education. It seemed to Bob that there was a need for a new breed of academic administrator in the schools—and he was more than ready to apply the theory he had learned at Syracuse to the classroom.

The field of deaf education was in a state of flux. William E. Stokoe's work establishing American Sign Language as a legitimate language was gaining increasing attention in schools serving deaf children. The Babbidge Report had concluded in 1965 that the current educational system (with its emphasis on speech, speechreading, and use of residual hearing) was a failure.[1] Meanwhile, "Total Communication," a philosophy which not only took into consideration the heterogeneity of students and their preferred means of communication, but was said to have promise in the teaching of English, was being advocated by many educators.

Total Communication was still in its infancy in 1972. In 1968 the philosophy and instructional methodology of Total Communication had been introduced at the Maryland School for the Deaf. Until that time, teachers of deaf students used sign language only as a supplement, and in many programs it was allowed strictly with the students considered to be "oral failures," or who had multiple disabilities. English was still the dominant language—in fact, English was the only recognized language in schools for the deaf even though American Sign Language (ASL) was used in the dorms among students and of course among deaf staff.

David Denton claimed in his advocacy for Total Communication that by using signs in English word order and speaking simultaneously, along with amplification and speechreading, deaf students could acquire the tricky syntax of English. One underlying assumption was that it was possible to sign while retaining normal English syntax, and that speech and signs were compatible.[2] Although linguists were to later challenge and, in the eyes of many, disprove this assumption, the concept was very attractive to educators of the deaf who for many years had recognized that deaf children readily used sign to acquire and understand language (in the more general sense) and academic content, but continued to struggle with poor achievement when learning through primarily oral-based efforts to teach English.

Within this overarching philosophy, a technique known as "simultaneous communication" developed, a practice of combining manual components (signs and fingerspelling) with the use of speech at the same time, usually in English word order.

Having grown up hearing for his first 11 years, Bob naturally adopted the "simultaneous communication" technique, most often signing and speaking at the same time. His Spanish seldom entered the picture, other than through the distinct Spanish accent in his English pronunciations, a constant reminder of his linguistic background and heritage.

Bob and Donna had not anticipated the number of attractive employment offers that would soon come his way. They had planned to move back to White Plains with their family, where Bob would resume his career at Fanwood. The house they had temporarily rented out to a Fanwood teacher in Elmsford was ready for their return. However, numerous promising opportunities called for a re-evaluation of their thinking. Bob first considered an offer at California State University at Fresno to serve as chair of the deaf education program. In need of a Ph.D. for the position, Cal State officials enticed Bob with a full professorship and the promise of tenure after a year. The offer was very tempting, given that both his and Donna's families were located in California. At that time there were almost no other deaf individuals serving as faculty members in teacher preparation programs and certainly none as department chairs. To hold a position as chair would have indeed been another milestone.

During a visit to Gallaudet College, however, Bob ran into John Schuchman, the college dean, who also made him an attractive offer—to become an associate professor in Gallaudet's graduate school with the additional responsibility of reestablishing the undergraduate teacher education program which had been discontinued about 15 years earlier. Gil Delgado, now dean of graduate studies, was the driving force behind the effort to convince Bob to come to Gallaudet. Delgado had been watching Bob's progress as a deaf Ph.D. student working his way through Syracuse University and knew that Gallaudet would be lucky to have him as a faculty member. Delgado convinced Gallaudet to make a counteroffer—and Bob accepted. Gallaudet was his alma mater and he and Donna had many friends in the D.C. area.

Shortly after this, Donna returned to Elmsford alone and prepared the house for sale. She and 12 year-old Brent and 15 year-old Brian spent several months there as Donna educated herself about real estate by reading up on the topic. Their house was sold on the same day she put it up for sale!

After the family moved to Gallaudet in 1972, Bob became so engrossed in his work developing an undergraduate education major and teaching courses in that program that he was unaware of the political issues Gallaudet was facing in relation to parental dissatisfaction with Gallaudet's Kendall Demonstration Elementary School (KDES), a day school serving 125 students who resided in the Washington D.C. metropolitan area. One day while Bob was watching a televised news report he realized the extent of the problem. At the time, KDES had a student population that was nearly 90 percent African American, while the faculty was about 95 percent white. Parents were concerned that the cultural, ethnic, language, and parental education needs of the students and their families were not being adequately addressed. Bob knew that many KDES students were not high achievers and were not being accepted to good high schools, including the Model Secondary School for the Deaf (MSSD), also a demonstration school on the Gallaudet campus. Parents felt the administration was detached and uninvolved. When recruitment for a new director began, Bob was encouraged to apply.

The Kendall School actually predates the establishment of Gallaudet College. It is named for Amos Kendall, a journalist who held several federal government positions, including postmaster general under President Andrew Jackson. Kendall was the legal manager for Samuel F. B. Morse (of Morse telegraph code fame) when he donated land to support the establishment of a school for deaf and blind children in 1856. KDES and MSSD, along with Gallaudet, are authorized by Congress to function through the Education of the Deaf Act. Gallaudet operates the model schools through an agreement with the U.S. Department of Education.

In 1974, after only two years on the Gallaudet campus, Bob was appointed director of KDES. The responsibilities for this new position, however, became an "add-on" in that Bob never gave up his faculty appointment in the education department of the college. It was important to him as a professional educator, though quite a challenge while serving as director of the Kendall Demonstration Elementary School, to continue to teach and serve on Gallaudet faculty committees and earn his tenure and later promotion to full professor. There was no requirement that he do both and no extra compensation for doing so.

When Bob began his new post in late May, 1974, the first thing he learned as he arrived in his office was that his administrative assistant, a pleasant woman, could not sign. She had been at Gallaudet for 15 years. After months of working together trying to find a comfortable way to communicate, the administrative assistant resigned. Bob went to Carl Kirchner, the principal who had been Bob's first hire, and asked if he could borrow his administrative assistant, Fran Parrotta, who could sign. Bob was so impressed with Fran, however, that he offered her the post permanently. She was so capable and efficient that she freed him of many time-consuming tasks, which allowed him to visit classrooms, talk with students, teachers, and other staff, and make additional management changes. That was the beginning of a wonderful professional relationship that would last 18 years.

Bob also hired a secretary, Lynel Spencer, who came to work with him without any previous experience with deafness but willingly learned sign language to become a very dedicated employee. Lynel, too, would continue to work for nearly two decades with Bob as he took on new professional challenges.

ॠ ॠ ॠ

Busy as he was with his work at Gallaudet, this was also a time when his sons needed Bob for advice. Brian originally didn't want to go to college. Looking back on Bob's views on his sons' education, Brian summarized, "I guess as long as we were working and staying out of trouble that kept my father happy. He was concerned about grades. A 'C' was not really acceptable. We would get rewarded if we got good grades and it was always money. I guess money talks."[3] Brian remembered that when he completed high school his father had a talk with him:

> I wanted to be an auto mechanic. I can remember taking our family car engine apart in the garage and putting it back together because it needed a valve job. I was sort of like a self-taught mechanic. So it was a crisis of sorts when I finished high school. My father, being the first college graduate in his entire

family, felt that there was no way his son was going to be an auto mechanic. But he did compromise and that is when I took him up on his compromise. He said, "Do this Brian—just go and get the degree, and after you get the degree you can do anything you want, but you will always have that degree to fall back on." So I did go to college and get the degree and never did become an auto mechanic."[4]

Brian left home to attend the University of Maryland in 1974. Brent lived on the Gallaudet campus with his parents while attending high school in nearby Maryland. When a KDES construction project started up in the spring with Bob as the program officer overseeing the university's interests, Brent asked him if he could find a summer job at the site. Bob asked the head engineer, who was in need of construction laborers. The pay was good and no real skills were required, so Brent went to work for the contractor, Turner Construction. Later during the school year, he was hired part-time as mail room supervisor at Turner's K Street office, and when he graduated from the University of Maryland, he went to work full-time for Turner. He later became a vice president and construction controller with the company.

Brian heard about Brent's job and came over to see his father and ask whether he could help him get a construction job, too. Bob again talked to the head engineer, who joked about bringing on all the family because they needed laborers. Brian loved the work so much that he decided to go back to the University of Maryland after earning one BS degree to study for a second one in civil engineering. He became a director of special projects for a large engineering company in Silver Springs, Maryland, and also the owner of a cement company in partnership with his wife, Ruth, who is also an engineer.

Brent also recalled how he needed guidance about his college studies:

My father would say "Get the degree; put it in your back pocket because they can never take it from you." He never pushed me on what to major in college. He just said education first and sports second. It didn't matter what I did but school was first, then I could play baseball or basketball or whatever I wanted to do.[5]

Brent reflected further, "I will say this, we knew when dad meant business because we had that much respect for him. He never ever had to go any further than just giving you a stern look."[6] Brian added, "And then my mother got smart about that and then all she ever had to say was: 'Your father is real angry about this.' She always had to say his name so we would just stay in control."[7]

ə♭ ə♭ ə♭

By November 1974, Bob had prepared a position paper to share with the Kendall School faculty and staff. He had been hired to bring stability to the school community and he built upon the "Master Plan Report" previously defined by Gallaudet. He was faced with such tasks as developing a strategic plan and architectural designs for a new 125,000 square foot facility, recruiting minority teachers, establishing positive home/school relations and a new curriculum, and tying sign language skills to tenure awards. He candidly told the staff he would do everything in his power to assist the school to fulfill its mission; and that the chaos, frustration, and personal anxiety they experienced would continue, and, most probably, increase.

Three of Bob's strongest character attributes were honesty, commitment, and loyalty. Bob was so committed to these values for achieving the goals of the Kendall Demonstration Elementary School and the Model Secondary School for the Deaf that he unconditionally demanded them from his faculty and staff. They did not always respond enthusiastically, especially some middle level management staff who were not used to Bob's hard driving work ethic and his unwavering commitment not only to the schools' mission and his superiors, but to the children. There were many battles, and as a consequence some faculty members developed the perception that Bob had a rigid and uncompromising administrative style. But others were more accepting and understood that his style grew out of his intense commitment to education, the very process that had enabled him to earn advanced degrees and be in a position of authority at Kendall. His style reflected his desire to have each and every deaf child succeed through education as he had done. While he had many strong supporters, unfortunately the negative perception that some people held of his management style, fair or not, was to persist and follow him for many years.

In the midst of grappling with school politics, Bob never forgot that he was looked up to by many of the deaf children of color enrolled at Kendall. He had plenty of experience with deaf minority students at the New York School for the Deaf at White Plains and at Kendall, too, he was reminded of his own experience when young—few minority teachers for the children to hold up as "models," and few deaf teaches, minority or white. At Kendall, the children searching for a successful Hispanic deaf adult had to look to the director of the school.

Fina Perez, a young deaf girl from Guam, attended Kendall for awhile in the early 1970s. Her father, originally from Spain, was in the Department of Defense and the family moved around frequently. In 1975, Fina again enrolled at Kendall at the age of ten. She recalled her experience with Bob as an administrator there:

> It was a bit of a shock. Nearly all Black, a few white, and me. Back in Guam we all looked much alike, but here I was different and people looked at me. Then I met Dr. Davila—his skin was like mine, and he was Deaf! In Guam none of the teachers were deaf. He was also warm. He didn't keep himself separate from the students; he interacted with all of us. He would say to me many times over the next years right through high school at MSSD that I should think about going to college.[8]

With a predominantly minority enrollment, Bob nevertheless was undaunted by the challenge of raising the standards to give these children the opportunities they deserved. He was certainly no stranger to poor families and the special needs of parents to be able to support their children's education. As Bob worked on changing the policy that required Kendall students to compete for admission into the Model Secondary School for the Deaf, he also addressed the qualifications of the staff, especially their sign language skills. He told them, "It is in your best interest that you join with me in developing assessment procedures for determining competency in manual communication."[9]

Requiring competency in sign language was not an insignificant move—while many staff signed fluently, not all did. Total Communication was still relatively new and English was still the primary language of instruction, not only for the purpose of learning English itself, but in content areas as well. Assessment instruments or protocols like the Sign Communication Proficiency Interview or the American Sign Language Proficiency Interview had not yet been developed and the suggestion of formally assessing the sign language skills of teachers in a school for the deaf was a novel one, and for some, uncomfortable. In response, Bob established staff training programs in sign language at both Kendall and the Model Secondary School for the Deaf to support the staff in improving sign communication skills.

Bob took charge of Kendall at a time when the school faced increasing competition for enrollments resulting from the growth of suburban school programs in deaf education, which took away from Kendall's ranks. Public Law 94–142, the "Education of All Handicapped Children Act," had been signed by President Gerald Ford in 1975, the year after he became president. The legislation had just been passed, however, and local public schools had yet to establish strong programs or to hire adequate support staff. Most educators in schools for the deaf were either unaware of the potential threat to their schools or were aware of it but chose to think that somehow their schools would remain insulated from the national trend.

P.L. 94–142 mandated that all children with developmental disabilities, mental retardation, emotional difficulties, learning disorders and other handicapping conditions receive a "free, appropriate public education" (FAPE); furthermore, this education had to occur—regardless of the level or severity of their disability—in the "least restrictive environment" (LRE). The law applied to those between the ages of 3 and 21 and addressed key issues regarding the education of children with disabilities, including the provision of federal funding to the states to partially support special education services and establish of "individualized educational programs" (IEPs).

For over a century, deaf and blind children had enjoyed access to special state-run or state-supported schools, opportunities not available to other children with disabilities. In fact, at the time P.L. 94–142 became law, approximately 80 percent of all students who had a profound or severe hearing loss were educated in special schools. Every state in the U.S. with the exception of New Hampshire had at least one thriving school for the deaf, with many of the larger schools having enrollments that exceeded 400 students. Even deaf students who lived in the same city as a school for the deaf were enrolled as residential students and at best, went home only on weekends or during school vacations.

However, the general interpretation of LRE was that children with disabilities should attend the schools closest to their homes, being integrated with children without disabilities, whenever appropriate. Thus, parents who wished to have their children educated closer to home and who had "mainstreamed" their children as it was called, were now looking at alternative arrangements, and had a federal law which supported their efforts.

A key component of LRE was the categorizing of the continuum of services, with local public school classes defined as being the least restrictive and hospital and prison schools as the most restrictive. To the consternation of many in the deaf and blind communities, residential schools were placed toward the restrictive end of the spectrum, thus immediately saddling these institutions with implied poor standards and creating the motivation on the part of local education agencies to deny placement in these schools and to start local programs.

In general, parents of children who had high incidence disabilities (e.g., learning disabilities, behavior and emotional disorders, mild mental retardation, and communication disorders) were pleased to have their children in regular schools with boys and girls who were not disabled. To them, the social value of their children mixing with non-disabled children often outweighed academic expectations and goals, whereas parents of deaf and blind children often valued the acquisition of academic skills over socialization with non-disabled peers. For parents of children with low-incidence disabilities such as deafness, there was much greater dissatisfaction. There was also considerable consternation in the deaf community, which saw mainstreaming as a threat to their beloved schools for the deaf. The new law, and LRE in particular, quickly became heated topics in the field of special education and certainly in the education of deaf children, and would play a most important role in Bob's future.

Over the next two years, Bob immersed himself deeply in these issues. In 1975, he was elected president of the Convention of American Instructors of the Deaf (CAID). He held this leadership position for two years, guiding educators of deaf children through challenging changes. Then in 1978 he was elected president of the Council on the Education of the Deaf (CED), an organization which maintains standards for professionals in deaf education and evaluates university professional preparation programs.

Ə Ə Ə

Also in 1978, after four years as director of Kendall School, Bob was appointed by Gallaudet President Edward C. Merrill to the vice presidency of the college for Pre-College Programs. It was through his duties in that position that he first appeared before Congressional appropriations and oversight committees to discuss issues pertaining to the civil rights and education of deaf people and to help present and defend the Gallaudet College budget requests. Responsible for coordinating administration, policy development, long-range planning, and outreach, he represented both the Kendall Demonstration Elementary School (KDES) and the Model Secondary School for the Deaf (MSSD) as the college interacted with federal agencies and the public. He developed effective methods of service delivery; provided programmatic, personnel, and fiscal supervision; and managed a budget and staff which represented approximately 30 percent of the college's annual budget and work force.

KDES served more than 200 deaf students locally and MSSD more than 400 deaf adolescents from around the United States. Their primary enrollment area incorporated the District of Columbia, Maryland, Virginia, West Virginia, Pennsylvania, and Delaware. The schools had been mandated to serve as a national resource on education for deaf students and were charged

Vice President Bob Davila meeting with Audiology and Technical Support Staff to discuss new equipment at the Kendall Demonstration Elementary School. Courtesy of Gallaudet University Archives.

with developing, evaluating, and disseminating materials and techniques for use in schools and programs across the United States. Because of their broad missions and federal support, both schools were tuition-free.

The presence of the KDES and MSSD on the Gallaudet campus and the development of pre-college outreach programs brought Bob a status equivalent to that of a "superintendent" of a school for the deaf. This affiliation with Gallaudet made him potentially one of the most powerful deaf educators in the country. Deaf education was dominated primarily by hearing people, and from at least some perspectives, decidedly paternalistic. Bob strode confidently into this new leadership role, an energetic deaf leader in an era where there were very few deaf superintendents. In some ways he personified Total Communication with his preference for simultaneously speaking and signing, and with strong views as to how he thought not only the KDES and MSSD, but also all of deaf education, should move into the future. As he applied these strong views to effect changes, he predictably won the support of some, and alienated others. Nonetheless, during Bob's tenure as vice president for Pre-College Programs, those programs were substantially improved and Gallaudet assumed a position of national leadership in pre-college programming.

Bob's pursuit of his Ph.D. in educational technology had been a result of his fascination with the technological revolution occurring at that time and its potential impact on education. While overseeing the two model schools, Bob had ample opportunity to apply the knowledge he had gained at Syracuse. His mindset and its potential impact on education led to his embracing and upgrading technology at a level nearly unprecedented in similar programs serving deaf students, particularly in the areas of instructional television and computers. His training in educational technology had truly paid off.

He also applied the knowledge and skills gleaned from his work with the annual technology symposia in Nebraska, making sure a variety of classes, especially in science and mathematics, made full use of computers. To address literacy, he also implemented enhancements of the language curriculum, library and media resources to prepare students for work after graduation. A keyboarding class was included to prepare the high school students for college or direct employment. Bob also established a transition policy that assured that the elementary students could move into the high school unopposed. This change included improving the options to accommodate a wider range of student abilities.

Focusing on student development was another important part of Bob's work at the model schools. His Pre-College Programs encouraged students to take an active part in the world outside "Kendall Green" (Gallaudet's campus) by attending off-campus activities, such as theater and dance performances, where the use of interpreters allowed them to enjoy cultural experiences within society. Working with professional actors, musicians and hearing students from the Washington, D.C.-based Duke Ellington School for the Performing Arts, the high school students also performed popular musicals in sign language each spring. MSSD was fortunate to have outstanding faculty members in its theatre and drama program, namely, Tim McCarty and Eric Malzkuhn.

Bob knew that other schools for the deaf were in transition too, and many needed additional resources and technical assistance. He began to develop outreach services for them, often hosting regional meetings, providing in-service training at no cost for both schools for the deaf and public schools, and otherwise supporting the field of deaf education in general. The current Clerc Center and its national mission are an outgrowth of the process Bob started when he became vice-president for Pre-College Programs.

Fina Perez was one of the students who looked up to Bob. When she was in 8th grade, Fina's family had to move to St. Louis, and there was the question of where she would attend high school. She wanted to be home with the family, but at the last minute she agreed to stay in the dorms and attend MSSD. Fina recalled just walking over to Bob's house:

> I would ring the doorbell light and someone would come to the door—his wife or kids—and I'd ask to see Dr. Davila. Now we who lived in the dorms were not supposed to do that but I did, and he never turned me away. He would ask how I was and how my family was and we would chat a little.

His boys could sign and they would tease me. Looking back, I was so im-pressed that he was deaf. Dr. Davila never talked about being Hispanic or a minority. He played an important role in getting me into college.[10]

Bob recalled that, from the beginning, he was very interested in Fina and her family:

They exemplified the family unity, language environment, and support sys-tem that we in America strive to develop. Fina was a motivated student who bonded with me and through time I bonded with her entire family. The Perez family reflected the Spanish word *capacidad*, empowering support so critical to fostering a young deaf child to succeed.[11]

᪑ ᪑ ᪑

At the New York School for the Deaf at White Plains, where Bob had begun his career as a teacher, John Dean, president of the board of trustees, realized that there had never been a deaf, nor Hispanic, board member in the school's 170-year history. Bob was appointed to address this disparity, and he immediately impressed the board members with his expert knowledge of educational issues. His leadership in deaf education was expanding rapidly and, having been promoted from his faculty post at Gallaudet to become a program director and then a vice president, by 1980, two years short of his 50th birthday, Bob had essentially reached the pinnacle in his career.

Or so he thought.

That same year, amid the Cold War and the hostage crisis in Iran, Ron-ald Reagan had been elected to the American presidency and federal appoint-ments were being made. Bob's name was taken into consideration, and he was contacted as a possible candidate for a position as part of the incoming Rea-gan administration. A White House representative told Bob that if he was interested, he should come to an interview and bring a copy of his resume and other credentials. No details were provided him but, out of curiosity, he decided to respond to what seemed a rather informal and unbuttoned invita-tion. He could only wonder what was going on.

Bob had always been a Republican. He had voted for the first time when he was 21 years old while teaching at the New York School for the Deaf. Westchester County, where the school is located and where he resided, was a conservative district, which had further guided his political views. But Bob had never been very active in the Republican Party. This was the first time in his life that he would venture beyond private voting and commit to a political office. Nor had he given any consideration to leaving Gallaudet, especially since he was enjoying the prestigious office of vice president and the challenges associated with leading the model schools. However, he had always practiced a personal policy of not closing the door on any opportunity until given a chance to examine it in detail.

After much thought, Bob asked Gil Delgado, then dean of Gallaudet's graduate school, to accompany him to the interview as his interpreter. The meeting did not proceed in a manner either of them could have anticipated.

First, Bob and Gil went to a large hall in downtown Washington, D.C. that had temporarily been landscaped into numerous little office spaces, each one occupied by a young-looking interviewer. The young lady with whom they met took an immediate interest in sign language and the half-hour allotted for the meeting was consumed in animated discussion about signs and ended up being a quasi-sign language lesson for her. After 30 minutes, a monitor interrupted to let them know that their time was up. The young lady apologized and said that she was going to make sure that Bob's credentials went to the "right people"—he should be hearing from someone soon. Bob recalled:

> I left feeling that the session had not been a waste of time inasmuch as she seemed very enthusiastic and had promised to follow up. The truth of the matter is that I never heard again from anyone in the Reagan administration for the entire eight years they were in office.[12]

Soon forgetting the strange interview, Bob returned to his Gallaudet responsibilities. His national and international leadership activities brought more honors to him. He received the Leadership Award from the Gallaudet Alumni Association in 1983.

Few people know that Bob was the first deaf person ever to apply for the Gallaudet presidency. In 1982, the campus was shaken by Dr. Merrill's announcement that he would be retiring from the presidency of Gallaudet in 1983. The campus was alive with discussion and rumors about who would succeed Dr. Merrill. It was well known that Dr. Merrill himself was very keen on the idea of a deaf person becoming president of Gallaudet, stressing that "Gallaudet College will assist her graduates to break into professions where deaf people have never served before."[13] President Merrill thought that Bob was a likely candidate and on several occasions he talked to Bob and encouraged him to apply. He also thought that several other deaf professionals were ready for the challenge. And so, Bob did apply.

As the world would learn from later events, Merrill's sentiment was not shared by the board of trustees or its leadership. It soon became evident that even though he had support from several stakeholder groups, notably the students, he also had significant opposition primarily from hearing board members whose images of deaf people did not match reality. The board's resistance appears to explain why Bob did not advance in this search process as the only deaf candidate in the pool. He later reflected, "I applied because I was not privy to all these perceptions at the time and I believed that if a deaf person was actually selected that I would have a chance."[14]

While Merrill, as well as several people in the deaf community, suggested that a deaf president might be worth considering, there appeared to be no widespread support. One problem Bob had at the time was that his name was mentioned often and openly. Some board members thought that the decisions were being made external to the board, and this led to some anger. Another issue was, of course, the fact that Bob was deaf. While Dr. Merrill and many others supported his candidacy, there were many who still believed that a deaf person could not effectively be the president of a university. During the interview, Bob was drilled with questions and one of the interviewers actually got up out of his chair and paced the room, listening to Bob's voice from different locations, evaluating his ability to articulate orally. Bob very quickly realized after this interview that the board was not in the mood to give a deaf person that much responsibility. The deaf community was not ready for a protest such as happened five years later. Bob knew that his throwing in his name had been just a practice exercise for him.

Sure enough, Bob did not make it into the final pool. W. Lloyd Johns, then president of California State University at Sacramento, was named the fifth president of Gallaudet. However, Johns held the post for only a few months and resigned for personal reasons before he was officially inaugurated. The board of trustees then selected Dr. Jerry C. Lee, vice president for Administration and Business, in 1984 as interim president and he was subsequently installed as the college's sixth president without a new search process, thus effectively ending the conversation about whether a deaf person could serve as president of the world's only university for deaf people. Who could have predicted then that a similar scenario, this time played out in the eyes of national and even international media, would take place only a few short years later?

CHAPTER 9
Blessed and Tormented

"**I** WAS SURPRISED BECAUSE I WAS A TEENAGER and had never really gotten to hear my father speak Spanish," Brian recalled about a family vacation to Puerto Rico in the mid-1970s when his father had lost the keys to the hotel room.[1] Bob had gone around asking people in Spanish if they could help the family look for the keys. The experience was also an awakening for Bob. As he says, "It made me realize that it was important to me to find my roots again."[2]

He had never abandoned his Hispanic roots, of course. There always had been reminders of his heritage in both social and professional circles. Bob's friend George Propp remembered the Convention of American Instructors of the Deaf (CAID) meeting in Los Angeles in 1977 when a Mexican buffet banquet was served aboard the ocean liner *Queen Mary,* a tourist attraction docked at the Long Beach pier. The ticket price was a then-exorbitant $25 and several deaf friends who had congregated at one point during the banquet commented a bit negatively on the flavorless Mexican cuisine. Bob promised them a true Mexican fiesta the next day if they would meet him after the morning sessions. When they did, Bob took them down several blocks from the convention location to Olvera Street, where he had killed time as a kid while traveling to Berkeley. The restaurant was still in operation in the barrio district and, as Propp recounted, "We all had a lunch that was twice as copious as the banquet dinner and set us back something like $1.80, which I believe included beer."[3]

Bob and Gil Delgado also continued their close friendship, highlighted by professional trips to Spain, Argentina, Puerto Rico, the Dominican Republic, and Brazil. In the Spanish-speaking countries, they presented as a team, usually to educators. Neither Bob nor Delgado knew the sign languages of these countries and they met primarily with hearing persons. There were no deaf leaders like Bob to be found in these Spanish-speaking countries, and the hearing professionals were amazed to see Bob representing a college and holding such a leadership position. The fact that Bob also could speak Spanish was even more impressive. Bob, of course, faced this language barrier with his usual energetic style. Since he did not know their sign languages, Delgado interpreted spoken Spanish into American Sign Language.

During their first trip to Madrid in 1985, Bob was slated to give a presentation to an elite group of Spanish educators of deaf students. The evening before, he was practicing the presentation in the hotel room, reading it out loud in Spanish. Dr. Jorge Soler, a native Spaniard, and Delgado were listening as Bob came across the word *obstáculo* (obstacle) and pronounced it with the accent on the "u" instead of the "a." What Bob didn't know was that when pronounced in that manner, the word took on a vulgar meaning (*culo* being street Spanish for "ass") and should not be spoken in public. Bob turned around, completely puzzled over why Soler and Delgado were laughing so hard. Needless to say, the three of them found another word for *obstáculo* in Bob's presentation!

In Argentina, also in 1985, Bob was the main guest of a group of deaf persons in Buenos Aires for a *barbacoa* (barbeque). The dinner was held outside on a deck and the guests were served *morcillas*, or blood sausage, considered a delicacy in that country. Naturally, the guest of honor was given the first two *morcillas* with much flourish. A wary Bob asked Delgado what it was and was told, "blood sausage." Bob, being somewhat finicky about strange foods, smiled, thanked the chef and when no one was looking, pitched the sausages over his back to the street below.

Seeing none on his plate a short time later, his hosts were delighted that he was enjoying the dinner. They brought him more. The same sequence of events occurred with Bob tossing them and being given more. Bob remembers that the dogs on the street below the deck had a feast that evening.

Despite his wariness of some culinary items, gratitude for Bob's support of the Hispanic community came in many forms and from many voices. Perhaps one of the finest tributes he received was from the Spanish Association of Educators of the Deaf and Language Disorders, which recognized him in 1985 as the year's "Member of Honor." Bob was the first non-Spaniard and first deaf person ever inducted.

ॐ ॐ ॐ

Bob was happy that Gallaudet had installed tennis courts. When he was a student there, he could not even afford a racquet and the college had decided not to install the courts he had discussed as a sportswriter. Now, he eagerly played whenever time permitted. It was a nice escape for him.

Meanwhile, Donna was teaching sign language at the Model Secondary School for the Deaf. She had initially agreed to take the job for only a short time, but the allotted three months turned into years. In addition to teaching sign language, she evaluated faculty for tenure considerations with regard to their signing ability. During earlier years, Donna had not accompanied Bob when he left for his summer studies at various universities around the country. She had always wanted to be there when the boys came home from school and, since Bob's positions required him to be away from home a great deal in the evenings, she assumed the majority of the responsibility in raising Brent and Brian. Looking back at how the family had had to move around, and how the boys had attended a number of different schools, she was glad she had made the decision to spend substantial time with them.

After both Brian and Brent left for college, Bob, as vice president, was required to live on campus. Now, in the midst of Bob's overloaded schedule, which included international travel, he and Donna were nagged by the feeling that they had not spent as much time as they would have liked with their respective families. Since his aged mother, still living in California, was unable to continue with the restaurant she had run for many years, Bob sent her occasional financial assistance.

Brent had married Mary Jane Boyer a year earlier, in 1984. They had met in a sign language class as high school sophomores in Riverdale, Maryland. Parksdale High School was one of the first to offer sign language as an option in the foreign language department. Their meeting in this class was the beginning of a lasting relationship. They graduated the same year and attended the University of Maryland together.

Bob was extremely preoccupied by the required response of Gallaudet's Pre-College Programs to the National Commission on Excellence in Education's *A Nation at Risk,* an alarming federal report which claimed that American students were not being taught the right subjects and were not learning enough. The report had also expressed concern that many teachers were ill-prepared. Little had been done to improve the educational system, and notwithstanding advances in civil rights, most children of color were still doing poorly in school compared to their white peers. In addition, Congress appointed a Commission on the Education of the Deaf (COED) chaired by Frank Bowe to determine the state of education for deaf children as a follow-up to the 1965 Babbidge Report.

As a member of the Conference of Educational Administrators of Schools and Programs for the Deaf (CEASD)[4] for 14 years, Bob recognized the importance of this report. One of his first acts when elected as CEASD's first Hispanic and first deaf president in 1986 was to collaborate with Oscar Cohen, superintendent of the Lexington School for the Deaf, on writing a position paper, "Current and Future Needs of Minority Hearing Impaired Children and Youth," to be presented to the COED. The paper pointed out the deaf/hearing achievement gap, the gap between deaf children of color and their white peers, the dearth of professionals of color within deaf education, and the phenomenon of institutional racism within the deaf community. Deaf children of color were thus suffering doubly—as a result of being deaf and being members of a minority. Their math and reading levels were significantly lower than their white deaf peers and drastically below all their hearing peers. Yet, few people in deaf education were talking about this disparity.

During that fall of 1986, there occurred another moment of truth in Bob's life. Writer Philip Garcia from the Hispanic Link News Service discovered Bob and realized the potential of his life story. He asked Bob to draft some biographical material and he subsequently published it in the October 20 issue of *The Hispanic Link Weekly Report*. It was in this article that Bob stated boldly, "To be both Hispanic and deaf is to be blessed, as well as tormented."[5] In discussing his roles as a leader at a college and in the deaf community, Bob now publicly recognized that he was "inextricably a product of dual heritage."[6] Being Hispanic, he explained, means more than having a Spanish surname. Similarly, being deaf implies more than an inability to hear. "Hispanics share a common culture and language," he pointed out. "Deaf people, too, know the influence of indigenous social standards and a unique mode of communication."[7]

Garcia's article, titled "Robert Davila is Quietly Opening Doors," led to a ripple of publications in a variety of other Hispanic newspapers and magazines providing exposure of Bob's success to the public beyond the deaf education community. An issue of *El Hispano* revised the original article and published it with a similar title, as did *The San Antonio Express-News* and *The New Mexico Progress*. In an article in *Vista*, titled "Focus on Hispanic Americans," Bob described with some reticence his life as a pioneer in the struggle to overcome "the difficulties of being both Hispanic and deaf in an environment that is largely neither."[8] He acknowledged that he felt comfortable using three distinct languages: his native Spanish, American Sign Language, and English, which he considered his third language."[9]

There were few Hispanic educators following Bob's lead in attempting to effect change in the education of deaf children of color. He reported that hearing Hispanics formed a minuscule group of about 90 educators of deaf students. "But what kind of deal are Hispanics getting? Who is sticking up for them?" he asked. "People look at me as an exception. It shouldn't be that way." Bob emphasized that deaf children who come from Spanish-speaking families do not even have Spanish-language competence. He pointed out that, "It's not a question of bilingualism. Many don't have a language to begin with."[10]

Bob's own experience, as he described it, had always been "sink or swim." Now, in 1986, there were only 25 Hispanic students enrolled in Gallaudet—a disproportionately low number.

Bob emphasized again that at no time during his education did he have a Hispanic teacher, let alone one who was a deaf Hispanic. He acknowledged that his experience was painful at times. "It is important to appreciate your background, to feel good about yourself," he affirmed. Hispanics "have to be at the forefront, fighting for their rights, asserting themselves."[11] Bob recognized the need for change on various fronts. "My greatest hope," he asserted, "is that both groups—the Hispanic and the deaf—will come to appreciate each other and work together for all of us whose identities are firmly rooted in both cultures."[12]

ૐ   ૐ   ૐ

In 1986, Bob added to his laurels when he was elected president of the Conference of Educational Administrators of Schools and Programs for the Deaf. It was during his presidency that Bob met Susan Murray. CEASD and the Convention of American Instructors of the Deaf (CAID) maintained a national office in Washington, D.C., the costs of which were shared equally by both organizations as well as the *American Annals of the Deaf*, the official organ for both organizations. Murray was hired to replace the director of the national office, who had depleted the organization's funds. She came into a struggling situation and was able to keep the national office open and functioning for a short while, but Bob and CAID president Richard Steffan were unable to find a permanent solution. Bob went to see Gallaudet President Jerry Lee, who allowed him to hire Susan as one of his assistants. They decided to close the national office and an old friend of Bob's, a lawyer, provided pro bono support. This move by Bob essentially saved the two organizations. In the process, Bob and Susan established a working alliance that lasted almost two decades.

At Gallaudet, Bob was one of the few senior administrators who taught classes on a regular basis, although there were some years when he could handle just one course per year. Only a few weeks after Susan was hired in the fall of 1986, Bob asked her to cover his early morning graduate-level psychology class one day, as he would be out of town on business. He suggested that she use the time to familiarize the students with the professional organizations in education of the deaf, the major publications, and related issues. Susan recalled:

> I was pretty intimidated by him at that point and was afraid the students would report back to him if my lesson fell below the mark, so I prepared like crazy. I had a bad case of nerves that morning as I approached the classroom about 20 minutes early, but at least Dr. Davila wouldn't be there so I felt I could at least get through the session. WRONG! I opened the door to what should have been an empty classroom, and who was sitting there with a big thermos bottle in front of him and a grin on his face?[13]

Bob told Susan that his plans had changed and he did not have to go out of town after all. She offered her notes and transparencies for him to teach the class, secretly relieved, but he would have no part of it. Then, to make matters worse, he opened up the thermos, pulled out two styrofoam cups, and offered her a cup of steaming coffee. He looked so pleased to have this treat to offer that she could not even tell him that she absolutely hated coffee. She recalls, "Instead, for the first time in my life I gulped a big cup of strong black coffee. That was just the first of many times over the next 15 years that I simply completely followed Bob Davila's lead."[14]

Over the next two years, Murray learned to "read" Bob's administrative style very well. The Davilas had owned a townhouse in Ocean City, Maryland for several years but found little time to use it. Bob always looked forward to going there on vacation. He would talk about all the books he was going to read, all the videos he had packed away to watch, and how he was going to love taking it easy for two full weeks. At Gallaudet, his staff looked forward to it, too—until they realized that he never stayed on vacation more than a week. "It never failed," Murray remembered. "We would show up for work one week before his vacation was due to be over, and he would already be back in the office, arriving earlier than any of us, to boot!"[15] Bob said he loved the idea of "taking it easy," but, in reality, it was much too boring for him. It would prove to be a recurring pattern in his life.

During his four decades as a deaf community leader, Bob interacted with many other deaf leaders. American deaf community leaders pictured here are receiving recognition at the World Federation of the Deaf Congress in Japan, 1991. Left to right are Phil Bravin, Robert R. Davila, I. King Jordan, Merv Garretson, and Yerker Andersson with the Japanese host.

Thus, as 1988 approached, Bob reached a point of convergence in his identity as a professional. Heretofore, he had been highly recognized and respected as a leader in deaf-related organizations. Since he had left his home in the barrio in 1944, he had slowly drifted away from his Hispanic world. However, there were four powerful forces now tugging at him. First, the scarcity of deaf Hispanic professionals and the increased exposure Bob had received in the Hispanic professional community over the past two years had now provided him with a new frontier in his career—applying his skills and knowledge as an academic administrator to addressing the special needs of minority deaf children. Second, his firsthand experience with minority deaf children at the New York School for the Deaf at White Plains, the Kendall Demonstration Elementary School and the Model Secondary School for the Deaf had reconnected him to his past. Third, his experiences with Gil Delgado, especially with organizations serving deaf people in other countries, emphasized further the better opportunities deaf Hispanic children *could* have in the United States, and how unique Bob was as a deaf Hispanic leader, not only in his country, but internationally. And fourth, Bob's work with Oscar Cohen in the CEASD on the needs of minority deaf children held the potential to effect powerful changes in American schools if the position paper could be translated into procedures and policies.

CHAPTER 10

Deaf President Now

EVER SINCE THE EARLY 1960S when Dr. Ray L. Jones directed the National Leadership Training Program in the Area of the Deaf (NLTP) at California State University at Northridge (CSUN), there had been formal opportunities for qualified deaf persons to develop leadership skills. Many deaf men and women who participated in this program pursued successful careers as administrators in vocational rehabilitation programs, schools for the deaf, and in other services in the deaf community and deaf education. The dream of a deaf person leading one of the premier postsecondary institutions such as Gallaudet University or the National Technical Institute for the Deaf at Rochester Institute of Technology, however, was one that remained distant—until the spring of 1988.

Despite the success of NLTP graduates and other deaf men and women, there always seemed to be a message to deaf applicants for such positions. They "came close, but did not meet the requirements."[1] Bob had experienced that in 1983 when he was the only deaf applicant considered qualified for the Gallaudet presidency. He was among the five semifinalists, but did not make it to the final three.

When Dr. Jerry Lee resigned as president of Gallaudet in 1987, a period of great turmoil within the institution began. Although his administrative experience was predominantly over the Pre-College Programs, Bob felt highly qualified for the presidency. By 1988, he had held a high level administrative position there longer than any other deaf person, serving as vice president at Gallaudet for 11 years. "I have really grown in my position," he said in 1988, "made contacts, learned from my mistakes." And he admitted, "I have made a few. There is no other way I could have acquired my skills and knowledge except through the experience of having the job."[2]

99

Still, in his heart, Bob believed that his candidacy for the Gallaudet University presidency would be a political exercise in futility. When the search was first begun, there were many people who expressed their opinion that the time was right for a deaf person to lead the university. Bob believed that by not picking an acting president who was deaf, the board of trustees sent out a message. He reasoned:

If individual members still had concerns and reservations about the ability of deaf people to do the job, the best way to resolve that concern would have been by picking a deaf person as acting president, and see if they developed the ability to do the job. If they were willing to do it for Lee, why not for a deaf person?[3]

Years later, Bob expressed disappointment and anger that the hearing members of the board of trustees, while he was an administrator, appeared to have no real desire or interest in hiring a deaf person as president.

As a senior officer of the University, I had a lot of interaction with and reporting responsibilities to the board. I got to know them as individuals. All of the hearing members, without exception, knew little if anything about deafness or deaf persons; they rarely, if ever, visited programs on campus and appeared vulnerable without a battery of sign interpreters handy.[4]

Bob had spent many years representing the university to potential benefactors, as well as consulting with outside organizations to promote university goals related to universal improvement in the education of deaf students, monitoring compliance with University standards and policies within Pre-College Programs, completing internal budget and strategic planning, responding to Department of Education mandates and to recommendations from national advisory boards, and assisting in the development and implementation of University-wide personnel and compensation policies. He had also served as a member of the president's central administration and as chief administrator for media and technology programs, including the computer center, television studios, art and graphics production centers, and the media and telecommunication equipment distribution and maintenance center.

The initial field of 87 candidates for the Gallaudet presidency had first been narrowed down to 17, and after interviews with these individuals the field was further reduced to six. Along with Bob, there were two other deaf candidates, I. King Jordan, dean of Gallaudet's College of Arts and Sciences, and Harvey Corson, the superintendent of the Louisiana School for the Deaf and a member of the University's board of trustees. There were also three hearing persons: William Dill, president of Babson College in Massachusetts; Humphrey Tonkin, president of Potsdam College of the State University of New York; and Elisabeth Zinser, vice-chancellor of the University of North Carolina at Greensboro.

After the February interviews, Bob was cut, along with Tonkin and Dill. Bob was the deaf candidate with the most experience as an administrator on the university level. But his insider status and prior decisions as a manager at Gallaudet for 18 years had apparently eroded his support among his colleagues. "I have made decisions that have affected certain individuals," he reflected, "and those types of decisions always come back to haunt me. But that is my job. I have to let the chips fall where they may....I think being a minority member didn't help either."[5]

Understanding that racism, discrimination and prejudice do not require intent, Bob further explained his belief that racial discrimination may have been a factor. "How large a factor it may have been with my candidacy, I don't know, but it was probably a factor with the board and some individuals in the deaf community."[6]

This left Harvey Corson and I. King Jordan, both of whom were deaf, and Elisabeth Zinser, a hearing candidate, in the running. "I was disappointed, yes; shocked, no," Bob said in an interview a short time later. "I have served my profession well. I have received just about every honor there is in my profession, but that wasn't good enough to make the final three. From the way the consultants talked and wrote things down, it was obvious to me that interviewing me was part of an exercise."[7]

Much has been published about "The Week the World Heard Gallaudet" and the "Deaf President Now!" (DPN) protest that occurred that spring. After the University's board of trustees selected Zinser as the college's next president—over the two deaf candidates—the campus erupted in anger and spawned widespread protests that captured the world's attention.

ề» ề» ề»

During the height of the protest when the campus was closed and entry was severely restricted, Bob, being a vice president living on campus, nevertheless had free run of the place. Furthermore, he was one of four senior administrators chosen by the board to run the University during the crisis. The Central Administration Management Team, which was set up during this upheaval immediately after Lee left the post, also included the Gallaudet provost, Catherine Ingold; Merv Garretson, a special assistant to the president; and James Barnes, vice president for administration and business. The Central Administration Management Team included representatives from the three major divisions of Gallaudet—academic affairs, Pre-College Programs, and business and management. The team agreed to meet with the executive committee of the board on a regular basis. Although there were two official meetings, Bob knew that there was other communication between the two hearing members of the Central Administration Management Team (Barnes and Ingold) and the chairman of the board of trustees. One of them summarized to Bob some of the exchanges he had missed by not having been invited. He was angry indeed. Having been eliminated as a candidate was upsetting. But he was still a member of the Central Administration Management Team!

The uproar at the selection of Zinser was not surprising. When the protest began, Barnes and Ingold found themselves barred from the campus by the students. They relocated to downtown Washington with some key board members, and attempted to manage the chaos engulfing the University as best they could from afar. Ruder Finn, a public relations company, had been hired by the board of trustees to manage the publicity related to the presidential announcement and protest, and several members of the Central Administration Management Team were staying at the Ruder Finn office. Garretson was away on vacation and thus missed out on the events. Until eventually approached by President Zinser, Bob was never asked to join Barnes and Ingold at their downtown location, and so he remained on campus.

Bob received a call from a friend who was at the University of North Carolina at Greensboro. His friend cautioned that Zinser was very aware of everything that was happening on campus and she was coming to take over. He also told Bob that Zinser suspected Bob had been a leader in the demonstrations and was concerned about his role. When Bob became angry and explained that as a member of the Central Administration Management Team he reported directly to the board and could not lead demonstrations, although he supported a deaf president, his friend suggested that he send Zinser some flowers.

"Are you crazy?" Bob demanded to know. "You know what my value would be when people hear about that? No, sorry, I can't do that." He was no longer a candidate for the presidency himself and he could voice his opinions openly. "I support the demonstration and I will have to take my chances with this," he told his friend.[8]

Bob was only peripherally involved in the DPN activities that closed down the campus and temporarily made the University the media magnet of the world. The protesters had no quarrel with him, nor he with them. In fact, he had a number of supporters among protesters. He was not to remain in the dark from administrative matters for very long, however. As he remembers:

> One day of the protest, I was walking down from my campus home behind MSSD to the front gate to visit with the protesters marching up and down the street when two Gallaudet campus security officers pulled up in their squad car and told me I was being summoned by President Zinser. I had never met her; in fact I had never seen her. Nor did I even know where she was. They asked me to get in the car and they would drive me downtown.[9]

When the squad car brought Bob to the Ruder Finn office downtown, he saw Provost Ingold, Barnes, and Gallaudet's lawyer, who were among those ensconced in the offices of the public relations firm. There was no interpreter. The only other deaf member of the Central Administration Management Team, Merv Garretson, was still out of town. During an interview shortly after the protest, Bob recalled:

> They tried to help me out by signing as they spoke. I think the reason they called me was because they realized it was a mistake to leave me out. I was a full fledged member of the [Central Administration Management Team]...I think it might have bothered them a little bit. They were meeting without me and that practice was exactly what we were protesting against![10]

They were all eating take-out Mexican food. "They made a big thing out of that, tried to make me feel comfortable, but I wasn't really involved in anything else," he remembered.[11] When Bob asked why they had not called him, they explained that things had been hectic and they were happy someone was on campus. But Bob had been in the dark with no one contacting him up until that point.

In addition, Donna had had eye surgery that week. She had suffered an injury to her left eye that became infected and endangered the sight in that eye if not her life as well. Nothing is more frightening for a deaf person than to have one's eyesight threatened. Bob was taking care of her as best he could during all of this turmoil. When he was offered a hotel room to be available to participate in deliberations with the board, he declined for that reason.

The next day, Bob was called back to the Central Administration Management Team at the office downtown. Zinser and Spillman, the chairperson of the Gallaudet board, were there. When Zinser approached him, she could not use sign language and she had an interpreter ask if she could speak to him. After they introduced themselves to each other, she attempted to obtain his support. As he explains:

> She said that she wanted me to know that she was president and had all the authority that goes with the position and that included assigning tasks and responsibilities to all administrators. She then asked me to identify a small group of highly respected, capable and articulate alumni leaders to be asked to go into the Deaf community to counter the negativism being expounded by the protesters. She asked me to find 10 or 15 deaf leaders who would speak positively of her and help change the views of those protesting. "I am the president now and you work for me. Can I depend on you to help me with this?" she asked. But I had to respond candidly. I told her there wasn't anyone left who didn't support the protesters. I could think of no one who would support her approach, let alone even agree to participate. She got up and walked away and that was the only time I ever spoke to her.[12]

Bob remembered Zinser as "polite, very determined, honest and sincere."[13] He had made it clear to her that afternoon that there was no hope for her. "Voices were strong," he warned her, "unity unbroken, and...few would elect to step out of line."[14] After Zinser also met with the student leaders, she knew that the student demands were inflexible and that the whole affair would not blow over. The students felt no remorse and had no second thoughts. Everyone in the know had instinctively understood that the campus would explode if the "wrong" decision prevailed. The board, with its perpetually closed eyes, had walked right into the disaster. Zinser resigned that evening.

The search committee was aware of the perspectives of the deaf community, the university's faculty senate, and others who had been involved in the on-campus interviews. After the protest began, the National Association of the Deaf, the National Fraternal Society of the Deaf, and the Gallaudet Alumni Association included Bob in their recommendations for alternative choices.

Like most others close to the process, Bob believed that the protest at Gallaudet had been inevitable. Campus groups were divided over their support for several deaf candidates. As the board subsequently considered reopening the search to allow other candidates to be considered again, one deaf colleague in support of Harvey Corson came to Bob's home and attempted to convince him to decline if he were offered the presidency. Bob had been told about the cliques formed in support of other candidates, but he was certainly surprised over the arrogance of this faculty member. Bob responded, "You are here to discriminate against me! This is the very thing we are protesting! You're wrong!"[15]

The colleague backed off. It was nevertheless recommended that the search would not be reopened.

The vested interests within the DPN movement events certainly did not help Bob, and he realized that he would have been a more attractive candidate had he come from outside the university. "But I can live with myself," he summarized in 1988. "I do my duty the best way I can. When I look in the mirror in the morning, I like what I see."[16]

Two days after Zinser resigned, I. King Jordan was selected as Gallaudet's eighth president.

The Deaf President Now protest was a major turning point for deaf people throughout the world. It was a statement that deaf people wanted control of their own destinies. "It was terrible that we had to go through this experience for things that should have been given to us a long time ago," Bob said shortly after the event in 1988. "On the other hand, it's a good thing it happened. It has created positive change. You expect that the future will be better."[17]

For many others, what happened to Bob was puzzling. In a chapter titled "The Dr. Robert Davila Mystery" in his book *Triumph of the Spirit: The DPN Chronicle,* Angel Ramos writes, "Years later, many questions about events that occurred during the DPN movement remain unanswered. Some may always remain unanswered....One question that should be answered, and which no one has been willing to shed light on, is why Dr. Robert Davila...was not included among the final three candidates."[18]

As for Bob, the events of that week represented yet another moment of truth—for he realized, without question, that he would need to leave Gallaudet University if he were to further advance his professional career.

CHAPTER 11

Momento de Verdad

BEING THE FIRST DEAF PERSON and the second person ever to be elected to the top post of all three major professional organizations for educators serving deaf students—the Conference of Educational Administrators of Schools and Programs for the Deaf (CEASD), the Convention of American Instructors of the Deaf (CAID), and the Council on the Education of the Deaf (CED)—was indeed a great accomplishment for Bob. Other honors came in quick succession, including election to the Alumni Hall of Fame at Hunter College and the Daniel T. Cloud Leadership Award from California State University at Northridge. Disappointed as Bob was with not winning the Gallaudet presidency, he had no time to think about it.

The final report of the 1988 Commission on the Education of the Deaf (COED), established by Congress in the Education of the Deaf Act, had painted a dismal picture, similar to what the Babbidge Report had presented 23 years earlier. The COED Chairman Frank Bowe, a deaf regional commissioner of the Rehabilitation Services Administration (RSA), held the highest position ever attained by a deaf person in government—up to that time. The COED report concluded: "The present status of education for persons who are deaf in the United States is unsatisfactory. Unacceptably so."[1]

Bob concurred with the COED report. Responding to this report had provided him with the opportunity to lead the Gallaudet Pre-College Programs in remaining current with the state of education of deaf people in the United States. Noting how other countries were effectively diagnosing and identifying deaf infants and establishing early intervention programs and preschool education, COED recommended improved early intervention programs for deaf children in the United States.

It is commonly known that most children born deaf have difficulties learning to read. The COED report indicated that while progress had been made since the 1965 Babbidge Committee Report, it was not satisfactory. The report also noted that the federal government was doing much more for high-achieving deaf students than for those whom the nation's schools had failed. The ironic result was that those who needed the most aid received the least. With its numerous recommendations, and its recognition of the unique language, communication and cultural status and needs of deaf children, the COED report was to become the blueprint for the reform of deaf education.

As an administrator responsible for K–12 schooling in model programs within the Gallaudet campus, Bob had been deeply enmeshed in these issues. His national advisory boards for the Kendall Demonstration Elementary School and the Model Secondary School for the Deaf often grappled with these concerns and he discussed them in depth with his friends and colleagues. Bob felt there was an acute need for better leadership in the government agencies regarding the education of children with disabilities.

ê» ê» ê»

Historically oppressed, the deaf community was implementing its own coming-of-age civil rights agenda. Research was helping achieve the recognition and legitimization of American Sign Language (ASL) as a language and as an appropriate medium by which to teach. Leaders of the deaf community, asserting "Deaf power," were focusing on having deaf persons play greater decision-making roles. For all intents and purposes, the struggle centered on power-sharing between deaf and hearing persons, with the education gap between deaf and hearing children a major target. Deaf leaders decried decades of inadequate education of their community's children resulting from the near exclusive decision-making by hearing persons. Bob had been at the forefront as a deaf leader for years. Now, as his term as president of CEASD came to a close in June 1988, William P. Johnson, Superintendent of the Iowa School for the Deaf, wrote to him and expressed appreciation for an outstanding job. "Without your diligent efforts, extraordinary commitment, and perseverance to seeing a successful conclusion to many critical activities, the organization would not be in the excellent position it is in today," Johnson affirmed. "I want you to know that many of us truly appreciate what you've done with, and for, our organization."[2]

Meanwhile, Bob was closely following the 1988 presidential race and he was particularly interested in how the candidates expressed support for disability groups. On April 14, 1988, only a week after the Deaf President Now events, Bob wrote to Vice President George H.W. Bush, the Republican national candidate, noting, "I am delighted to support you in your desire to serve our nation as President and want you to know that your statement on the disabled strikes the right chord." In his letter, Bob explained that he had been proud and pleased when Bush became the first public official to endorse the selection of a deaf president for Gallaudet University, saying, "When you had to call your shot, you did so decisively and without hesitation."[3]

Bush, busy with his campaign duties, didn't write back to Bob until June 30. In that letter, he congratulated Bob on his recent induction into the Hunter College Alumni Hall of Fame. The vice president wrote:

> The credentials you are continuously acquiring establish you as a role model, not only for the deaf and handicapped, but for all youth everywhere. Your helpful comments regarding our mutual belief that, with the right kind of assistance, the disabled are capable of achieving goals, deserve further study.[4]

At the time, Madeleine Will was assistant secretary for the Office of Special Education and Rehabilitative Services (OSERS) under President Ronald Reagan. Will was the parent of a child with Down syndrome. As such, Mrs. Will was very supportive of having all children with disabilities in regular classrooms. She also strongly supported the so-called Regular Education Initiative (a movement initiated by special educators), an approach that was originally designed to keep all learning disabled students in regular classrooms but was now being applied to all students with disabilities, including deaf students. Her entire time as assistant secretary was extremely contentious, and for groups such as CEASD and other deafness-related organizations, quite trying.

Over the months to come, Bob watched Senator Tom Harkin, D-Iowa, chairman of the Senate Subcommittee on the Handicapped, challenge Will. Harkin was concerned about the COED recommendations and the progress she was making toward addressing them at the federal level. This included the recommendation concerning screening procedures for high-risk infants and young children and the importance of English language acquisition as a subject of government-funded research. There was also a recommendation that deaf education might be considered more of a bilingual education issue and that deaf education programs be eligible for support under the Bilingual Education Act, a recommendation that Bob supported.

When George H. W. Bush won the presidency in November 1988, defeating Massachusetts Governor Michael Dukakis, many federal positions opened up as his new administration took over the White House. The stage was being set for Bob's next adventure.

ə๖ ə๖ ə๖

In January 1989, Bob received a phone call from the U.S. Department of Education. Would he be interested, the caller inquired, in coming over to discuss a possible position in the new administration under President George H. W. Bush?

He remembered thinking at first, "I've heard this one before." It had been a waste of time to go through the interview a few years earlier. But, with the search for the new Gallaudet president over, thereby eliminating any possible promotion for him within the university, he reminded himself about his policy of "never closing doors."

He accepted the invitation.[5]

At the meeting, Bob was accompanied by Fran Parrotta, his assistant and interpreter. Having developed intelligible speech in Spanish prior to his deafness and in English following, Bob generally communicated orally with hearing people, either in English or Spanish as the need arose. However, speechreading (lipreading) was especially difficult in situations involving several languages and an interpreter was needed to translate into sign language what other people were saying. Present at the meeting from the Bush administration were Bill Phillips, chief of staff to Secretary of Education Lauro Cavazos, and Becky Campoverde, deputy chief of staff. Bob spent about an hour answering a wide range of questions that included probes into his professional expertise, his educational, political and personal philosophy, his voting record, his personal life, his work on behalf of his political party, and his career.

Becky Campoverde wrapped up the meeting by saying she had to ask every potential candidate three significant questions: Have you ever been arrested? Have you ever been audited by the IRS? Have you done anything in your private life that if it became public knowledge would embarrass the president?

Bob responded "No" to all three. With these questions, the meeting ended. Bob was told that if his candidacy moved forward, someone would contact him. He thought it very strange that at no time was any particular job mentioned to him, nor was he asked for which position he would like to be considered.

Much to his surprise, Bob learned about a week later that he would be meeting with Secretary of Education Lauro Cavazos. Dr. Cavazos, former president of Texas Tech University, and himself Hispanic, had recently been re-appointed as a holdover from the Reagan administration. As Bob recalls, "I almost didn't believe it!"

To prepare for that meeting, he carefully studied the organizational chart of the Department of Education and scoured the program listings in each of the major divisions, especially those under the Office of Special Education and Rehabilitative Services. He once again asked Fran Parrotta to accompany him to the meeting as an interpreter. He also thought extensively about the kind of job or jobs for which he would like to be considered. Boyce Williams, a deaf man, had once served as chief of the Rehabilitation Services for the Deaf Branch, and Bob used this position as the standard to determine which positions he would consider should any be offered.

"Are you nervous?" Fran Parrotta asked as they entered the Department of Education that afternoon.

"Who wouldn't be?" he signed as the elevator door slid open.[6]

Bob had an established habit of always preparing extensively for meetings, and that was the case for this interview. He knew that Cavazos, like himself, had served in a variety of professional and administrative positions and, also like himself, was the first Hispanic to hold a high-level office at his own alma mater. Even before meeting Cavazos, Bob felt a sense of kinship and of a developing bond. The secretary had received an award from President Reagan for "Outstanding Leadership in the Field of Education," and the National Hispanic Leadership Award in the field of education from the League of United Latin American Citizens. These were interests Bob had spent much of his career promoting. Here, in Cavazos, was a man for whom he could work with pleasure.

Fran Parrotta interpreted into ASL the questions asked by Cavazos, one by one, some of them repeated from the previous interview. "Have you ever been arrested?" "Have you ever been audited by the IRS?" "Have you done anything in your private life that if it became public knowledge would embarrass President George H. W. Bush?"

Bob responded "No" again to all three. He now felt relaxed, hoping that the uncomfortable part of the meeting was over.

Bob didn't have to be a rocket scientist to know that he had not been invited to meet the Secretary of Education to discuss a job at a low or middle management level. Ever since Madeleine Will had left the post of assistant secretary for the Office of Special Education and Rehabilitative Services (OSERS) as part of the change in administration, Bob had occasionally allowed himself to think about serving in that position. After all, he was a scholar known throughout the United States and around the world. Mostly through matters related to deafness, he reminded himself cautiously. He had also served as associate editor of *Exceptional Children,* a journal that publishes original research and articles on professional issues relevant to the educators of children and youth in special education, and his master's degree was also in special education. He had authored many reports and articles in educational journals, and led almost every deafness-related national organization in the United States. He felt that his credentials were at least as good as those of Madeleine Will.

Bob's moment of truth in this meeting with Dr. Cavazos came when he asked Bob directly if he had given thought to any particular position for which he might wish to be considered in President George H. W. Bush's Department of Education.

Bob had to think on his feet. Show self-confidence. Convince the secretary of education that he was the right person for such a distinguished post—all within a few minutes.

Bob expressed his interest in the assistant secretary position in OSERS.

Cavazos agreed that he was not only qualified for that post, but also for the equally respected assistant secretary positions for elementary/secondary education and for post-secondary education. With this exchange, Cavazos turned to Bill Phillips, his chief of staff who was in the room with them, and asked him to clarify the next steps. Phillips replied that they would need to send Bob's name and credentials to Pendleton James, President Bush's transition director of personnel at the White House.

On the way back to Gallaudet in the taxi after the meeting Bob was justifiably pleased. He turned to Fran Parrotta and just nodded, "Whew!"

Fran looked at Bob, smiled, and signed, "Today, Gallaudet...Tomorrow, 'Good Morning America!'"[7]

On January 30, 1989, ten days after Bush's inauguration, Bob took the action needed to make his candidacy official. He wrote to the Honorable Chase Untermeyer, newly-appointed director of presidential personnel: "After much reflection, I submit to you my name for consideration for the position of Assistant Secretary for the Office of Special Education and Rehabilitative Services, U.S. Department of Education." In his letter, Bob also noted, "Personally, I have myself experienced both ends of the least restrictive environment continuum, allowing me to understand objectively the merits of the various options which should be available to all disabled students in America."[8]

ॐ   ॐ   ॐ

Bob was confronted with his first political firestorm before he was even in office. The California School for the Deaf yearbook fantasy about his being a boxer attending a White House reception now seemed to have a prophetic quality. In real life, however, he had a different kind of battle to fight. Bob knew there would be certain groups in the disability community that would object to his nomination. He had heard about the concerns that he was "a single disability person" seeking to manage cross-disability programs. When the White House sent up the trial balloon to test public reaction to Bob's possible nomination as OSERS head, the White House switchboard lit up like a Christmas tree as people called in to object to his appointment.

While Madeleine Will may have also been a "single disability person," several factors may have caused such a reaction in 1989. There was now much more interaction and collaboration among organizations advocating for distinct disabilities. Most people involved with deafness did not work in consort with those associated with other disabilities, and thus they were not regarded as team players.

The White House staff members were surprised at the intensity of the reaction. Bob had great credentials, but the fragmented disability community politics created a degree of opposition that certainly merited their attention. Although it bothered Bob that people were protesting his appointment, he knew those who were calling and writing didn't know him personally.[9] Some people were objecting simply because they did not want anyone outside of their own disability community to have the job. In essence, it seemed as if one of the primary objections to Bob's appointment was that he had attended a special school himself—even though that special school had been so essential to his monumental achievements!

Not only was the reaction to Bob's nomination intense, but also it was very well organized. For example, an organization called TASH (The Association for the Severely Handicapped), who opposed Bob's nomination because they feared that he was not adequately supportive of inclusion, even mounted a telephone campaign. Jeanne Glidden Prickett, later the Superintendent of the Iowa School for the Deaf, was working that time at Gallaudet's National Center of Deaf-Blindness and recalls the following:

> The TASH office folks mounted a calling campaign to members and called me at my desk at Gallaudet. The line the young man was clearly reading from a script went like this, "Please call this White House number and express

your opposition to the nomination for Assistant Secretary of Mr. Robert Davila, a blind man who does not support inclusive programs, because he went through segregated special education programs." I was incensed and stopped the young man. I told him that Dr. Davila is a DEAF man who went through a doctoral degree in a mainstream program [Syracuse University] with little support and they had better get their story straight. The number they had given me was indeed a White House office exchange. I called Merv Garretson [a respected leader in the Deaf community] and asked him what to do. He encouraged me to call back, talk to a person at a higher level, and get the exact position.[10]

Bob conceded that their concern was valid, but he knew that if anyone could develop knowledge and understanding of the needs of diverse constituencies in a hurry, he was the person. Fortunately, the White House agreed and decided to go all the way with his nomination. As preparation, he read everything he could get his hands on about other disabilities. He could have contacted individuals in the areas of blindness, autism, mental retardation, and other disabilities, but he chose not to do so. He didn't want someone reporting later that he had been asking around for very basic information while he was being considered for this extremely important position in the disability field. He knew how potentially damaging such a revelation could be.

Complaints about his possible appointment were also flooding the Department of Education. Ultimately, Bob was informed that he might have a problem. The Department of Education advised him to arrange meetings with board members and leaders of many national organizations serving persons with various disabilities in order to understand each organization's perspectives about their group's needs, their political connections, and their perceptions of other organizations, and of him.

These meetings were not always friendly. During a visit with the board of directors of the Detroit-based Autism Society of America (ASA), he was asked to make a 10–15 minute statement about his credentials, experience, personal attributes, philosophy, and plans, and then to answer questions. The supposedly brief meeting stretched into hours. As he still remembers vividly: "It was, to say the least, a harrowing and traumatic experience but one that I knew I had to go through—and leave behind a positive impression."[11]

During the exchange Bob had with the ASA board members in Detroit, one asked him to describe his disability experience. Knowing that some were concerned about his single disability background, he responded that his experience was both personal and professional. Professionally speaking, he had a master's degree in special education and he had also taught and/or worked with multiply-handicapped deaf students and adults. On the personal side, he had a cousin who was blind, a nephew with Down Syndrome, a niece with autism and a grandmother with mental illness. He concluded that disability knows no barriers; and he felt this statement had come across well.

However, toward the end of two hours of grueling questions, Bob kept making eye contact with an elderly woman with gray hair and a very serious look on her face who was seated directly in front of him. When the time for the last question arrived, she made a big display of wanting to ask it. She explained that she had been listening to him for almost two hours and had not heard anything different from what she had heard from many government officials in the past. "You haven't addressed any of the issues and problems which my husband and I have to deal with in caring for our adult autistic daughter," she argued. "Frankly, I am disappointed in you." She said that she wanted the last question because she planned to ask if Bob knew the last thing that she and her husband did before bed every night. Bob was really thrown off by her statement. He said, "No, ma'am, I have no idea what that would be. Why don't you tell me instead?"[12]

She replied, "The last thing we do every night is pray that we will still be alive in the morning because that means we will have one more day to care for our daughter. What is going to happen when he and I are gone? Will you take responsibility for caring for our daughter? Why should you be assistant secretary if you can't or won't?"[13]

In the 30 or so seconds that she required to make that statement, Bob experienced yet another moment of truth. His life flashed by in an instant as he looked back on its major events. He recalls, "It struck me that this lady's life and times revolved around worry about dying and leaving her autistic daughter unattended."[14] Compared to this lady, he thought, the parents of deaf children do not have any problems. In his mind, he realized his mother never had had to worry about what would happen to him or who would care for him as an adult.

Bob was very candid and direct, explaining that it would not be within his scope of responsibilities as a federal official to assume responsibility for her daughter. Big government could not do that either. What he *could* do was work with her and other advocates to improve services and supports for persons with disabilities, for their personal assistants and for their parents and guardians. "I could see people in the room nodding as I was speaking, which told me that I had answered correctly," Bob remembers. At the conclusion of the questioning, however, the chairman of the board of the ASA asked if he would leave the room for a few minutes so that the board could discuss its position on his possible appointment. "I went out with my interpreter for a few minutes," Bob explained. "Then I was called back and informed that the board had decided that they could *not* support my candidacy for reasons related to my long service in "segregated programs," my lack of cross-disability experience and the absence of any previous government experience." The board added that their decision was not personal. They admired Bob for his achievements and believed that he would be able to make important contributions in various roles—but not as assistant secretary of OSERS.

They finished by graciously saying that they would make every effort to work with Bob if he was appointed despite their dissent.

"And that is exactly what happened," he recalls with relief. "I did work well with the ASA and its key leaders. I believe that part of their willingness to set things aside and endeavor to work with me was related to the fact that one of my nieces has autism." At the time this meeting occurred, however, the exchange Bob shared with the elderly lady served as a powerful antidote to his limitations as a "single disability" educator. Bob explains, "It made me realize that not all of my views and experiences could be generalized across disabilities. I realized I had much to learn and I set about learning it. I probably studied harder when I was preparing for, and serving in, OSERS than when I was in my doctoral program."[15]

᠗᠙ ᠗᠙ ᠗᠙

Then came the vetting process. On April 25, 1989, Bob was formally nominated by President Bush to serve as assistant secretary of the Office of Special Education and Rehabilitative Services. Gallaudet University President I. King Jordan immediately sent out a memo to the Gallaudet community, "This is an unprecedented honor and we wish Dr. Davila every success."[16] Bob immediately began meeting with high-level Department of Education personnel who would steer him through the confirmation process. These included Philip Link, from the Secretary of Education's office, and Patty Guard, director of policy and evaluation (later promoted by Bob to deputy director of the OSERS' Office of Special Education Programs). Link and Guard were knowledgeable advisors who prepared Bob in terms of engaging dialogue, winning over dissenters, advocating certain positions and philosophies, and learning he should acquire before the confirmation process.

"Vetting," the careful examination of the qualifications of persons being considered for governmental posts, is a very political process. In Bob's case, this included an FBI check on his qualifications and a whirlwind of interviews with select people, including various White House personnel. President Bush's intention to nominate Bob was made public and thus covered in the media, including in the *New York Times*, in order to see the reactions.

Clearance by the FBI is a standard procedure for persons nominated to high-level government positions. Bob was fingerprinted and required to list his memberships in organizations, including foreign ones, as well as all his travels to foreign countries. Indeed, as an administrator for Gallaudet and as president of several national organizations, he had journeyed abroad extensively, to Canada, Finland, Sweden, Denmark, Germany, Austria, Switzerland, France, England, Spain, Italy, Brazil, Argentina, Greece, New Zealand, Australia, Hong Kong, Japan, the Dominican Republic, the Philippines, and Yugoslavia.

During the Bureau's clearance process, Bob was also asked to describe possible opposition to his appointment. Bob cautioned that because he was deaf, some might incorrectly assume that he would not support the full integration of students with disabilities with their non-disabled peers. "Nothing could be further from the truth," he wrote in his statement to the FBI. "These few individuals assume that all deaf people and educators of the deaf are opposed to integration. This is a misinformed and erroneous view."[17] Indeed, Bob firmly believed (and does to this day) that the "bottom-line goal" of special education and rehabilitation is to assist individuals with disabilities to develop personal independence and integrate themselves as contributing members of their communities:

> The manner in which programming is planned and designed and resource support allocated must keep this basic goal as a guide. I see no problem, whatsoever, in allaying any concerns a few individuals may have regarding my special education philosophy and my position on integration and the least restrictive environment provision of Public Law 94–142.[18]

Bob Lennan and his wife Mary, whose friendship with the Davilas dates back to the days when both men were teachers at the New York School for the Deaf at White Plains, can still recall a visit to their home by an FBI agent who was investigating Bob. When Bob's friends finished giving their upbeat description of Bob's personal and professional qualifications, the agent commented that Bob must be a very special person because everyone she had interviewed had painted a very enthusiastic and positive picture of him.[19]

Oscar Cohen, superintendent of the Lexington School for the Deaf, who worked closely with Bob in establishing the CEASD Ethnic and Multicultural Concerns Committee, recalls his phone conversation with the FBI agent who was following up on Bob's nomination. The agent repeated almost verbatim what was said to the Lennans—that in all the years of conducting background checks, he had yet to find such a positive and unanimous out-pouring of support for a nominee.

Taras Denis told the FBI agent that although he and Bob were friends, he often got upset at Bob when he would not bend in order to benefit from some decision. "This guy is as straight as an arrow!" he told the agent.[20] They asked no more questions.

With the support of his references during the vetting process, Bob was placed onto the road toward a presidential appointment. Ahead were several additional meetings with Pendleton James in the White House as well as with Congressman Steve Bartlett (R-Texas) and Senator Orrin Hatch (R-Utah), Bob's Congressional sponsors. He still had to "sell" himself to them, and they in turn sponsored his appointment and assured the administration of the nec-essary votes within the Senate to ensure his confirmation. Since no one in the Senate questioned his qualifications, a confirmation hearing was not necessary; however, Bob was subject to a series of meetings with very tough questions.

During one interview with Congressman Bartlett, Bob was asked: "How can you direct policy development for multiple disability groups when your experience has been in only one disability field (deafness)?" "Are you sufficiently conservative that you won't badger the Congress for unrealistic budget increases that cannot be appropriated?" "There was recently a story about a *Washington Post* reporter who was found to have included several falsehoods in her resume. I need to ask you if there is anything in your im-pressive resume that you need to change before we go any further with your nomination?" "Can you make decisions without regard to their impact on Gallaudet University?" "How are you going to travel around the country to speak to divergent audiences on issues of great importance without convey-ing the impression that it is your interpreter who is speaking?" "Tell me your vision for handicapped people in the future and how you will work to fulfill it while serving as OSERS assistant secretary."

Tough questions! Each and every one. He answered them impressively. Bartlett grabbed a note pad from his desk and took notes, nodding his head as Bob responded. Turning to Bob, Bartlett told him that he appeared to be a very strong candidate.[21]

Many more meetings followed these initial sessions with his sponsors, including the White House Seminar for Prospective Presidential Appointees in May. In June, he was making a round of courtesy visits on Capitol Hill and stopped in to see Strom Thurmond, the senior senator from South Carolina better remembered as a notorious former segregationist. The 88-year-old Senator asked Bob who he was and became confused when he saw Bob speaking directly to him but, with Fran Parrotta interpreting when he spoke to Bob. He then asked Bob, "Do you speak English?"

As Bob began to explain the position for which he was nominated, he mentioned vocational rehabilitation services as being among the responsibilities of the Office of Special Education and Rehabilitative Services. Senator Thurmond abruptly interrupted him, saying "You'll be responsible for vocational education? That's in the Agriculture Department, right?"

Thurmond's aide attempted to explain that Bob was not involved in vocational education. He was applying for a post related to vocational rehabilitation, but the Senator, still puzzled by the signing that was going on, kept focusing on vocational education. A few times, the aide looked at Bob, whose deafness and struggle to find an opening to get in a word made the situation even more humorous. When Bob finally had a chance to reply, he began to speak and sign when the Senator suddenly ended the interview. He looked at Bob and said firmly and dismissively, "I don't have anything against you." He then gave Bob and Fran each a key chain souvenir. They thanked him and left his office.[22]

A much tougher challenge came on June 30, 1989 when Bob responded to a set of questions from Senator Harkin, chairman of the Senate Subcommittee on the Handicapped. Members of the subcommittee asked him to describe his vision for people with disabilities; what role the Office of Special Education and Rehabilitative Services would play in making his vision become a reality; the major objectives he had set for himself for the next 12, 24, and 36 months for the divisions of the Rehabilitation Services Administration, the National Institute on Disability and Rehabilitation Research, and the Office of Special Education Programs; his plans for continuing the major policy initiatives developed by Madeleine Will; his plans for his own policy initiatives; and his positions on affirmative action and the least restrictive environment provision of P.L. 94–142.

The Senate Subcommittee also asked him how he thought parents should be involved in the education of their children, how special education should be monitored, and how he would strengthen the interface between special education and adult services, all of which seemed to be the priority management issues facing the Office of Special Education and Rehabilitative Services.

Since the Office of Special Education and Rehabilitative Services monitored the supervision of Gallaudet University, Bob agreed that he would have to recuse himself from decisions relating to or affecting the University for the period of one year. In the interim, other officers would be able to handle matters pertaining to Gallaudet.

Donna was very much Bob's partner and fellow sufferer throughout the confirmation process. The criticism coming from other disability groups bothered both of them. The worst scenario running through Bob's mind was that the White House might back off its support for him. As he recalls, "That would have hurt my professional image and I would never have gotten such an opportunity again."[23] While Secretary Cavazos and Bill Phillips, his chief of staff, were committed to Bob's appointment and masterminded his vetting throughout this difficult period, Donna discussed a wide range of other scenarios with him. Not surprisingly to Bob, Donna considered him the perfect choice and had no doubt about his ability or qualifications for the appointment.

CHAPTER 12

Assistant Secretary!

O N JULY 13, 1989, the *Congressional Record* reported that the Senate had confirmed Robert Refugio Davila, of the District of Columbia, to be Assistant Secretary for the Office of Special Education and Rehabilitation Services, Department of Education.

Donna's undying faith and support came forth teasingly that evening, "See, I was right!"[1]

On July 31, Vice President Dan Quayle administered the oath-taking ceremony for Bob's formal inauguration. Several hundred representatives and invited guests from the disability communities as well as deaf leaders witnessed this historical ceremony, at the White House. Donna and Bob's two sons attended the ceremony. Brian was a civil engineer, and Brent an accountant. Brian and Brent were pleased with the recognition given their father, although none of the family realized how much of an "insider" Bob had become until the first White House Christmas party where the President, Mrs. Bush, cabinet officers, and various others walked around shaking hands with the Davilas and eating Christmas cookies! At that moment, Bob realized he had attained goals beyond his wildest dreams.

Brent's wife also attended the oath-taking ceremony. Brent recalled, "Mary Jane was real nervous. Afterwards, you could go up and shake Dan Quayle's hand and there was a photographer there. My wife went up to Dan Quayle, she was young at the time, and she said, "Mr. Quayle, nice to meet your hand!"[2]

Friends and family reacted with delight over Bob's appointment. He was inundated with congratulatory notes. Bob's 87-year-old mother, who was recuperating from knee surgery, was navigating comfortably with a walker and the assistance of a nurse and a therapist who came to the house three

Robert R. Davila, Assistant Secretary for Special Education and Rehabilitation Services, U.S. Department of Education, 1989.

times a week. Soledad didn't understand the intricacies of the term "assistant secretary" and for awhile she thought Bob had somehow been demoted.

Praise and support came from many national and international deaf leaders and from a wide range of professional organizations, as a result of Bob's having acquired a reputation through his adept and sensitive handling of the various positions he had held over the years. Fred Weintraub, assistant director of the Council for Exceptional Children, said that Bob "didn't get the job solely because he's deaf. He's a person who is deaf and who is also terribly competent.... Bob becomes a role model instead of a token."[3] In announcing Bob's appointment, the World Federation of the Deaf News noted that, with his considerable experience in both classroom teaching and educational administration, Bob would "certainly make an impact on the education of disabled persons."[4]

Bob was now occupying the highest ranked federal position ever held by a deaf person. In this position, he oversaw an annual budget in excess of $5 billion for special education and vocational rehabilitation programs aiding more than eight million children and 28 million adults with disabilities. His authority for federal involvement encompassed the education of the nation's 36 million people with disabilities. Some experts considered this post the "most difficult job in education."[5] Bob, however, remained undaunted. "This opportunity is more than I ever dreamed," he said. "I believe I really can make a positive difference in the lives of children with disabilities and their families."[6]

But making progress would not be easy in light of the skepticism Bob continued to encounter during the early months in his new post. He had to deal with assumptions, often incorrect, about his viewpoints and possible favoritism toward deaf people, and with worries of opponents who were unfamiliar with his past record or his ideals as a person. During that first fall in office he saw, under the surface, "a lot of feelings, a lot of emotions."[7] Similarly, several disability groups expressed their fear that he would be too "conservative" on integration. They thought that he would promote segregated educational programs for children with disabilities, even though he had repeatedly avowed his support for mainstream programs.

"Mainstreaming"—the education of children with disabilities in public school settings with their non-disabled peers—had long been controversial in the deaf community, mostly because it threatened to dismantle the traditional residential-based system serving deaf children. The Congressional Commission on the Education of the Deaf (COED) had called for caution to ensure that deaf children did not fall through the cracks in the rush for placement in least restrictive environments. Bob did not consider the issue of least restrictive environment to be the real problem. He acknowledged the fears of some who believed that integration was often placed ahead of a student's welfare while pointing out that not every deaf person should be in a special school. He emphasized that the law was clear that a continuum of program services was needed.

Despite going out of his way to be impartial, Bob was occasionally shocked at the lack of tact he encountered. During one meeting in the office of the executive director of the United Cerebral Palsy organization, someone asked Bob if he realized how lucky he was that Senator Harkin had a deaf brother. Puzzled, Bob asked him in what way would he be lucky regarding that? "The Senator had something to do with your appointment, didn't he?" came the reply. The assumption was that Harkin would never have supported Bob if his brother had not been deaf. Bob was tempted to give a lesson on how the political process is not so easily manipulated, but of course, he restrained himself.

In time, many of the critics who had opposed his appointment came to support him when they found him to be an open, fair ally and representative. His efforts to examine opposing views and find compromises and worthy solutions were well reflected in his comments when he delivered the commencement address at his alma mater, Hunter College in New York, in 1990. "Honest differences of opinion are the lifeblood of a democracy," he said. "We must work to transform these controversies into opportunities for collaboration."[8]

Bob maintained his characteristic concern and forthrightness as he continually reassured others that he would study each issue individually. Paul Leung, editor of the *Journal of Rehabilitation*, who interviewed the new assistant secretary during his first month at OSERS office in the Switzer Building, affirmed these qualities in his article. He found Bob "gracious and personable" with a "comfortable, confident and upbeat demeanor."[9]

ঌ   ঌ   ঌ

One of Bob's first interactions with the White House occurred when he was asked to review and comment on a draft of President Bush's State of the Union Address. Bob noted that the president did not mention persons with disabilities and in his three-page response, he suggested that the president should comment on the need to bring persons with disabilities into the mainstream of American society and to help them acquire full rights, accommodations, and access to public and private institutions and employment. President Bush did mention in the address his commitment (and our country's) to providing full civil rights and access to persons with disabilities.

In August 1989 Bob was invited to meet with President Bush and Roger Porter, assistant to the president for Economic and Domestic Affairs, regarding the proposed Americans with Disabilities Act (ADA). As the highest ranking disability-related officer in the government during the time that the ADA was framed, Bob served as a resource person available to Congressional and administrative personnel as they drafted the various sections of the Act. In an August memo, Porter wrote to Bob:

> You and many others in the disability community have worked tirelessly to move this legislation to the point where it is today. We are pleased to see that the consensus we have reached with key Senators is one which you can join us in supporting. The obvious support you gave the President was much appreciated. Both the Nation and the disabled community will benefit from the enactment of legislation that has the broadest support possible. I am confident that the understanding formed in our Friday meeting will stand us in good stead as we work together to move the Americans with Disabilities Act through the legislative process and on to the President's desk.[10]

Thus, immediately following his appointment, Bob had been thrust squarely into the planning stage of one of the most significant pieces of legislation in history for people with disabilities, an act that established a clear and comprehensive prohibition of discrimination on the basis of disability. This first civil rights measure on their behalf promised to thoroughly address the discrimination facing the disability community.

When Bob testified for the first time before Congress on September 7, 1989, he summarized that his position was, in his mind, a chance to repay the country for meeting his own special needs. His educational background, he explained, had undoubtedly shaped his perspectives relevant to his new post. He was himself a product of the special education and rehabilitation systems, including his elementary, secondary, and postsecondary education, which had been supported by a vocational rehabilitation grant. "I believe I have gotten about as good an education as any American citizen can get. I feel that the sacrifices I had to make because of circumstances...were well worth it," he asserted.[11]

In a sense, Bob's appointment was a fulfillment of a fantasy he had held since he was a young man in his late 20s. At that time, he had been inspired by the autobiography of Pulitzer winner Carlos Peña Romulo, *I Walked With Heroes,* the story of a man who had grown up in the slums of Manila in the Philippines, and had overcome economic adversity to rise to the rank of Brigadier General in World War II under General MacArthur. Romulo also served as president of the University of the Philippines, and he had distinguished himself as U.S. Secretary of Education. Romulo had then entered politics and, as the first president of the United Nations General Assembly, mingled with kings and queens and other great leaders. Yet, he never lost his common touch.

ॐ ॐ ॐ

Bob set out immediately to put his "stamp" on the Office of Special Education and Rehabilitative Services. Prior to his appointment, the General Accounting Office (GAO), at the behest of the House Subcommittee on the Handicapped, had identified worrisome problems related to an excess centralization of authority at OSERS, a lack of cooperation and deficiencies in meaningfully shared decision making, poor communications internally and externally, and difficulties obtaining and allocating organizational resources. The GAO report revealed that unfilled positions had been informally occupied for long periods on an "acting" basis. There was also a lack of staff competence and a high staff turnover rate. Bob had a formidable challenge ahead!

Bob was expected to address these issues. Several months later, Representative Major Owens of Brooklyn, chair of the committee and a Democrat, gave Bob a grade of "A" for making great progress in resolving these problems. This regard was representative of the bipartisan support Bob enjoyed from the Hill throughout his tenure at the Office of Special Education and Rehabilitative Services.

As part of his management plan, Bob also addressed the provision of technical assistance to individual states. The Office of Special Education Programs (OSEP), located within OSERS, had initiated efforts to review the roles played by informational clearinghouses, institutes, regional resource centers, advisory boards, and other mechanisms that provided technical assistance to the field of special education.

Bob's management team included three strong senior managers with extensive experience in state government, who helped improve relations with state agencies. These three persons were Nell C. Carney, commissioner of the Rehabilitation Services Administration; William Graves, director of the National Institute on Disability and Rehabilitation Research; and Judy Schrag, director of the Office of Special Education Programs. Fortunately, Bob had a friendly and supportive association with these top managers. He personally interviewed them and had a say in their appointments. He met on a regular basis with them to review OSERS-wide issues and problems.

At this time, telecommunications technologies were rapidly expanding in the deaf community, but no telephone relay service was available yet. Fran Parrotta, who had relocated with Bob from Gallaudet's Pre-College Programs as his administrative assistant, had an excellent unobtrusive style and helped Bob with receptive communication in many one-on-one meetings. Lynel Spencer, his secretary, who also came with Bob from Gallaudet, assisted him with telephone calls. In meetings, Bob usually spoke for himself, his speech being intelligible due to the late onset of his deafness, and either used Department of Education interpreters or hired certified interpreters from agencies to facilitate communication. Bob also taught sign language to everyone on his personal staff.

As with most other high level political appointments, the position imposed tremendous demands on both time and energy. With his staff, Bob was constantly on the move and obligated to attend meetings and functions, often resulting in 10–12 hour workdays. Bob was out of town an estimated 40 weekends per year and when in town there were endless piles of memos, reports and documents to read. Understanding and accepting of the demands of Bob's job, Donna looked forward to their spending free evenings together. The couple learned to cherish these free moments during these hectic years, because they were few and far between.

Always strong and decisive in his roles as vice president at Gallaudet, and president of national organizations, Bob now found himself addressing the dismal General Accounting Office report and overhauling the way OS-ERS was managed. By September 1989, he had conducted a one-day retreat with his senior management team for the purpose of developing goals and objectives and establishing a management system to measure the teams' success in achieving those goals. He would need to plan corrective actions to reinvigorate the ailing office even as OSERS continued to award and administer program appropriations. At this retreat, he developed a new set of goals in full consultation with his senior staff, and with the input of the rehabilitation, special education, and disability research communities.

Also in September 1989, Bob was a member of the Department of Education team that accompanied President Bush to an education summit meeting with 50 state governors. Comfortable with the goals President Bush and the governors agreed to pursue, he assured the audience that whatever flexibility is created, no child with a disability would be deprived of the appropriate support. Bob looked forward to a future when all Americans, regardless of their special identity and distinguishing characteristics, would have equal access to opportunities in education, training, employment and community life. "This is the vision that has guided my own personal outlook and which will continue to guide me as I begin work in my new position," he promised.[12]

When Bob arrived at OSERS, he was surprised that although the department was supporting a network of parent training centers around the country whose responsibility was to provide orientation, referrals, information and training assistance to parents of children with disabilities, the department was not providing such support to parents of deaf children. In addition, many cross-disability conferences did not include deafness. Parents of deaf children were either not invited or not being informed about the conferences. Bob initiated a Family Leadership Conference and made sure that deafness was included. He subsequently informed his staff that no meeting involving cross-disabilities should be held without including representation by deafness personnel, professional and family.

By January 1990, Bob had established a new set of priorities and presented them to many parents and other representatives from groups such as the Epilepsy Foundation of America, the Learning Disabilities Association of America, the Spina Bifida Association of America, the Autism Society of America, and the American Society for Deaf Children. He promised the participants at the Family Leadership Conference that he would increase the ability of communities to include people with disabilities and provide technology so that students with disabilities could take part in an integrated education and culture.

Bob's position also allowed him to have a dramatic impact on the education of minority students with disabilities. Previously, minority individuals needing special education often were not identified until they entered school at age five, but P.L. 99–457, passed in 1986 and which expanded P.L. 94–142 to include infant and toddler programs, had changed that. These children now could be identified at a younger age. As Bob summarized, "This will no doubt make it possible for many more individuals with disabilities to become effective learners from the day they enter school."[13]

Although there had been a marked increase in minority parent involvement regarding decisions about their children's educational programs over the previous few years, Bob stressed that there was still "a long way to go before this form of collaboration is fully realized."[14] Outreach to minority communities would be important. Residents of these communities needed to be made aware of the provisions of the Individuals with Disabilities Education Act and the Rehabilitation Act. Many families hesitated to become involved because of language and/or cultural differences. Some individuals didn't receive services simply because they were unaware of their existence. The burden was on the professional communities to make their services accessible to all parents.

Many parents knew little or nothing about their rights to acquire a free, appropriate, public education for their children under key federal laws. Bob saw this lack of knowledge as a major stumbling block to collaboration between parents and educators. In response to this need, the Office of Special Education Programs funded a network of parent centers, each offering assistance to parents of individuals with disabilities, including information and training regarding their rights under P.L. 94–142.

While schools needed to be open to input from all parents, parents also needed to develop skills in advocacy for their children and opportunities to network. Alone, schools and parents can only do so much. Together they can make a huge difference. Bob's own family and his schooling had made him the strong person he became and this experience shaped his leadership. Remembering how many other deaf Hispanic children had very different experiences as compared to his own, he emphasized that educators were teaching minority *individuals*. "We must increase the number of persons from minority groups who pursue careers in special education and related fields," he argued.[15] He spoke from personal experience: "Minority students are directly and positively affected by the presence of minority teachers in the classroom [and] children with disabilities from minority backgrounds need role models every bit as much as other children."[16]

There had been times in his life when he actually believed that an individual with a minority background could not be a teacher. "As the son of Mexican immigrants who were migrant farm workers," he recalled in a 1991 OSERS publication, "I know first-hand the obstacles that all too often prevent minority individuals from benefiting from special education and rehabilitation programs. But I also believe I understand the problems that professionals must overcome to make such programs responsive to these individuals."[17]

Bob saw both the benefits and the limitations of home and school environments. Growing up a migrant farm laborer, he learned the value of hard work. This lesson was largely the reason he was now in a high-level government position, making decisions that would influence the education of other minority children with disabilities.

Clear in his intent to reach out for increased parental support, Bob recognized the need for an increased involvement on the part of the parents of children with disabilities, and increased funding for expanding OSERS Parent Training Centers.

ஒ ஒ ஒ

Bob strongly embraced the Americans with Disabilities Act (ADA), a landmark piece of legislation enacted on July 26, 1990. He was present at the signing of the ADA on the White House lawn. Bob was thrilled with its promise, which he wrote was "to eliminate discrimination in employment, in the provision of services by public agencies, in public accommodations, and in access to telecommunications services." He saw how it could revolutionize the status of persons with disabilities in society by providing "a powerful tool for enabling people with disabilities, including those from minority backgrounds, to reach their full potential."[18]

In comparison with the ADA, for which he did not author any specific sections but had only provided advice, the re-authorization of the Individuals with Disabilities Education Act (IDEA) in 1990, relied on Bob's guidance. This was an enhancement of the original legislation (P.L. 94–142) enacted in 1975. Whereas IDEA went from the Office of Special Education and Rehabilitative Services to Congress, ADA had been developed *in* Congress.

Bob was both excited and proud to work on two important aspects of the 1990 re-authorization of IDEA. First, the name was changed from "The Education for All Handicapped Children Act of 1975" to the "Individuals with Disabilities Education Act." Second, a transition requirement was added which focused on coordinating services for students. This promoted transitions to post-secondary education, vocational training, integrated employment, and/or continuing and adult education. The path chosen would take into account the individual student's needs, preferences and interests. Bob contributed greatly to the Individualized Transition Plans (ITPs), a hallmark of IDEA. The introduction and inclusion of this transition service attempted to strengthen the structure of the Individualized Educational Program (IEP). Post-secondary activities could include college education, vocational training, integrated employment, continuing and adult education, and independent living or community participation.

Bob wrote that "the very heart of the Individuals with Disabilities Education Act is individuality—individual need, individual services designed to meet those needs, individual education goals, and individual paths. It was this very vision—individualized programs designed to meet individual needs— that served as the basis for the IDEA."[19] He saw "appropriate education" as a powerful concept, providing the foundation upon which individualized programming and the delivery of individualized services are built. He explained that an appropriate education not only accepts but also embraces the unique needs of each child. It is a flexible education made up of high quality services, tailored to the child's needs. "To my mind," he said, "it is this concept of appropriateness that is the very hallmark of special education."[20]

Anthony Shriver, a nephew of President John Fitzgerald Kennedy, was head of "Best Buddies," a college student organization he had founded to mentor developmentally disabled children living near college communities. Bob was delighted in July 1990 to attend Rose Kennedy's birthday celebration, and be seated at a table with Shriver, his sister Maria, and her husband Arnold Schwarzenegger, along with other guests. Bob and Schwarzenegger were "probably the only Republicans in the whole room." About 250 persons—a host of government personages, corporation/business bigwigs, and political leaders invited from all over the world—were at the reception under tents on the lawn of the Kennedy compound in Hyannisport. Among them was Michael Dukakis, who had lost in the most recent race for president. With Fran Parrotta helping with the interpreting, Bob had a nice chat with Dukakis and then roamed over the lawn, mingling with other dignitaries while spending time with Secretary Lauro Cavazos and his wife.

The real surprise for Bob was that he was one of the 50 special guests invited to the sit-down dinner that followed. The Kennedy Foundation paid for his expenses, including airfare and hotel. As he recalls, "Unfortunately, the invitation was for two people and I could not take Donna and an interpreter so I decided to be practical: I took the interpreter. (And lived to tell about it!)."[21] Donna understood how important the event was to Bob. After this celebration, he and Anthony Shriver continued to work together on disability issues and developed a friendship.

Despite missing the party at Hyannisport, Donna had ample opportunities to mingle with other dignitaries and official events. During one dinner, Tennessee Senator Al Gore saw Bob and Donna signing and came over to talk with them through an interpreter. Donna found him to be very nice and, having read about Gore's six year-old son who had been hit and critically injured by a car outside a baseball stadium in Baltimore, she asked the senator about the boy's progress. Gore was so surprised and grateful that Donna asked about the boy that he held her hand for a long time. Donna reflected, "Can you imagine being fawned over by a good-looking man who years later came so close to getting elected president of the United States? That was a great honor and thrill!"[22]

Over the next six months, Bob continued to develop programs and services to support his newly-established priorities. His dream of making a difference in the education of students with disabilities through this post in the Department of Education was temporarily delayed in December 1990 when Lauro Cavazos, who had given him such vindication in his pursuit of these goals, resigned as Secretary of Education. There was a distinct possibility that the assistant secretary posts might be assigned to others under Cavazos's replacement. "I want you to know," Bob told Cavazos, "that one of the greatest privileges and honors accorded to me was the opportunity to serve in your administration...your legacy will be reflected by the energy and dedication of those of us who remain."[23] Over the first year of Bob's tenure, the two Hispanics had established a congenial relationship and so Cavazos's departure was acutely felt.

The following month, January 1991, President Bush selected Senator Lamar Alexander, then president of the University of Tennessee and former governor of the state, to replace Lauro Cavazos as Secretary of Education. Word spread that Alexander had agreed to take on the position on condition that he be permitted to select his own assistant secretaries. President Bush was reported to have assented to that request. Rumors and news travel fast in the labyrinths of government buildings. Even though Bob and the other assistant secretaries had all been informed at a White House meeting on the eve of their appointments that they had no job security and could be replaced at any time for any or no reason, Bob was caught unprepared by the news because he had not considered that he might serve for less than the president's full term.

Within a month, Alexander arrived in Washington and sent word to the assistant secretaries that he would be evaluating their work and deciding which ones he would invite to serve on his team. The first couple of officers he called in stayed for no more than a few minutes, just long enough to be told that he or she was not going to be invited to remain. After each "termination," word spread through the hallways like wildfire. A shiver of insecurity came over Bob as he thought about the perception some naïve friends might have should he be deemed a "failure," not understanding the political steps that are common when a high-level post is filled in the government. He had weathered the disappointment of not reaching the pool of finalists for the Gallaudet presidency, and he had overcome the challenges of earning a Ph.D. in a period when there were few resources to support him. Each time, he had his lifelong companion's support, however, and, once again, Donna calmed him when she saw his fear. "You will be good," she told him. "And you can live with the consequences. I will know the reason you may have to leave, and that is all that counts."[24]

Bob received the call at work one morning from Secretary Alexander's office, informing him that the secretary desired to see him the following day at 10:00 a.m. Bob deplored the agonizing wait till the next day. He remembered a famous Spanish saying, and whispered it to himself—"Si me van a matar mañana, que me maten de una vez. (If they are going to kill me tomorrow, let them do it right away.)"[25]

The next morning, he arrived at Alexander's office exceptionally early after a sleepless night. He had decided that he would not make a fuss if he were not invited to stay. Rather, he was determined to wish Alexander well and to let him know that he fully supported the new secretary's right to select his own staff of assistants. So Bob committed a short speech to memory and at the appointed time, appeared at the secretary's door in company with his trusted assistant/interpreter, Fran Parrotta.

They were ushered into the secretary's office and as Bob entered, Alexander caught him gazing at the photos, paintings, and artifacts that he had displayed around his new office. He was sidetracked and started the meeting by giving Bob a short tour. He showed Bob his family photos and explained some background on each member. Then they sat down. Bob thought that Alexander was very good at dealing with these situations. Ruefully, the nervous assistant secretary reflected, "He makes you feel comfortable and appreciated just before he pulls the trap door lever." Bob was about to give the secretary his rehearsed speech, but Alexander beat him to the punch: "Bob, I have heard many good things about your work and I want you on my team. What do you say?"[26]

"I was speechless," Bob recalled. "My throat went dry and I lost my nerve a bit." The shock must have shown on his face because after a moment of silence, Alexander asked, "Bob, are there any questions you want to ask me about my offer?" A relieved Bob responded: "Sir, you have already answered the only question I had."[27]

Alexander was to prove a truly supportive colleague and Bob benefited from his wisdom and guidance. Bob said of his new boss, "He was also super smart and I learned a lot from observing him and listening to him speak."[28]

CHAPTER 13

The Second Firestorm

B Y THE SPRING OF 1992, only occasional whiffs of smoke and a few glowing embers remained from the initial firestorm over Bob's ability to represent all disabilities. More than two years earlier, Bob had begun his work as a member of President George H. W. Bush's administration thinking a great deal about what his legacy would be. Bob wished to be remembered as a leader of all people with disabilities and not just deaf people. He consulted in the development of the ADA and took a lead role in developing Individualized Transition Plans, Parent Centers, and the cross-disability coalitions, which could then be used as a model for other groups. While some disability groups continued to believe he was anti-inclusionist, and though he actually did have many concerns that mainstreaming and inclusion would not meet the needs of *all* deaf children, he saw the concept of inclusion with an appropriate support system as one that could work well for many children and adults with disabilities.

Never did he imagine that his article in the Spring 1992 issue of the OSERS newsletter would fan the embers into a second political firestorm—this one over the issue of inclusion. In the newsletter, Bob stated that inclusion "transcends the idea of physical location and incorporates basic values that insist on participation, friendship, and interaction in all aspects of education and community life." In other words, Bob was saying that a child's feeling of comfort and security should be weighed as an important factor in determining his or her educational setting. Bob used a young deaf woman as a case study in his article.[1]

Bob's article was read and discussed all over the country. Many people were enraged. People associated with other disabilities wrote to him that the cultural issues surrounding the deaf community make it a somewhat unique situation. There is no culture of severe mental retardation, one individual complained, nor is there a unique language base for these individuals. Writers argued that discrimination was rampant throughout the school system, and change was desperately needed. They argued that Bob was in a critical position to promote that change. Many parents disagreed with Bob's interpretation of inclusion, hoping that he would take the time to have more discussion with those who were puzzled by his position. The letters urged Bob to reconsider his opinion that inclusion can happen in segregated settings. Some felt that any placement except for the regular public school setting was simply not inclusion and would further separate individuals and families from their right to a full and happy life.

On the other hand, people also wrote to Secretary Alexander in support of Bob, expressing concern that he had been criticized for his remarks that one placement, the regular classroom, might not necessarily meet the needs of all students. These writers urged Secretary Alexander to support Bob in the face of this opposition. Letters came from organizations serving students with other low-incidence disabilities, arguing that ultimate integration in adult society is not the result of integration in educational programs, but depends on the development of skills. Many of the unique needs of these pupils cannot be mastered in integrated placements, but nevertheless must be met as a prerequisite for successful integrated functioning, both socially and academically. Some supporters of Bob believed that there was nothing that deaf students needed more than a peer group with whom they could communicate fluently and easily, and that center programs and residential schools were the genuine LRE for many deaf students. Many parents saw their deaf children's residential school environments as far more supportive than mainstream programs, and some argued that residential schools were instrumental in the acquisition of language and the social and cultural tools needed for their children's educational growth.

The dilemma facing Bob was that the "rush to inclusion" did not consider the unique communication and socialization needs of deaf children. Theoretically, an "inclusive" environment was one which addressed the needs of every child with a disability. In reality, there were outspoken advocates who did not seem to care that some children would likely fall through the cracks. Even though IDEA allowed for a continuum of program placements, the regular classroom was generally seen as the least restrictive environment.

ॐ   ॐ   ॐ

Indeed, inclusion, early intervention, family support, and empowerment were hallmarks of Bob's work in the Office of Special Education and Rehabilitative Services. He saw an inclusive environment as being one in which no child or adult would have to bear the unfair burden of being present but still absent in terms of the benefit that comes through authentic interaction with peers. He argued that the U.S. leads the world in integration, including individuals from diverse backgrounds in all aspects of American life. To Bob, people with disabilities should expect no less.

Contrary to what some feared from a man who had worked for decades in special schools for deaf students, Bob cast himself as anything but an isolationist. Whether he was talking about programs for students with disabilities or the role of OSERS itself, he stressed the need to participate in the mainstream.

Bob's perspective, however, was not staunchly inclusionist. His refusal to endorse the blanket statement that *all* children should be in regular classrooms was a decision that caused him much grief. His position was that there was a need to recognize a continuum of program placements for children with different needs.

ॐ ॐ ॐ

Bob thought he would have eight years at the Office of Special Education and Rehabilitative Services during which he could develop his legacy in special education. To his disappointment, he discovered firsthand the unpredictability of politics. During the spring of 1992, the president's popularity soared to an astonishing high of nearly 90 percent due to successes in the Gulf War. However, when the economy took a nosedive later that year and reelection began to look questionable, Bob became worried about completing many of the programs and services he was working on. Multiple and extensive discussions were held on this topic.

During the first years in his post as assistant secretary, he had worked hard to open minds and change perspectives. In prior efforts to implement Public Law 94–142, some educators had interpreted LRE to mean that every child with a disability should be placed in a regular class without exception, with alternate placements considered only after evidence of failure. *In other words, a child had to fail in the regular classroom before being placed elsewhere.*

This critical issue had caused Bob great stress during his term in office and often placed his educational philosophy and his interpretation of the law's actual intent in conflict with extremists' views. He was sensitive to the views of many in the low-incidence disability fields such as deafness and blindness, which valued center-based or residential school programs because such programs created the critical mass of students required to develop comprehensive quality programming. He was convinced that these programs were not about segregation or integration; they were about quality and successful outcomes. He did not question or dispute his predecessor's dedication and commitment, but feared that many children, including deaf and blind children, would "fall through the cracks" should his predecessor's narrow agenda be pursued. He firmly believed that this had never been the intent of the law.

ﻛﻛﻛ ﻛﻛﻛ ﻛﻛﻛ

Although all disability policies were theoretically "cross-disability" in nature, policies which had been coming out of OSERS were not addressing the needs of deaf children. Bob recognized the needs of deaf children as unique, but the government did not. Bob very much wanted to leave a legacy of support for them. He was disappointed with his earlier efforts to have ASL recognized as other languages are in government policy, and he now envisioned his legacy in the form of a "policy guidance" for deaf students that might be completed before his term was over.

The policy guidance that Bob had in mind would ensure that deaf children would be provided with a free and appropriate public education (FAPE), a mainstay in IDEA legislation. This would be accomplished by providing background information and an outline of steps to state and local education agencies. Bob's plan would also identify procedural safeguards to assure that parents understood their rights throughout the decision-making progress by public agencies regarding their child's placement.

Bob had made every possible effort to enhance the educational opportunities of *all* children with disabilities. The policy guidance for deaf students was needed to address their special needs for a communication-rich, non-traditional classroom environment. Although the firestorm over his being viewed as a single-disability person was still fresh in his mind, Bob could not allow the "fail-first" mandate to continue without an attempt to further support the parents, educators, and children who he felt were being unfairly treated through misinterpretations of the legislation.

Bob asserted that all persons involved in the process of developing the IEP of a deaf child should examine certain factors. These included communication needs and the child's and family's preferred mode of communication; linguistic needs; severity of hearing loss and potential for using residual hearing; academic level; and the social, emotional, and cultural needs of the child, including opportunities for peer interactions and communication. He saw a need to include specialists in these fields as part of evaluator teams. This would ensure a proper understanding of the child in question, thereby better addressing his or her needs.

That spring of 1992, as Arkansas governor Bill Clinton's campaign for the presidency gained momentum, Bob was invited to give the keynote address on the topic of "least restrictive environment" at the July National Association of the Deaf (NAD) Convention in Denver. Home with his own people, Bob believed that he owed it to them to summarize what he was doing to change policies, despite the likelihood of criticism by other disability groups. At the NAD conference Bob described the growing concern, particularly by many in the deaf community, that school districts were interpreting the "least restrictive environment" provision of IDEA to mean placement in or close to the regular classroom. The overgeneralization being made was that these placements were inherently less restrictive. He emphasized again his belief that this was often not the case, *especially for many deaf children,* particularly when nothing was being done to allow them to communicate and interact with other children. He encouraged the NAD to redirect some of its efforts toward helping school systems provide appropriate support services for deaf children.[2]

The NAD speech was enthusiastically received and the deaf community was elated that the Office of Special Education and Rehabilitative Services was moving in this direction.

News of the speech quickly reached the larger disability community through the disability press, however, and touched off a vigorous letter-writing campaign from individuals and organizations, led by The Association of the Severely Handicapped (TASH), in opposition to Bob's position. People were afraid that adopting the policy for deaf children would ultimately lead to its imposition on all children with disabilities and overturn their long-time struggle for inclusion of all children with disabilities. Strangely, these people did not show that they understood the reverse effect of their views, i.e., the negative impact on the education of deaf children. While the Association for the Education and Rehabilitation of the Blind and Visually Impaired supported Bob's perspective and began its own letter-writing and lobbying campaign calling for a similar policy for blind children, the reaction by other disability groups, in turn, triggered a vigorous counter-response by the deaf community.

The Maryland Coalition for Integrated Education and the organization Schools Are For Everyone (SAFE) served as TASH's leaders in the lobbying effort, urging calls and letters to Secretary of Education Lamar Alexander, Congressional representatives and the White House. They implored the secretary, Congress and the president to stop Bob, arguing that the proposed policy was inconsistent with IDEA and would bring the Education Department into direct conflict with the Office of Civil Rights. By August 1992, their strategy was to slow things down by asking the White House for a review of the pending policy. The groups felt that if the White House ordered a review, sufficient influence could be exerted to kill the policy, or at least to stall it until after the election. Interestingly, while arguing against the policy guidance for deaf and hard of hearing children, not a single one of the organization's leaders could communicate effectively with a deaf child.

Bob had done his homework in first obtaining the backing of the Education Department's general counsel, confirming that his strategy would pass legal muster. As fall approached and President Bush's re-election became less certain, the White House stood resolutely by Bob's position. At the same time, Bob supported President Bush in every way possible during the campaign for re-election. President Bush was certainly appreciative of Bob's efforts. He sent Bob a letter on September 22, 1992:

> Please accept my sincere appreciation for assuming a leadership role in the Americans with Disabilities for Bush-Quayle '92 Coalition....Your individual support and endorsement of our efforts mean a great deal to me. Your collective endeavors with the community of Americans with disabilities are critical to our success in November. We must finish the mission begun four years ago.[3]

Once TASH and its supporters understood the extent of Bob's backing within the White House, they shifted strategy from trying to stop the policy and instead lobbied for a letter in place of a discrete policy in the federal register. The letter would carry less weight and have a much narrower distribution. There were only weeks left before the election. Bob knew that writing the *Deaf Students Education Services Policy Guidance* would not be difficult. The problem was that Bob's own staff ordinarily sent policy drafts to OSERS' policy office and legal team for review and rewrites. Revised versions were then sent to the Education Department's general counsel for clearance before going to the secretary for final approval.

Bob knew that sending the draft to his own policy people would likely kill any chances of it reaching the secretary before the November election, since groups opposed to the policy would likely have lobbied his staff to either make revisions or stall its moving on. The stakes were too high for the policy to be "penciled to death" by his own lawyers. In a rare move, Bob bypassed his own policy office and submitted the policy directly to the office of whose support he was assured, the general counsel of the Education Department.

Bob did not want to have his name as author of the policy guidance because he felt he did not have sufficient clout and that having his name on it would dilute its potential influence. There was also concern in the White House that his intent of issuing a policy guidance under Lamar Alexander's name would be controversial and might cause problems with the president's re-election bid. The White House wanted Bob to agree to wait until after the election. "I refused on the grounds that if the president lost the election, then the policy guidance would be watered down and of little value," Bob explained. "It needed to have the backing of a sitting president and his secretary of Education."[4] In the end, Bob had the support of Bobby Silverstein, Senator Harkin's director for disability policy, who agreed to help avoid political conflict.

Secretary Alexander asked Bob if this was what he really wanted to do. When Bob said yes, the Secretary told him to go for it.

On October 30, five days before the 1992 presidential election, Secretary Lamar Alexander signed the *Deaf Students Education Services Policy Guidance*, which was published in the Federal Register. Among the key statements in this policy guidance was the following:

> The Secretary is concerned that the least restrictive environment provisions of the IDEA and Section 504 are being interpreted, incorrectly, to require the placement of some children who are deaf in programs that may not meet the individual student's educational needs. Meeting the unique communication and related needs of a student who is deaf is a fundamental part of providing a free appropriate public education (FAPE) to the child. Any setting, including a regular classroom, that prevents a child who is deaf from receiving an appropriate education that meets his or her needs, including communication needs, is not the LRE for that individual child.[5]

About a year after he had begun his work in the Office of Special Education and Rehabilitative Services, Bob had hired Susan Murray, a former Gallaudet colleague, to be the Director of Public Information. Her expertise enhanced Bob's impact as he broke ground with many new projects, including the Deaf Initiatives Project of the National Association of State Directors of Special Education (NASDSE). Through Murray's capable assistance, Bob's determination to meet the needs of families was enabled. She also assisted him with a variety of other challenges, including increasing the interaction between those in deaf education and their counterparts in other areas of disability and special education.

Murray remembers the 1992 policy guidance work as one of Bob's most significant accomplishments as assistant secretary. It was an example of his resilience and hard work—pulling off a most challenging task in the face of organized resistance. She reflected that while Bob did most of the work, he had his eye on the prize—publication of the policy guidance as an edict from the U.S. Secretary of Education—and this goal elevated the process beyond the issue of whose name was on it. Murray said that the plan succeeded because Bob was the right person, in the right place at the right time, and because everything came together. As she remembered:

> I truly believe that it was all the better because it had so much more clout...a really positive thing because it encompassed the whole department....It was masterful on Bob's part how he did this. And, I think the fact that it later became statutory under a Democratic administration is very interesting....This is a great legacy for him because this would never, ever, ever have happened otherwise if it were not for him.[6]

Murray believed that Bob's own experience was critical to this accomplishment—"as a deaf person, and as an educator, and as somebody who can cut through so many layers of what really needs to be done."[7]

Bob's hard work was further cemented when, after the presidential inauguration, the Clinton administration converted the *Deaf Students Education Services Policy Guidance* into federal law.

ə✸   ə✸   ə✸

Bob had one last honor bestowed on him during his final months in office. Ten years earlier his deaf colleague Frank Bowe, a professor at Hofstra University, had spoken at the United Nations General Assembly to open what was internationally designated as the "Decade of People with Disabilities." As the decade officially ended, the White House wanted an American with a disability to be its speaker at the closing ceremonies. While there was a lot of competition for this honor, Bob was the highest-ranking administrative officer in the nation fitting that criterion at the time. He was invited to speak.

On October 12, 1992, Bob stood before the 47th session of the United Nations General Assembly and presented a plenary address at the conclusion of the United Nations' Decade of Disabled Persons. "We are pleased to share the results in America with our partners throughout the world as we work toward the goal of increased participation of people with disabilities in every aspect of life," he told the audience. "Mr. President...we are proud of our accomplishments, and look to the challenges of the next decade, and the next century, with optimism."[8]

Bob had not realized how significant this event would be until he arrived at the United Nations building. He stood there looking at the delegates and visitors, and for a moment the thought flashed through his mind that a former Napa Valley fruit picker had made it all the way to a podium at the United Nations General Assembly. Shortly after the United Nations address, he reflected, "As I spoke, the whole world learned that individuals with disabilities from minority backgrounds can have a leadership role if they have the skills, knowledge, and ability."[9]

ॐ ॐ ॐ

During Bob's term as assistant secretary, four major federal statutes enabling programs and services for individuals with disabilities had been successfully reauthorized: the Individuals with Disabilities Education Act (1990), the Infants and Toddlers with Disabilities Act (Part C of IDEA), the Rehabilitation Act of 1990, and the amendments to the Education of the Deaf Act (1992). Bob had undertaken what proved to be the effective promotion of greater public awareness of the needs and capabilities of individuals with disabilities, both nationally and internationally. He fostered awareness and implementation of the Americans with Disabilities Act, and he developed and promoted a national agenda for persons with disabilities within the scope of federal laws as administered and regulated by the Department of Education. His colleagues in many government programs were inspired by his tenacity and outlined to him their own plans to hire qualified professionals with disabilities to fill substantive, relevant positions.

Resigning as assistant secretary was difficult. Bob had invested so much of his time and energy into this work, and was hoping to have another term to capstone these accomplishments. On January 7, 1993, following the formality expected after an election, he wrote to the defeated President George H.W. Bush:

> This letter tenders my resignation as Assistant Secretary of Education for the Office of Special Education and Rehabilitative Services effective 12:00 p.m., January 20, 1993. It has been a great honor and pleasure to serve in your

Administration. Your appointment of me to this position has given me the opportunity to work to bring together individuals and groups with widely divergent views, and to develop public policy that addresses both the commonalities and the differences among the 43 million Americans with disabilities.... My selection to represent the United States before the General Assembly of the United Nations at the Close of the Decade of Disabled Persons is indicative of the commitment of our country, under your leadership, to recognizing the potential and productivity of every American.[10]

As he prepared to leave public office, Bob wrote to his friend Gil Delgado: "It was an experience of a lifetime and something I will treasure in my memories. Your own support throughout my service sustained me in times of difficulty. *Muchísimas gracias, amigo* [many thanks, friend]."[11]

Warm and friendly letters were also written to Bob—from parents, advocates, professionals, and persons with disabilities who had appreciated his efforts on their behalf. He was especially commended for the many contributions he had made to enhance opportunities for *all* students with disabilities.

Rep. Major R. Owens (D-New York) looked back at Bob's tenure as assistant secretary. "He had a mess to clean up," acknowledged Owens, chairman of the House Education and Labor subcommittee.[12] "The whole atmosphere has changed in terms of morale. It's much better."[13] When Bob left office in January 1993, he left behind a well-oiled and effectively-managed Office of Special Education and Rehabilitative Services.

Senator Paul Simon (D-Illinois) wrote to Bob:

We don't often enough let people know when we appreciate the job they've done, so I want to thank you for your service as Assistant Secretary....You should be proud of the job you did. All of us who are concerned about high standards for government programs, particularly programs serving people with disabilities, can be grateful for your dedication and hard work.[14]

Colleagues within his office also described him as a fence-mender both within the department and in Congress. Even with conflicting views among disability groups and special interest groups, Bob was able to forge consensus. Philip Link, an executive administrator in OSERS, reflected: "Senators on both sides of the aisle found him a very charming individual and put aside their partisan differences."[15]

CHAPTER 14
Fiercely the Product of Both Cultures

WHEN THE DEMOCRATS CLAIMED THE WHITE HOUSE, Bob began spending time reacquainting himself with his computer and enjoying with Donna the longest "vacation" they had had in many years. After leaving his office at high noon on January 20, they traveled to the West Coast for a restful vacation there, and then spent some time at their beach condo at Ocean City, Maryland.

Bob had married a woman of Swedish descent whose prelingual deafness hindered her acquisition of Spanish and, thus, he used his native language only occasionally, mainly at conferences overseas. He was now overjoyed to have the opportunity to converse occasionally with a family member in his first language. This was Ruth Amaro, a civil engineer from Caracas, Venezuela, whom Brian had married in June 1992.

Ruth came from a professionally trained family. Her father was a medical doctor. She had obtained a position in Brian's company, Charles P. Johnson Associates, an architectural/engineering firm in Silver Spring, Maryland. Shortly after starting out, she noticed Brian's nameplate and, assuming he spoke Spanish, addressed him in her native language. Ironically, neither Brian nor Brent had ever learned Spanish. This first encounter between the co-workers led to a close friendship that culminated in marriage.

Donna and Bob had first become grandparents in February 1990 when Mary Jane, Brent's wife, gave birth to a son. In June 1993, Ruth gave birth to twin daughters, and Donna and Bob then had three grandchildren to enjoy. Within a short time, Brian and Ruth sought Bob's advice on the language their twin daughters should learn first. Bob advised them, without hesitation, "Teach them English first. They can learn Spanish as a second language."[1] Throwing a third language into the mix, ASL, when the grandchildren were old enough, was a nonissue, Brian recalled. When Bob and Donna wished to talk directly to the young children, their son explained, "My father basically did the same thing to them as he did with my brother and me—dangling a little money in front of them—boy they learned fingerspelling real quick!"[2]

The grandchildren were indeed a joy in their lives. While Bob was working for the Department of Education, Brent's young son developed a special liking for the tags found on mattresses and cushions that say, "Do not remove under penalty of law." Little Brian (named for his uncle) would tear a tag off and rub it incessantly between his fingers as a means of self-reassurance, akin to sucking on a pacifier. Brent recalled:

> My wife and son went to a Christmas party at the White House. I couldn't make it that year. [During the party they] went on a tour of the White House. This was not the same tour the general public would go on. So they walked through a room the general public never visited. While you are on the tour, you are not supposed to sit on the furniture. I don't know if it was the Jefferson room they just came out of, but my son had this tag and he was running it through his fingers. Fran Parrotta asked him, "Where did you get that tag?" Young Brian explained, "It's from the couch." My wife and Fran freaked out thinking he had ripped the tag from one of the couches in the White House. In fact he [had] brought it from home. Fran told me I should have seen the look on Mary Jane's face![3]

At another time, Bob and Donna's grandson walked into a roped-off area near a huge Christmas tree in the White House. Mrs. Bush walked under the rope, picked Brian up, and carried him around for a few minutes. Bob was thrilled.

While Bob traveled during his OSERS years, Donna spent a great deal of time with the children and grandchildren, all of whom lived nearby. She took up hobbies, including ceramics and jewelry making. She also went to Ocean City and took walks on the beach. Once a year, Bob and Donna spent about a month in August there, gathering crabs, walking and relaxing. Donna loved to read as a hobby, especially about medicine. When friends became ill, she usually had an article that she could share with them on the topic. She also enjoyed gardening. She accompanied Bob on some trips to Europe and especially enjoyed visiting England, France, and Germany. They also visited Mexico several times. Her favorite trip was to Sweden, a "quiet and beautiful country."

It was not until they were adults that Brent and Brian became better acquainted with members of their father's family. Once Brent and his wife Mary Jane went to Carlsbad, California for a business meeting at the LaCosta

Spa and Resort, located about a half hour's drive from San Diego. The retreat lasted three days. While Brent was in a meeting, Mary Jane heard someone knocking on the hotel room door. The gentleman at the door asked her, "Are you Brent Davila's wife?" After she acknowledged that she was, he explained, "I'm his Uncle Ray."

"My wife didn't know whether to believe it or not," Brent recalled.[4] Ray was retired and working as an electrician at the hotel. Brent had not seen his uncle in over three decades.

Brian also had a unique experience with his relatives from California. He took his wife and twin daughters there for ten days and sought out his father's family. Brian remembered, "My father's brother Gabe....You would have thought they were twins. Now you have to remember this is the first time I had seen any of these people in 33 years!"[5] Brian stayed with his Uncle Gabe for two days. The elder man had some souvenirs from World War II and talked about the War like it was just yesterday. Gabe had fought in the Battle of the Bulge.

ॐ ॐ ॐ

Bob was delighted when Judy Heumann, vice president of the World Institute on Disability, was nominated to succeed him in the Office of Special Education and Rehabilitation Services post. "She is dedicated, knowledgeable, experienced and enthusiastic and will continue to strive for an improved quality of life for persons with disabilities," he said.[6] Heumann, who has a physical disability and uses a wheelchair, had been legislative assistant to the chairperson of the Senate Committee on Labor and Public Welfare in 1974, and had contributed to the development of the Individuals with Disabilities Education Act. Along with the National Council on Disability and others, she had also assisted in drafting the Americans with Disabilities Act, regulations for Section 504 of the Rehabilitation Act, and federal and state legislation that led to the creation of more than 200 independent living centers nationwide.

It took time to adjust to a life out of government, but Bob was indeed proud of his contributions. Phillip G. Vargas, president of Human Research & Development, an international consulting firm in Arlington, Virginia, wrote in 1991 in *The Washington Post* that many Hispanics "remain mostly in the shadows of our society." But Bob had distinguished himself in a very visible role. Vargas emphasized that the invisibility of Hispanics was largely because they were "among the most poorly educated Americans."[7] Only about half of the Hispanics over the age of 25 in 1990 had completed high school (compared with 79 percent of non-Hispanics), and about 56 percent of Hispanic adults were functionally illiterate in English. Vargas, in arguing against bilingual-bicultural education, reiterated a point made by Richard Rodriguez in his book *Hunger of Memory*:

> To Hispanics, Spanish is the language of the family, of friends, of the community. It is also—like any other personal language—warm, intimate and easy. English, on the other hand, is the language of "out there," outside the home and the barrio, the language of the school and the workplace, a language of discomfort, "impersonal, brassy, powerful," and also cold and difficult.[8]

Vargas stressed that preparing to function productively in American society does not mean one must give up love for a language, or for family or culture. But he saw advocates of bilingual and bicultural education as cultural victims. "They love their culture so much they are unable to see that they may be helping to hold back our children from moving forward," he wrote.[9]

Rodriguez's description of the emotional value that Spanish has for Hispanics is similar to the passionate sentiments that Bob witnessed during his OSERS years on the part of deaf people for ASL. However, unlike Vargas, Bob believed that bilingual education was good, and began to work towards having ASL recognized as one of the 100 languages covered by the Bilingual Act. More than twenty years earlier, the Bilingual Act of 1968 had acknowledged the special education needs of children with limited English proficiency, but its goal had remained the teaching of English using the native language of the child. The act provided for the funding of bilingual programs.

Throughout his years in OSERS, Bob also had done everything in his power to provide support to Hispanics and other people of color. Not long after he assumed his leadership role in the Department of Education, he met Rita Esquivel, who proved to be willing to support him in this endeavor. Esquivel was director of the Office of Bilingual Education and Minority Language Affairs (OBEMLA). She had been confirmed several months earlier than he, and so already knew the lay of the land of the Department of Education. Fran Parrotta called their friendship the "Hispanic connection:"

> Rita and Bob hooked up immediately. They went to all the presidential and Department of Education Hispanic events together and went out of their way to get the other political appointees to participate. They met to discuss areas of interest to both of them, including bilingual education and American Sign Language, and particularly Bob's interest in getting ASL included in the Bi-

lingual Education Act. Rita was a good friend and a wonderful supporter. She liked him, she liked his Hispanic background, and she promoted him in the Hispanic community.[10]

Bob's desire to investigate solutions to long-standing concerns in deaf education was behind his discussions with Esquivel. Various scholars were advocating for bilingual education to be used as the core language development model for teaching children who became deaf before they had developed language skills ("prelingual deaf"). Other scholars had fostered recognition of American Sign Language as a true language and of deaf persons as a distinctive cultural and linguistic minority. Bob approached his new friend and asked her if she would be willing to support a proposal of his to include ASL among the more than 100 languages covered by the Bilingual Act. He was delighted that Esquivel supported the idea, going so far as to recommend that Bob meet with Jim Lyons, the executive director of the Bilingual Association of America.

Bob met with Lyons, a pleasant man who received him warmly. He listened respectfully, and after asking a few questions for clarification, concluded that Bob had made an excellent case for including ASL. However, Lyons then shocked Bob by explaining that he would nevertheless be unable to support the inclusion of ASL in the Act for one reason—limited funding. He further elucidated that the entire bilingual budget was less than the amount provided annually for Gallaudet University and the National Technical Institute for the Deaf combined, which together served about 2,500 students at the time. Whereas he and the Bilingual Association had to meet the language and cultural needs of millions of children and train their teachers. "All the time he was telling me this," Bob reflected, "he never lost his poise or his smile. This was a man also on a mission, but one who had done his homework."[11]

As disappointed as Bob was, he decided he would nevertheless make inquiries with the department's general counsel to see if ASL was in fact eligible for inclusion under the Bilingual Act's criteria. After a few months examining the issue, the general counsel informed him that ASL, despite having a unique syntax and grammar structure, was legally ineligible. The present law included a two-pronged test of eligibility. First, the language under consideration had to be the language spoken at home. Second, there had to be agreement that within three years of starting a bilingual program, students would switch to the exclusive use of English in the classroom. Neither of these conditions could be met in all cases for deaf students whose primary language was ASL.

When word got out about the negative ruling, predictably there was some anger expressed by persons in the deaf community who earnestly believed that deaf children using ASL and English were bilingual and thus justified to be included. Some people suggested that Bob had not advocated the cause to a sufficient extent. To address this concern and advocate more comprehensively for ASL to be included under the Bilingual Act, Bob decided to set up a meeting with the general counsel's staff and selected deaf leaders, including bilingual advocates, in order that they may ask questions and receive a full report from those whose job it was to interpret educational law. The meeting was helpful in defusing tensions, but the entire process left Bob with a feeling of loss. He had gone as far as he could in his endeavors with Jim Lyons and upon the advice of his general counsel that ASL was not eligible, he realized, to his acute frustration, that he would only be fruitlessly spinning his wheels if he pursued this crusade any further.

Bob's efforts during his OSERS years to increase awareness and support for the needs of Hispanic Americans in the workplace included serving on the Hispanic Employees Council in the U.S. Department of Education. Its goals were to foster and promote the interests of Hispanic employees within the department, including its regional offices; to increase awareness among program managers of the educational needs of Hispanic youth and adults; to help officials address the needs of Hispanics in the nation; and to promote awareness among Department of Education employees and others of Hispanic culture, language and heritage. Bob was also invited to various performances in the Barnard Auditorium in the main building of the U.S. Department of Education on Maryland Avenue as part of the Council's efforts to recognize the accomplishments of Hispanics.

Valuing diversity had also been a key thread that was woven into much of Bob's committee work during these years.[12] This was essential to President Bush's priorities, too. Since 1989, President Bush had retained or filled about 280 positions with Hispanic appointees, more than in any other previous administration. Approximately 120 of these, or about 43 percent, were Hispanic women. Two were cabinet secretaries (Secretary of the Interior Manuel Lujan, Jr., and Education Secretary Lauro Cavazos), seven Hispanics were in the executive branch, three were ambassadors, and, along with Bob and Rita, eight were assistant secretaries.

Perhaps some of Bob's most influential and effective opportunities to make a difference during the OSERS years came through his invitations to address various multicultural, Hispanic, and disabilities organizations as a keynote speaker. Such opportunities included the Conference on Multicultural Deaf Children at San Diego State University; the First Annual Hispanic Conference on Independent Living in Washington, D.C.; the 7th Annual Bilingual Special Education Conference in Rochester, New York; the Conference on the Hispanic Deaf Experience: Excellence and Equity, in San Antonio; and the 15th Annual California Fiesta Educativa Conference, in Los Angeles. His papers often had such titles as "Educating Hispanic Youth" and "Meeting the Needs of Hispanics with Disabilities." At the Fiesta Educativa Conference, the theme was "Family, Culture, and Solidarity." In Bob's presentation there, he suggested that these titular concepts provided the most important foundations for a fulfilling and happy life for all people, including individuals with disabilities. Bob stated:

> By being grounded in one's family, we gain strength. By being strong in one's culture, we gain identity. By working hard toward achieving solidarity with those with whom we come in contact, we gain unity. This is the essence of empowerment in the making.[13]

Since the National Council of La Raza (NCLR) was headquartered in Washington, D.C., Bob and Fran Parrotta were able to do a lot of work with NCLR leaders Raúl Yzaguirre and Rene Cardenas on behalf of the Hispanic community. Established in 1968, the NCLR was a leading national organization that advocated for civil rights and also engaged in policy analysis and advocacy on national issues such as education, housing, immigration, and free trade. Yzaguirre, Cardenas, and Bob all shared the common desire to see the NCLR assume a significant role in addressing the needs of Hispanics with disabilities. At one point at the annual NCLR convention in Anaheim, California in 1991, they successfully convinced the NCLR program committee to include some offerings addressing disability issues. Angel Ramos, Art Montoya and Bob were on the program. In 1992, the year Bob left OSERS, the NCLR presented him with their Triumph of the Spirit Award. That same year he received the Shining Star Award from the National Hispanic Council of the Deaf and Hard of Hearing. Both awards recognized his pioneering work to support Hispanics with disabilities. That year, Bob also spoke to an audience in the U.S. Department of Education for Cinco de Mayo on the topic of "The Battle of Puebla and Hispanic America's Quest."

Much more than simply reaffirming his Hispanic roots, by involving himself in these activities, Bob—who was the highest-ranking Hispanic in the Department of Education following Secretary Cavazos' resignation—had applied his leadership skills to support and motivate organizations in effecting change within educational systems serving Hispanic students.

Prior to and throughout his OSERS years, despite the demands on his time resulting from his responsibilities, Bob also continued to contribute substantially as a leader in the deaf community. At the urging of Dr. Oscar Cohen of the Lexington School for the Deaf (New York) and a handful of other supporters in 1988, Bob, as president of CEASD at the meeting in Providence, Rhode Island, had established the Ethnic and Multicultural Concerns Committee. At the time, the differences between minority deaf children and white deaf children were not well recognized. In fact, the conventional wisdom was that a child's deafness somehow mitigated his or her racial, linguistic or ethnic minority background. However, it was also very clear to some professionals in the field that the academic achievement of Hispanic and African American deaf children lagged severely behind that of their white peers. Researchers at Gallaudet had found that students who were members of minority ethnic groups were likely to be exposed to less curriculum content and were more likely to be placed at a lower level in school. They also found that African American and Hispanic deaf students demonstrated significantly poorer achievement patterns in both reading and math comprehension as measured on the Stanford Achievement Test.

Although establishing the Ethnic and Multicultural Concerns Committee was not a particularly radical move, it nevertheless met with resistance. Because of the prevailing view that deafness overshadowed the effects of being born and raised in a minority family, some CEASD members questioned the rationale for establishing the committee. At one CEASD meeting, when the committee recommended the establishment of an annual $1,000 scholarship to be awarded to a member of a racial, linguistic or ethnic minority graduate student in deaf education, several members, including some board members, objected, stating that such a scholarship would drain resources away from deafness related projects. Bob's forcefulness as a leader, along with the support of Cohen, Gil Delgado and a few others, prevailed, and the scholarship was established.

The Ethnic and Multicultural Concerns Committee, under Cohen's leadership and with Bob's support, began to organize efforts to bring this glaring inequity to the forefront. In 1989 Bob was the dinner keynote speaker at the first of its kind CEASD-sponsored conference entitled "Black and Hispanic Deaf Children," held at Gallaudet University. He began his presentation with the following: "In the time it took us tonight to chat and eat our dinner, two American children died of causes related directly to their poverty. Can you guess what color those two children were?"[14] A stunned silence fell over the room.

Throughout the day the conference had enjoyed a very positive, even joyous theme. For the first time, a group of educators, many of them people of color, hearing and deaf, who had never before had been able to fully participate and feel comfortable at a conference, shared their struggles and celebrated their differences. Perhaps everyone was expecting a similarly uplifting keynote address. But Bob was intent on telling the truth, and it was not a pleasant picture. He continued:

> Do we need to wonder why our black and Hispanic children score more poorly on standardized achievement tests? Is it a surprise that only slightly more than half of our Hispanic children graduate from high school? Minority status should not be a handicap, but in fact it is. And what happens when a child whose family is already isolated from the mainstream American experience has a condition which we know can isolate a person even further?[15]

Clearly Bob was drawing on his own personal experience. He went on to further personalize his remarks:

> Please realize, when we begin to establish special programs for minority students, people may raise questions because what we are doing challenges the very American sensibility that in our democracy, all are created equal. We are saying in essence, "bootstraps" alone are not all that is necessary to elevate oneself. Very well-meaning people have questioned me on that issue. You see in purely demographic terms, I was born very much at risk. My parents came from Mexico to California to work in the fields before I and my seven brothers and sisters were born. When I was 8 my father collapsed in a fruit orchard, dead at the age of 48.[16]

For many, it was the first time they had seen or heard Bob tell this very personal story. The somber mood that Bob established with his blunt opening sentence continued to blanket the room. Bob went on to describe that his mother was too poor to visit him at school or to meet with his teachers and participate in his education. He also acknowledged that, while he personally had "pulled himself up by the bootstraps," this was not the case for everyone. In his keynote he reiterated what he had said in his work with Phil Garcia and the Hispanic newspaper articles: "I am very proud of what I have achieved, but I also regard myself as an incredibly fortunate exception. I would never assume that because I succeeded with very few support services, so should all others."[17]

Bob concluded his with the following:

> I stand before you a Hispanic deaf man and tell you quite honestly my identity
> is fiercely the product of both cultures. I, like my brothers and sisters, use main-
> ly English among ourselves and with our children. With my mother, however,
> we use only Spanish. Anything else would be disrespectful. My deafness makes
> me no less Hispanic than my Hispanic heritage makes me less deaf.[18]

It is through his presentations that a window into Bob's self-concept
opens. He was clearly proud of his achievements, but at the same time somewhat bitter about what he referred to in one presentation as the "assault on
our minority students' self-esteem,"[19] because despite his many successes, he
too had been a victim of that process. He also recognized the irony of pointing that out. For example, in his keynote presentation at the Black Deaf
Advocates convention in Atlanta, Georgia on March 14, 1992, he explained
that someone unfamiliar with the issues and concerns that had brought them
together might say, "'Minority deaf persons are doing well.' But, ladies and
gentlemen, sad to say, we are all there are.'"[20] He also noted that 20 years after
he had earned his doctorate from Syracuse University, "I remain the only deaf
Hispanic person with a doctorate, and the only black deaf American with a
doctorate is also in this room."[21] This was Glenn Anderson.

Bob's leadership in establishing the CEASD Ethnic and Multicultural
Concerns Committee was a major leadership contribution to deaf education.
While the inequities facing African American, Hispanic, Native American,
and Asian American deaf students have not been rectified, there is far more
attention being devoted to these issues than ever before, and that attention
would not have been possible without Bob's leadership.

Bob kept himself busy throughout the following year. In April 1993, Gil
Delgado invited him to Santa Fe, New Mexico to present at an Acton Seminar
and provide a national perspective on the Notice of Policy Guidance and what
was happening with full inclusion. Although about 50 percent of the population in Santa Fe was Hispanic and 10 percent American Indian, there remained
a need to better address the specific learning and cultural needs of this population. "As you know," Gil wrote to Bob, "Hispanics will soon be the largest
minority in America. NMSD [the New Mexico School for the Deaf] should
be the 'model' in this effort."[22] Gil felt it was important for hearing parents
of deaf children to understand deafness from the perspective of a deaf adult.

In January 1994, Raúl Yzaguirre, president of the National Council of
La Raza in Washington, D.C., invited Bob to be a panelist at an open forum

on disability issues in the Hispanic community, titled "The Emerging Role of Hispanics with Disabilities: Impact, Influence, and Involvement." This national event was attended by representatives of more than 100 NCLR affiliates and disability experts across the country, and provided a forum for Hispanic community-based organizations to focus on disability-related issues affecting Hispanics. It also created an opportunity for a diverse range of Hispanic groups to come together to develop a plan of action for their current and future roles in disability education and service programs. As Yzaguirre summarized in his letter to Bob,

> Involvement of community-based organizations is critical to enable Hispanics with disabilities and their families to make full use of their rights and available resources. Because of your continuing involvement in the field of disabilities, your remarks will be especially pertinent.[23]

In another keynote address at the Second National Multicultural Deaf Conference at Lamar University in Beaumont, Texas in 1994, Bob addressed the issue of role models and representation of minorities and deaf people in educational programs for deaf children. In his opening address to the conference he stated that he was not proud of the fact that he was never taught by a minority person—hearing or deaf—in any school he had ever attended from elementary to graduate school. He continued:

> In fact, I never even saw one in any capacity in the schools I attended....Is it any wonder that for many years while growing up I believed that Hispanics could not become professionals? During my early years all the Hispanics I knew, including my family, were fruit and vegetables pickers.[24]

CHAPTER 15
Return to White Plains

NOT SURPRISINGLY, BOB SOON BECAME RESTLESS after leaving OSERS. He updated his resume, giving absolutely no thought to retirement. He had many prospects in other cities but preferred to remain in Washington, D.C. Although gone from public service, he was not forgotten. He had an opportunity to buy into a consulting company, but declined because consulting was unpredictable and stressful. Bob did, however serve as a consultant to the National Captioning Institute (NCI) in Falls Church, Virginia. John Ball, the president of NCI, made an offer of a permanent, full-time job, but after four months of commuting in Washington-area traffic, Bob decided he didn't want to do that for much longer.

Despite having been away from the Kendall Demonstration Elementary School and the Model Secondary School for the Deaf for four years, Bob remained fully cognizant of the challenges faced by residential and day school programs serving deaf children. Although the New York School for the Deaf (NYSD) at White Plains (Fanwood) was steeped in a long and rich history, it now was in desperate need of strong leadership to move forward.

When Bob began as assistant secretary in the Department of Education, he had to resign from on Fanwood's board of directors. In the summer of 1993, he returned to the board. At that time, the school was having management problems and the board was considering making a change in the headmaster's position. The chair and president of the board called Bob in Washington, D.C. and asked if they could come down for a day to discuss the situation to obtain his advice. By the time the meeting was over, the two Fanwood board members were convinced that Bob should be offered the position himself. They returned to White Plains and obtained the board's endorsement. Shortly after this, Bob was hired as headmaster at Fanwood.

"Strangely enough, although I had taught and served as an administrator at Fanwood for 17 years, I had never stepped into the headmaster's house until the day I joined the board of trustees years later," he would recall. Bob had remained close to the school community, and he and Donna quickly reunited with old friends and made many new ones. "We loved White Plains," he remembers. "Both of our sons were born in the same hospital in that town and were delivered by the same doctor almost four years apart."[1]

Upon arriving again at the school, Bob asked many tough questions. As he had done within the Pre-College Programs at Gallaudet in the 1970s, he noted the number of long-time employees who could not sign fluently. He challenged the school as to how it could possibly prepare deaf students for a competitive workplace and a bright future if the faculty and its charges could not communicate effectively with each other.

Shortly after Bob began as headmaster, he hired Susan Murray as principal. She had worked for Bob at both Gallaudet and at the Office of Special Education and Rehabilitative Services. Murray reflected on Bob's changes in the organizational structure at Fanwood:

> Was the process painful, especially for those whose jobs were eliminated? Of course. Was it beneficial to students? Definitely. NYSD students had a strong affiliation with this headmaster, and the mutual respect was a driving force in many of the changes that happened on Knollwood Road. Did the changes help ensure the future of the school? Without question.[2]

Arlene Rice, the daughter of deaf parents and whose mother had attended Fanwood, had previously worked as the first female chairman of the Republican Town Committee in Brewster, New York. One of her first assignments was to work in the New York State Assembly for Vincent Leibell, who later became a New York State senator. Her experience with Leibell brought her into contact with then-Assemblyman George Pataki who asked her to head his campaign in Putnam County, New York, for state senator, and then to act as a key aide in his run for governor, which he won in 1992, shortly before Bob returned to Fanwood. When Leibell lost his re-election to a second term, Rice, tired of the daily grind of administrative work but needing two more years of work in the state's pension system to be vested, took a job as staff interpreter at Fanwood in 1993. Rice was intrigued by the prospect of the new headmaster. She remembered:

We were both registered Republicans, had held positions in government which came to an abrupt end, had a long history with the school, and were fluent in ASL and English. Fanwood had never had a deaf leader and, from what I heard, to get Dr. Robert R. Davila was a giant accomplishment. The buzz among the trustees was that they needed to quickly take advantage of George Bush's defeat by bringing "Bob" back to Fanwood.[3]

While hired as a staff interpreter and reluctant to assume office duties again, Rice said she would run the headmaster's office just for the summer while the search for a person to fill the executive assistant to the headmaster position continued. Her skill with sign language was certainly an asset.

"Bob usually got what he wanted," Rice recalled. "He made it clear after two weeks with me that he thought I would be perfectly suited for his office and did not envision me leaving."[4]

Rice remembered that Bob's focus was always "Students First." He brought many changes to the school and tried to change the culture in his own inimitable style. His decisions, although not always initially popular with the staff, usually had good long-term results. His decision-making process was always thoughtful and whenever possible, proactive rather than reactive.

Bob loved a challenge of any kind. On one trip with him to the state legislature in Albany, Rice recalls their sitting across from a man while waiting to see a legislator. Bob's speech was clear and he was speaking to Rice while she responded in sign language. Rice summarized:

After about ten minutes into the conversation, the gentleman across the room looked directly at Bob and said, "Gee, don't you ever get tired of explaining everything to her? What you do for her is so nice." Obviously he thought Bob was the hearing person and I was the deaf one! Bob calmly looked at the man and said, "Oh no, you get used to it after a while." When the man left the office, we both howled. That was Bob! He definitely had an impish, mischievous nature![5]

On another occasion, Bob was asked to serve as an expert witness on a case in Florida involving a developmentally disabled boy who was turned down for admission to a school for the deaf on the grounds that the school did not have specially trained professionals to address his needs. Bob requested that Rice accompany him as interpreter. They arrived in Florida on a Sunday afternoon and stopped for something to eat at a local restaurant. She recalled:

We were sitting in a booth waiting to be served and out of nowhere appeared one of our Fanwood students. It was not vacation or break time so Bob thought it was strange. The student [who had reported his absence from school due to illness] was shocked when Bob waved him [to come] over to our table, wondering what his headmaster was doing in Florida. Bob, with his quick sense of humor said "I knew if I kept looking, I would find you." The student explained he was with his mother and kept shaking his head all the way back to his table.[6]

Rice also described a trip with Bob to Albany to protest the governor's attempt to change the funding mechanism for New York State-supported schools for the deaf. The eight state-supported New York State schools known as the "4201 Schools," so named because of Section 4201 of the state education law, had been working to defeat the governor's proposal, as were members of the New York State deaf community, students' parents, teachers' unions and students themselves. The groups had come together to protest the change. Since Rice had a personal relationship with Governor Pataki stemming from her political activities in Putnam County, she arranged for Bob to have a meeting with him.

Although she knew Bob's tendency to be "bullish" at times when fighting for what he believed in, she knew that his strong political background would temper his comments with her Republican friend, Governor Pataki. Sure enough, Bob began with a casual comment. Smiling at Pataki, he said, "I heard that you know a few signs." Pataki responded, "Well, I have forgotten all the signs except one." Bob was curious, "Which one do you remember?" Governor Pataki looked at him with a smile and made the sign for "bull ____."

The ice thus broken, the Governor was most receptive to hearing Bob's criticism of the new funding plan and, although Rice was holding her breath, things went very well. At one point, Bob looked at the governor and said, "Governor, sir, please know that exactly what 'they' are telling you will happen will result in exactly the opposite. This proposal to change the funding will be detrimental to deaf students throughout New York State." Between that encounter and the pressure brought to bear by parents, the deaf community, teachers, unions, and the 4201 Schools Association, the Governor dropped his proposal.[7]

Bob thought about the days when he had worked at Fanwood under Dan Cloud and how his former headmaster had been so tough. Now, a broader knowledge of human resources and educational issues was required and he acutely felt the challenge of filling Cloud's shoes. Bob brought the same

Bob's mother, Soledad Trejo Davila, died in 1994 at the age of 92. Her work ethic had a powerful influence on his life.

open management style to the New York School for the Deaf that he had developed in the Office of Special Education and Rehabilitative Services. He had a profound respect and affection for Fanwood. At the same time, he knew that the school was at risk of losing not only its identity but its very function in a world that had embraced the concept of educational inclusion and which failed to recognize the unique role of these "center schools."

As a result of Bob's encouragement, families of students attending Fanwood became increasingly involved in making decisions regarding the school's welfare. Susan Murray remembered, "This new level of parent empowerment did not always sit well with staff, who found their long-standing job duties changed as a direct result of Davila's open management style and what his many years of experience had taught him about listening to the families of our students."[8]

In the midst of the many administrative changes at Fanwood, Bob's mother, Soledad Davila, passed away in 1994 in her home in California. He traveled back home to attend the funeral. His mother did not have much formal education, but she had possessed a tremendous work ethic and wisdom, which had rubbed off on him. Rice remembered that despite his accomplishments, Bob never forgot his roots. He loved to talk about how, as a child, he would ride the train four or five hours alone to get to his school in Berkeley. He also spoke fondly of his early family life, reminiscing how he looked forward to his visits to his family in Carlsbad. Rice reflected, "Whenever he spoke of his childhood, his eyes lit up. He always spoke about his favorite teachers at the residential school who took a special interest in him and how they helped him so much."[9]

Later, looking back on his mother's life, Bob remembered how a deafened person can sometimes identify voices from memories. "I do," he recalled, "and I would describe my mother's voice as soft and sad. She always had a ton of burdens weighing on her."[10]

Upon his return from California, he faced disagreement from the teachers' union, whose members were not pleased with some of the changes he had made. Bob demanded more from the teachers, including better preparation and more student-centered teaching. He set up a stricter evaluation process; by 1995 some Fanwood teachers were rebelling by interpreting the union contract more specifically. But, as Susan Murray reflected:

> [Bob's] leadership minimized these conflicts and any possible impact on the operations of the school....I believe he truly respected the professionals and paraprofessionals who were represented by the union, and that his words and actions communicated that respect to them. Without his strong and direct leadership at such a critical time, I'm not sure Fanwood would have moved into the new century as a viable educational institution.[11]

Bob had walked into a tense situation at Fanwood resulting in part from the previous administration not being able to garner substantial consensus and support from faculty and parents regarding these changes. He saw the need for changing the status quo quickly. However, he had had a long history with the school as teacher, supervisor and trustee and had just left one of the most prestigious education positions in the U.S. government. With these credentials, it was significantly harder for faculty to mount a campaign against what Bob stood for and aimed to obtain in the form of drastic changes and concessions. He was successful, although not popular initially.

Bob admitted to setting out such a large agenda for his work at Fanwood that, at times, he over-committed himself. "I do think," he reflected in a letter to a colleague, "we made some progress in establishing an enhanced school climate and culture, but the (real) payoff is still improved student outcomes." He explained that curriculum renewal, improved teacher skills, challenging subject matter, and higher expectations for students were but a few of the issues and concerns that they must continue to address. "The current budget crisis," he added, "has made it very clear that the public, in general, expects a greater return for its investment in special education."[12]

Bob at the New York School for the Deaf at White Plains posing with a group of students and teachers who won the Northeastern "Math Bowl" in competition with deaf students from 16 other schools, 1994.

Despite the challenges at Fanwood, Bob continued his leadership in the field of deaf education with scores of national and international presentations. These included advocating improved education for Hispanic students through the National Hispanic Council for the Deaf and Hard of Hearing Biennial Conferences in San Antonio, Hartford, and Boston and the Hispanic Deaf conference at Lamar University in Beaumont, Texas. At the August 1993 commencement exercises at Lamar University, Bob applauded Lamar's efforts to prepare a new generation of leaders and summarized:

> We are well aware that minority persons are under-represented in teaching and educational administration. So are persons with disabilities, including persons who are deaf. Lamar's effort to alleviate this situation reflects great credit on the university and meets a critical need in our nation's schools.[13]

At Fanwood, while still an avid tennis player, Bob decided he had better slow down and take up golf. Rice recollects that golf did not come naturally to Bob:

> One day he was grumbling about the game and I told him about a hypnotist who professed to be able to help golfers. Since he excelled in mostly everything he tried, he engaged the services of this "golf hypnotist" who came to the office for this one session. I'm not sure why it helped but I recall Bob's game improving. From my perspective, it was simply Bob's determination that usually made him succeed.[14]

Bob and Donna looked forward to spending time with their children and grandchildren. Bob never got into golf until he and his son Brent both pursued it. Brent discussed their get-togethers:

> I think these are real special moments to my father. My own son is an excep-
> tional athlete. He picked up golf when he was about 10 years old, and a year
> later he was good enough to play with adults. The three of us, father, son and
> grandson, have played 20 to 30 rounds of golf together. I shoot in the 90s, my
> dad shoots in the 90s, and his grandson also shoots in the 90s, driving the ball
> almost as far as we do.[15]

Brian added, "I bet it does disturb him, only because he likes to be the best at what he does."[16]

ॐ ॐ ॐ

In December 1994, William E. Castle resigned as Rochester Institute of Technology (RIT) vice president and director of the National Technical Institute for the Deaf (NTID), one of RIT's colleges. Bob had been invited by Castle that year to serve on NTID's national advisory group, which was mandated by federal legislation to advise NTID. Shortly after Castle's resignation, RIT President Albert J. Simone asked James J. DeCaro, the dean of NTID, to serve also as interim director of NTID and to assess whether there was a need for both a director and a dean for the college. After a year of study, DeCaro recommend to President Simone that, at that time, NTID needed both a director and a dean because of the budget circumstances in the Congress which called for a strong executive officer to represent the college on Capitol Hill and an operating officer to oversee the academic and operational side of the college. Simone accepted this recommendation and started a national search for a new director.

Several friends encouraged Bob to apply for the position Castle had vacated. A few years earlier, in 1991, Bob had received an honorary degree from RIT. He told the audience, "Receiving this recognition was one of the high points of my career. The message that RIT sent by giving me this award is that deaf people, to whom the Institute is so solidly committed, can achieve unparalleled success."[17] Bob had been nominated for the RIT award by NTID professors. His contributions to the field of education and to government policy, and his support for the use of technology in particular, related strongly to RIT's criteria for awarding honorary doctorates. As he received his honorary doctorate at RIT, Bob had said:

I have no doubt that the same forward, adaptive, and flexible thinking that has made NTID a success thus far will keep it flourishing as we embrace the world of the future. By staying relevant and keeping on top of the change that inevitably will become our present, NTID can help us be ready for the future as it rushes toward us.[18]

The favorable, initial impression that Bob left at the graduation ceremony led to his being invited back to RIT the following year to present the keynote address at NTID's national symposium: Educational Applications of Technology for Deaf Students. Now, as the search opened in 1996, Bob was not fazed by the fact he was in his 60s. He applied and was among a field of 30 candidates, deaf and hearing. Far from feeling that he was a shoo-in, however, he was uncertain about his chances until a formal offer was received from Dr. Simone. Following his interviews, he sent his former assistant Fran Parrotta an e-mail titled, "Ordeal by Fire:"

> Well, I have survived the process so far. Spent two and a half days being grilled, probed, poked and pinched by about 20 groups at NTID. Started as early as 7 a.m. and kept on going through 10 p.m. or so. Included interviews with RIT deans and VPs, the president of the univ. and board members, etc. I did my best and can only hope it works out. It's a great job. It would make up for all my past disappointments! But, I've grown, too. If I don't get it, it won't be the end of the world![19]

The audience for his presentation as a potential candidate had filled the impressive Robert F. Panara Theatre at NTID. Despite the grueling process, Bob told Fran, "I think I did well. I was very comfortable."[20]

Dr. Simone appointed Bob as the first deaf director for NTID and vice president for RIT. Bob liked President Simone, who reminded him of former Gallaudet President Merrill. He had the same professionalism, compassion, dedication, work ethic, and friendliness. On May 9, Simone wrote to Bob.

> The search committee, the NTID community, and the RIT trustees and vice presidents are all in agreement that you are the right person for RIT at the right time. We anticipate that you, through your vision, energy, and talent, will lead NTID to the next level of its phenomenal growth and development. In the process, RIT as a whole will benefit in a way which further establishes its own uniqueness. Together, NTID with RIT can make NTID and the rest of RIT even stronger.[21]

Bob responded enthusiastically. "I am delighted to be getting the opportunity to work with you and your administrative team to lead NTID and
RIT during one of the most critical and demanding periods of our country's
history," he wrote to Simone on May 13, 1996. "I commit myself to doing
all I can to fulfill the promise of NTID as the premier institution serving
deaf students....Thank you for the confidence you have demonstrated in my
potential to lead NTID."[22]

After the announcement of his new position, Bob was flooded with
congratulatory letters and cards. The Fanwood community generally wished
him well in his new leadership position at NTID. Gil Delgado wrote to him,

> Hey, *hombre*! How many miles in a milestone? Aside from all the honors you
> have attained in your profession, I am proudest of your image in the world of
> our Hispanic people and the model you are for Hispanic Deaf persons. *Mi
> buen amigo, te felicito en esta ocasión tan especial con un fuerte abrazo y un grito*
> [My friend, I congratulate you on this very special occasion with a big hug
> and shout]."[23]

Bob responded ruefully to Delgado, "I haven't had an easy job since I managed a salad bar at Lake Placid one summer years ago. Seriously...I am looking
forward to my new position and doing my very best to make a difference."[24]

But Donna did warn Bob that she wanted more time to visit family
and see their sons and grandchildren, who remained in the D.C. area. Ever
since the early Fanwood years, she essentially had taken on the primary responsibility of raising the two boys and running the household. She did not
want to commit too much to the social life associated with his new post. Every time Bob talked with Donna about the NTID appointment seeming a
formidable challenge, she said to him, "If the job was easy they wouldn't give
it to you!"[25]

CHAPTER 16

The NTID Years

BOB WAS FORMALLY INSTALLED into the office of vice president for RIT and director of NTID during a ceremony in the college's Robert F. Panara Theatre in October 1996. Among the guests on stage that day was Gallaudet University President I. King Jordan. Poking fun at the rivalry between the two colleges, Jordan began by quipping that he was proud to say that Bob was a Gallaudet boy.

Regardless of how people remembered Bob at Gallaudet, and the fact that he had recently received an honorary doctorate there, he was *now* an "NTID boy."

For more than a century, the American deaf community had been calling for a national technical college in order to provide deaf people with a broader range of opportunities than the liberal arts programs that Gallaudet had been offering with such excellence. NTID was established at RIT for the purpose of providing a residential facility for the postsecondary education of individuals who are deaf in order to prepare them for successful employment. In June 1965, President Lyndon Baines Johnson signed the NTID Act in the White House Rose Garden. The National Association of the Deaf was "immeasurably grateful and appreciative to Congress for its farsightedness and humanitarian awareness of the needs of the deaf, as evidenced by the law making NTID a reality instead of the dream it was."[1] The signing of the NTID Act was followed by a competitive bid among eight of the nation's top universities. RIT was the only institution that met all of the specific NTID Act requirements. Its competence in postsecondary technical education was widely recognized by the nation's employers. Furthermore, RIT's established reputation would considerably enhance the chances of employment for its deaf graduates.

Throughout its 40 years at RIT, the college of NTID has offered a variety of technical programs in business, engineering, science, and visual communications. Deaf students may also participate in approximately 200 educational programs available through RIT, providing them access to advanced technological courses of study at the undergraduate and graduate degree levels. NTID also offers a master's degree program to train secondary education teachers. In addition, NTID conducts applied research and offers training workshops and seminars.

Bob was at the pinnacle of his profession in 1996 with this post at NTID, one of the two most visible jobs in the field of U.S. postsecondary education of deaf students, the other being president of Gallaudet University. At the installation in October, he felt that he could accomplish good things. He had held the highest office in every major professional organization for educators of deaf students in the U.S. and now served in the highest post at NTID. The 63-year-old RIT vice president had high praise for NTID:

> The outstanding success and achievement of [its] graduates over the past 25 years attest to the excellence of its services, and I am honored to be asked to assume leadership at a time when a technical education has become so critically important.[2]

President Simone viewed his hiring of Bob as "one of the very best personnel appointments I have ever had the privilege of making."[3] He had first met Bob through the Fanwood headmaster's membership on the NTID National Advisory Group, finding him "quiet and respectful, very low key." There was a great deal of mutual trust between the two and Simone relied tremendously on Bob's insights into the deaf community. He found Bob able to negotiate with both the deaf and hearing worlds in ways he had never seen before. "He is a seamless ambassador in both worlds," the president of RIT summarized.[4]

Simone and Bob met almost weekly. Bob was very organized, always showing up for meetings with an agenda to cover. The president found himself agreeing with Bob on most decisions. "His philosophy, which I share, is to give a little more than you take without compromising your principles," Simone explained, adding, "He tries hard to be fair."[5]

Bob, of course, did not know the meaning of "slowing down" and viewed his new post as a great challenge. With his longstanding interest in technology, the notion of leading a technological college into the new millennium was a thrilling prospect. He had impressive credentials with which

*RIT President
Albert J. Simone
with Bob Davila
at the installation
ceremony in the
NTID's Robert F.
Panara Theatre,
October 1996.*

to maintain and enhance NTID's vitality as a leading institution in the postsecondary education of deaf students. Wendell Thompson, director of NTID Government and Administrative Affairs, recalled traveling with Bob to Washington, D.C. for annual meetings with the Department of Education to discuss funding for NTID:

> During the first visit I made with him, I felt like I was there with a celebrity. The Switzer Building (where the Department of Education is housed) was definitely HIS building. It really was remarkable walking through the halls with him—he knew everyone. Clearly, he had lots of friends in the government.[6]

The meetings were indeed routine for Bob. He had the advantage of knowing all the people he dealt with in the Department of Education and of also knowing most people forming the Congressional committees on the Hill. Ironically, at the tables for Congressional hearings, the assistant secretary for the Office of Special Education and Rehabilitative Services sits in the center, flanked by the Gallaudet and NTID witnesses on each side. When Bob was employed at Gallaudet, the Kendall Demonstration Elementary School and the Model Secondary School for the Deaf presented their budgets separately from the undergraduate and graduate programs, so as VP for Pre-College Programs, he had served as co-witness with the Gallaudet president at those hearings. Of course, he had also been present at these hearings as the assistant secretary of OSERS. One day, as Bob represented NTID during a hearing before a House committee, Congressman John Porter from Illinois accurately noted that Bob had rotated through each spot at the table.

Bob was nevertheless humble during these Congressional visits to his old stomping grounds. He would avoid identifying himself as a former assistant secretary of education, preferring to introduce himself as the NTID vice president. He shied away from opportunities to take advantage of his former connections. Thompson viewed him as being "very traditional" in demeanor during these visits, always arriving in town one day before the hearings so that they could study NTID's "Hearings Book," a comprehensive document containing key information related to budgeting, programs, and services, to prepare for the hearings in Congress. The book is assembled in anticipation of those questions that might be asked by members of the committee during the NTID testimony. Bob was always well prepared, as Thompson remembered, and was a "good talker."[7]

Louise Slaughter, a Congresswoman from Rochester, New York and a strong supporter of NTID, was a liberal Democrat and, of course, Bob was a conservative Republican. Thompson reflected,

> They knew that about each other and still got along fine. Slaughter would always make a point of talking about the Republicans in ways that would test Bob's mettle, and Bob would sit there with a soft smile as he watched the interpreter.[8]

What began as a business relationship between Thompson and Slaughter slowly evolved into a personal one that, in time and despite political differences, eventually included Bob. Representative Slaughter was always willing to go out of her way to support NTID.

ॐ   ॐ   ॐ

Bob had been an outside candidate for the NTID position, unlike his experience during the "Deaf President Now" event in the spring of 1988. Yet, even with his varied experience managing a huge budget with a complex structure of government bureaucracy at OSERS, leading Gallaudet's Pre-College Programs of Kendall Demonstration Elementary School and the Model Secondary School for the Deaf, and serving as headmaster for the New York School for the Deaf at White Plains, this NTID post *was* different. University faculty, especially at RIT, expected a good measure of grassroots involvement in decision-making. In fact, the NTID Strategic Plan, which was approved several years before Bob began, had flattened much of the administrative structure above the level of chairpersons. The plan called for a strong emphasis on a collaborative administration of the programs and faculty and staff of the college.

In addition, the deaf graduates of NTID would be employed in a rapidly changing technological society. Unlike when Bob was at Syracuse, deaf people now had easy access to the telephone because of relay services that allowed for enhanced communication with hearing people. The Internet, and especially email, provided even better opportunities for direct communication between hearing and deaf persons. Captioned television and the promise of hand-held pagers and videotelephony were technologies expanding at such a rapid rate that the playing field of telecommunications access was being leveled like never before.

While these were indeed exciting times, and Bob intended to work with a new dean at NTID to assure that the degree programs accommodated these changes, he was immediately beset with more global budgetary concerns.

As at Kendall, OSERS and the New York School for the Deaf at White Plains, Bob once again faced the task of having to make unpleasant decisions. When he began his residence as vice president, NTID was still reeling from budget cuts that had eliminated 117 of its 640 faculty and staff positions over the previous two years. The U.S. Congress, led by Newt Gingrich, had earlier proposed that the budgets of NTID and Gallaudet both be reduced by 10 percent. This was part of the "Republican Budget Revolution" of the 1990s; thus DeCaro, then interim director, had been forced to implement a series of budget cuts.

Then a "self-study" through the Middle States Association Commission on Higher Education took place, and another budget reduction resulted. The formal accrediting process done through self-regulation and peer review was intended to strengthen the quality and integrity of the college's programs. "While I am pleased that we have accomplished such a significant reduction in expenditures without negatively impacting on our students," Bob reported to Congress, "this did not occur without expending enormous institutional energy. It has required extraordinary good will, trust, and cooperation on the part of our faculty, staff and administration."[9]

With Rochester's large community of 10,000 deaf and 60,000 hard-of-hearing persons watching critically, Bob tackled these concerns head-on. During his first year, he presented to Congress a revised mission statement from NTID's strategic planning process in order for it to be incorporated into law. When the strategic planning process had been initiated in 1991, there was no crisis on the horizon. The plan served the institute well since the changes called for by the "budget revolution" were made in a systematic and logical fashion, utilizing the NTID Strategic Plan for reductions and for redirecting available resources to priority areas that it had identified.

The students were watching, too. Even before he set up his office on the RIT campus, Bob received email notes from Hispanic deaf students. Lori Leal, the student secretary of the Hispanic Deaf Club at RIT, wrote to him, "It is nice to have a Hispanic Deaf person taking the leadership at NTID." Leal wanted Bob to know that during the previous year she and Jaime Mariona had succeeded in establishing the Hispanic Deaf Club at RIT. Sadly, she would be graduating from RIT and would not see him in his new post. She encouraged Bob to support the club and attempted to set up a meeting with him during his next visit to the RIT campus.[10] Bob wrote back the next day, May 15, 1996, "Be assured of my interest in what you are doing."[11] He suggested that they meet even before he moved into his office.

During his years at RIT, Bob traveled more miles on RIT business—raising money for the college, courting corporate support—than all the other RIT vice presidents combined. Cheri McKee, his administrative assistant at NTID, noted that Bob never needed an alarm clock. He always naturally awakened at 5 a.m. "He would arrive at his office at 7 a.m. and leave long after I left at 6 p.m.," she recalled. "He would walk up to my desk to say 'Good morning,' and when he left, I had ten more things to do."[12] She described Bob as very task-oriented and productive. He liked to delegate work and wanted people to handle things independently. He had a place in his heart for alumni of the New York School for the Deaf and their families, and frequently saw students in his office. He was very caring and made connections for students and wrote reference letters for jobs. The vice president also gave his administrative assistant a great deal of freedom. Cheri recalled, "Bob was never threatened by my suggestions or edits. He made me feel empowered and valued."[13]

Bob also felt fortunate that Cheri was as outstanding an administrative assistant as Fran Parrotta at Gallaudet and the Office of Special Education and Rehabilitative Services, and Arlene Rice at the New York School for the Deaf at White Plains had been. "I feel that over the years I have been blessed with the good will and support of fantastic people to work with me," he said.[14]

President Simone described Bob's management style as follows:

> If someone is arguing a point, Bob tends to lean more than halfway over to show support for someone's point of view. He shows great empathy for someone else's position. He also can dig his heels in if he believes in something. He can be one tough hombre.[15]

Some faculty members at NTID, however, saw the "tough hombre" side of Bob too often. Many perceived his style of management as not process-oriented enough, and while input was solicited, there was still a sense that decisions were being made single-handedly.

Bob described this trait as being one of the many characteristics rooted in his past. Growing up without Hispanic deaf models to look up to, he had turned this absence into a personal goal. He explains, "That was probably the motivating moment of my life."[16] He pursued that goal relentlessly. "Not only did I become a teacher," Bob points out, "I became president of three national organizations in education. That's the kind of person I grew up to be: You challenge me, and I'll meet your challenge."

Bob was aware of how his words could come across, however, adding, "Perhaps I shouldn't say that, because it sounds egotistical."[17]

Bob's administrative style at NTID was indeed difficult for many of the faculty to accept. Bill Castle had focused primarily on external issues, allowing the dean to lead the programs within the college. Jim DeCaro had been very grassroots-oriented, although he had to combine the roles of vice president and dean. Bob brought with him a more straightforward approach to the vice presidency, based on his broad experience in leadership positions. He had inherited a mess as president of the CEASD and he almost unilaterally saved the organization. At the Model Secondary School for the Deaf and Kendall Demonstration Elementary School he had to bring calm and order to a tense environment. At the Office of Special Education and Rehabilitative Services, while he depended heavily on his managers, Bob knew he was ultimately responsible for many very important decisions and, again, demonstrated a very decisive leadership and management style. At the New York School for the Deaf in White Plains during the few years he served as headmaster, he had approached problem-solving in the same manner. "This is the way we do it," was the message he appeared to leave after meetings with NTID faculty.

Granted, Bob did seek advice from D. Robert Frisina, who had served as NTID's first director and vice president for RIT. Frisina was now the director of the International Center for Hearing and Speech Research. He had been the basketball coach at Gallaudet when Bob was a student there in 1950, and Bob had served as the team manager, traveling with the team and getting to know Coach Frisina. Over the years, they had maintained a close relationship. Now, at NTID, Bob would occasionally stop by Frisina's office late in the day to chat, ask for advice, share information and just relive old memories. Bob recalled that "Frisina never volunteered advice unless I asked for it—and

*Bob interacting
with NTID student
leaders while
serving as vice
president of RIT
and director at the
National Technical
Institute for the
Deaf at Rochester
Institute of
Technology, 2003.*

I did."[18] Looking back at the NTID years, Frisina summarized, "Bob Davila has overcome many obstacles that would discourage many among us. And for this I recognize and applaud his achievements."[19]

The students also recognized his leadership. In 1998, Victor Medina, a student leader, united the various ethnic and other student organizations in a fundraising effort to honor Bob as the college's first Hispanic deaf vice president. To outsiders, it may be somewhat of a surprise to hear that deafness does not necessarily have a unifying effect, but such was the case on the NTID campus during Medina's time there. He sought inspiration in how to solve these divisions and found it in his hero, Bob Davila. The fundraising campaign itself was a tremendous success, netting $2,500, which went towards creating a life-size bust of Bob Davila. On May 3, 1998, the various NTID deaf organizations turned out in record numbers for a Hispanic Deaf Club-hosted event where a surprised Bob Davila was presented with the bust.

ॐ ॐ ॐ

In July 1998, T. Alan Hurwitz, who had joined the faculty at NTID in 1970, was appointed dean to replace James DeCaro who had recently retired. The college now had a unique partnership in its first deaf director and deaf dean. Then in its 30th year, NTID, one of RIT's seven colleges, was a global leader in high technology and career education. The 1,100 deaf and hard-of-hearing students from the U.S. and other countries enrolled at NTID were actively integrating with RIT's 13,000 full- and part-time hearing students in nearly 200 technical and professional programs of study. Within a short

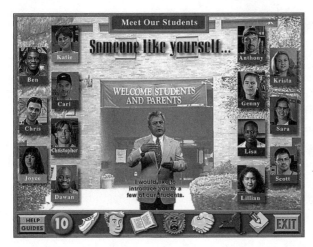

As a leader in educational technology, NTID has produced many forms of media over the years. Bob was involved in recruiting new students in this CD.

time of Hurwitz's hiring, he and Bob had formulated an ambitious agenda for maintaining the college's leadership in postsecondary education.

One item on both Bob and Alan's agenda was increased involvement in international programs. Following a needs assessment study that had been conducted in Hungary by former-dean of NTID James DeCaro and his colleague Ken Nash, a program entitled Project Access was funded by a grant from the Open Society Institute of New York in January 1999. Project Access created the first-ever Information Technology curriculum for deaf students in Central and Eastern Europe. By connecting schools for the deaf and hard-of-hearing to each other and to the world, and by providing graduates with greater access to high schools and the job market, Project Access had as a goal full access to information, skills and meaningful employment, something that had not previously been available to deaf and hard-of-hearing citizens of that region. Although Bob had reservations about NTID's involvement in elementary and secondary education in other countries, preferring higher education initiatives instead, he nevertheless supported the project and led a delegation to Hungary.

Professionally, Bob, despite approaching the age of 70, continued to be energized. He filled every moment of his day. He was invited to present at many conferences, workshops and other events, and always brought his message of the need for education, communication access and opportunities for post-secondary education, training and advancement. Among these many invitations and presentations, one of the most significant was the invitation to be the opening keynote presenter at the 19th International Congress on the Education of the Deaf in Sydney, Australia in July 2000.

The International Congress on the Education of the Deaf, or ICED as it is known, holds a very important, albeit controversial, place in the history of the education of deaf individuals throughout the world. At the 2nd ICED, held in Milan, Italy in September, 1880, the famous "Milan resolution" had been passed, which declared "the incontestable superiority" of articulation over signs in bringing deaf people to more fully integrate with hearing society and in giving them a fuller knowledge of language. This "oral method" was proclaimed to be preferred to that of signs by the Congress, and the simultaneous use of articulation and signs was thought to hinder the development of speech and lip-reading skills. Thus began a century of dominance by the doctrine of oral education, a position that was not challenged in terms of language until 1960 when Dr. William Stokoe, a brilliant linguist, empirically demonstrated that American Sign Language was a complete language in its own right. The oral method was subsequently challenged educationally in the early 1970s by the "Total Communication" approach and subsequently by American Sign Language.

Of the 164 delegates to the 2nd ICED in 1880, educators in favor of the oral method, primarily French and Italian, represented 74% of the vote. Only Britain and the United States voted against the resolution. Edward Miner Gallaudet had appealed to the conference not to dismiss sign language. He argued that a "visual method" combining signs and articulation offered great benefits to most deaf students.

Given this history, it was indeed significant that Bob was invited as the opening keynote presenter at the 19th ICED. Prior to Bob's keynote on the first morning of the Congress, the governor-general of the Commonwealth of Australia made a reference to Milan, noting that the Milan Decree was passed at a time when the education of the deaf was rarely a matter with which deaf people themselves were allowed to be concerned. Bob's selection as the keynote presenter, the first such address by a deaf person at the ICED in its history, was a testimony to the fact that now deaf individuals themselves were taking a leading role in determining their own educational destinies.

This theme was evident in Bob's address to the ICED, where he spoke of the dramatic change and progress resulting in the empowerment of deaf persons and improvement in the quality of their lives over the previous 40 years. But ever the realist, and perhaps thinking of his own personal experience, Bob also noted that as deaf education entered a new millennium, pride should be taken in the accomplishments of students but, "we must also temper the enthusiasm that derives from the success of a few and remind ourselves that there is much still to be done."[20] Although aware of the significance of his own selection as the keynoter, later that week while having dinner with a friend, Bob noted with dismay that even after all these years, there had been only one deaf plenary presenter at the ICED!

Nevertheless, Bob enjoyed his time in Sydney, meeting with long-time friends, and noting, as he did in his opening remarks, that "this is the seventh congress that I have attended and could very well be the last because I expect to be retired by the time the next one is held. I can think of no greater honor for an educator of the deaf to receive than to be invited to address this prestigious conference."[21] Always interested in new challenges, Bob concluded his week by completing the famous but arduous Sydney Harbor Bridge climb with two deaf colleagues.

ॐ ॐ ॐ

Throughout his years at NTID, Bob also promoted the quality education of deaf students in other countries, presenting keynote addresses in Tokyo, Japan, at NTID's sister college, Tsukuba College of Technology; and at the Sixth Asia-Pacific Congress on Deafness in Beijing, China. In 1993, The Nippon Foundation (Ryoichi Sasakawa Scholarship) of Tokyo had awarded both Gallaudet University and NTID two million dollars each to establish endowment funds to assist international students to attend Gallaudet or RIT with a view toward returning home to contribute to improving the quality of life for deaf and hard-of-hearing persons in their own countries. The Foundation emphasized that priority should be given to students from developing countries. Prior to this award, both Gallaudet and NTID were restricted to a 10 percent overall enrollment of international students, including Canada, which traditionally has sent many students to both colleges.

In 1998, Bob asked The Nippon Foundation for another award of two million dollars to increase the endowed fund because NTID was experiencing an increase in interest and applications from international students. International students were mandated to pay a surcharge of 90 percent above regular tuition charges and many of them were not able to enroll because they did not have the necessary financial assistance. The Nippon Foundation responded by saying that, before it could consider NTID's request, it would need to send a site visit team to evaluate the outcomes resulting from the original award.

The site visit "team" was made up of one senior administrator from the Foundation. The visit began with a lunch Bob hosted for him and about ten international students who were receiving assistance from The Nippon Fund. Before the lunch, Bob worried about what the students might say, and wished that he had had an opportunity to brief them on the purpose of the visit. However, they performed admirably and Bob was most impressed with their articulate responses and with their polite and courteous reception of the visitor. The visitor himself seemed to have enjoyed the exchanges and smiled constantly and asked excellent questions.

Following the lunch, however, Bob escorted the visitor to his office to review the balance of his schedule for the day and as soon as they sat down, the delegate spoke up and said, "Dr. Davila, please know that we are not going to be able to grant you any more scholarship support." Bob recalls, "His remark left me dumbfounded and speechless." Bob, of course, asked the gentleman why. The response was even more impacting. He said, "Because every student in that room was not telling the truth!" He explained that studies had been conducted of the outcomes of the Foundation's extensive support to international students to travel to the U.S. to study and the results indicated that too many of them did not return to their home countries. "This defeats the purpose of our intentions," he explained. "We are not providing funds to create more Americans. We want to be more direct in helping countries to help themselves."[22]

From this disappointing experience, Bob came to realize that The Nippon Foundation was on the right track in monitoring the effect of its substantial support to other countries. At that time, NTID was just beginning to develop the Northeast Technical Assistance Center (NETAC) program which was funded by the U.S. Department of Education as a regional resource center to assist colleges and universities in the Northeast in pooling knowledge, information and materials to improve their ability to serve deaf and hard-of-hearing students. NETAC was one of four regional centers funded by the Department of Education.

Not long after the disappointing news from The Nippon Foundation, Bob called in James DeCaro to discuss with him an idea he had that would utilize his engineering and educational backgrounds to develop a center to evaluate and adapt existing technologies to facilitate communication access by deaf and hard-of-hearing persons. From this brainstorming discussion, both Bob and DeCaro agreed that the NETAC service model was a wonderful concept that could work internationally as well as it was working in the Northeast region. Thus was born the idea of developing a proposal and submitting it to The Nippon Foundation. Bob and DeCaro agreed that if deaf and hard-of-hearing students couldn't come to NTID to study, NTID would assist in bringing education to them through collaborative efforts with existing universities in other countries.

During the 19th International Congress on Education of the Deaf, in Sydney, Australia in 2000, DeCaro and Bob hosted an officer from The Nippon Foundation, Mr. Y. Ishii, at an all-day session during which they walked this gentleman through the conceptualized features of what was to become the Postsecondary Education Network—International project (PEN-International). Ishii, a manager in The Nippon Foundation, was very impressed and promoted their concept upon his return to Tokyo.

Both Bob and DeCaro had received their PhDs from Syracuse University, where both were fellows in the Educational Technology for Educators of the Deaf Program, funded by the Media Services and Captioned Films Branch of what had then been the Department of Health Education and Welfare. The result of their collaboration now was a first-of-a-kind international partnership between colleges and universities serving the postsecondary education needs of deaf and hard-of-hearing students. Web technology, faculty development/training, telecommunications technology, information technology and instructional technology would be used to improve teaching and learning for students, increase the application of innovative technology, and expand career opportunities for deaf and hard-of-hearing people.

The same year the pair presented the concept to the Foundation, they received the first grant of five such grants that eventually totaled more than $5.8 million in support of PEN-International. Under DeCaro's leadership, the program has brought educational technology and faculty training/development for deaf education to China, Russia, Japan, the Philippines, the Czech Republic, and Thailand. The project has resulted in a tremendous increase of interest among other countries in emulating the NTID model of postsecondary education for deaf students. This ties to Bob's legacy, too. Both DeCaro and Bob have felt great pride in opening doors for deaf people around the globe.

ə๖   ə๖   ə๖

As vice president Bob was also responsible for establishing private fund raising efforts by NTID. His fund-raising prowess garnered $11.5 million dollars, which went towards financing scholarships, improving technological resources on campus, and furthering research and development efforts. He was particularly interested in finding funds for a student life center. He had found a donor, but the person died before an agreement could be finalized.

Then he went to see Joseph and Helen Dyer in Delray Beach, Florida, but the Dyers were not interested in supporting this center. Joseph Dyer was a retired mechanical engineer and a friend of Bob and NTID Dean Alan Hurwitz and his wife, Vicki. Helen was an amateur artist and both she and her husband had fought their ways through high school and college programs for hearing students. "These experiences became our motivation to help younger people along in order for them to establish themselves in a way that was not available in the old days."[23]

However, Bob noticed that the Dyers had many beautiful paintings and obviously appreciated the arts. He spoke in private to Mike Catillaz from NTID, who had accompanied Bob on the trip, and then outlined to the Dyers the dream NTID had for an arts center. Science and technology were very important, they explained, but deaf students should also attend college for other reasons, including learning about the arts. The Dyers agreed to support the establishment of a center to showcase artistic expression, while applying high-end technology in the process. "My wife and I were born long ago into an age when choices for deaf people were limited," said Dyer. "The founding of NTID gave deaf people many new chances to advance themselves. That's why Helen and I wanted to support NTID and its many contributions to deaf education, technology and the arts."[24]

On the way back to Rochester, Catillaz told Bob that he was asking for trouble. "Why?" Bob inquired. "The faculty won't let you cut down trees in their smoking area!" Mike smiled.

Sure enough, there was some resistance to the proposed location of the new arts center. More than a few people told Bob they were opposed to the elimination of the open garden that could be viewed from many areas of the academic building. Most, but not all, of these people later realized how beautiful and important the Dyer Arts Center had become. The 7,000-square-foot glass-enclosed Dyer Arts Center became the focal point of the Lyndon Baines Johnson Building. A glass roof bathes the exhibit rooms in natural light with the unique design accommodating the visual and communication needs of deaf people. In particular, the sight lines are excellent and allow visitors to view works of art from many vantage points. Bob considered the establishment of this Center a part of his legacy at NTID.

ತು ತು ತು

In 2002, Bob was in his 70th year; he had given six years of hard work to RIT, and he felt that it was time for a change. In April 2003, he announced his retirement. At this time, Bob looked back nostalgically at his career. He had spent 50 years of his life in professional service. "I figure that's two careers rolled into one and think it's time to stop while my wife (Donna) and I continue to enjoy good health and still have energy and enthusiasm to pursue our many and varied interests."[25]

He had run for student president at Gallaudet College and lost by two votes, and then he ran for president of his fraternity and lost by two votes. "That's when I decided politics was not in my future."[26] Yet, after graduating he had rubbed elbows with heads of state and many influential people. Politics did become very much a part of his career as it evolved.

Bob's parting words to the NTID community included praise for how the college in Rochester cultivated and nurtured deaf students to become tomorrow's leaders. "We do this through our cutting-edge academic programs that prepare our graduates to 'hit the ground running' and land jobs in fields that didn't even exist a decade or two earlier," he said. "We do this through the dazzling array of opportunities we set before them to help them become leaders, to grow and challenge themselves far beyond what they thought they were capable of when they arrived at RIT."[27]

He also reminded NTID students about how he had boarded the train as a young boy and waved farewell to his family—and to a life in the barrio. In letting go of that past, working hard, and developing resilience, Bob said, he managed to reach the top of his profession. He told the students,

> Use your talents well, never settle for less than the best, and always remember who you are and where you came from so that you can give back generously to the families, teachers, and communities who helped you get to where you are. To this new generation of leaders, I invite you now to get on board.[28]

Bob explained how his heritage, upbringing, and determination all helped to define who he was. "I leave NTID satisfied that I have contributed in a small way to this college's mission—to help young deaf people acquire knowledge and develop the skills they'll need to face's life's many challenges."[29]

❧ ❧ ❧

Bob's duties as vice president of NTID always kept him extremely busy, but he made it clear to his administrative assistant Cheri McKee that life would never be too hectic for him to see a student. Yet it soon became evident that the presence of a Hispanic deaf man in a position of leadership would positively encourage even the students who did not have direct contact with him—simply by virtue of his being there.

A Hispanic student Bob especially influenced was Kelly Lenis, who had been a student at the White Plains School during Bob's stint as headmaster there:

Dr. Davila was like a father to me. I was never afraid to come to his office to ask him anything, and every time I came, he always had a big smile for me. One time an article and photo of me being a storyteller at the local library appeared in my hometown paper. The next day, I received a note and a copy of the paper from Dr. Davila. He told me how proud he was of me and told me that I made the whole school proud. I never want to lose that note. I will always remember his advice to me: "Make the play first and protest the umpire's call later." It means you should reach your goals and finish your education and then become an activist later. This quote is important to me as I continue my education. I never had a Hispanic deaf leader in my life until I met Dr. Davila. Without him, I wouldn't have been a leader in school. He is what I want to be after I graduate.[30]

Bob often claimed that deafness was his greatest challenge. However, he also recognized that escaping the barrio and poverty were critical to his success. During one meeting at NTID with a large group of Hispanic high school students from the Illinois School for the Deaf, one student asked him what he considered to be his greatest challenge. "First," he responded quickly, "was overcoming economics to go to college, working in summers. I was too young to get a job. I worked hard and that was a big challenge."

Bob encouraged the students: "be proud of yourselves and who you are." When the students were about to leave the meeting room, Bob provided some parting advice. "One more thing: October is Hispanic Heritage Month, you know that?" he reminded them. "But celebrating only in October is a mistake."[31] He told them that when the month is over, people forget Hispanics and that Hispanic culture should be part of the curriculum twelve months in the year.

When Bob retired from NTID, his youngest sister, Mary Helen Moreno, still lived in Carlsbad. She could barely remember her brother from before he left for the California School for the Deaf at Berkeley. But she remembered the summers when Bob returned home, when he read to her and gave her nickels to buy candy at the neighborhood store. "He's been on his own from very early on," she said proudly. "He's been remarkable."[32]

As Bob brought his NTID career to closure, the NTID National Advisory Group established the Robert R. and Donna E. Davila Endowed Scholarship Fund, recognizing the couple's lifelong commitment to education for deaf and hard-of-hearing people around the world. Bob also received the annual APANSCE Award from Associació de Pares de Nens Sords de Catalunya (Association of Parents of Deaf Children of Catalonia). Catalonia is a region in northeastern Spain which includes the city of Barcelona as its capital. The APANSCE Award is given to an individual or institution that has worked to improve the education and lives of deaf children and their families in Catalonia. The association is dedicated to collaborating with associations of deaf people and promoting technology to improve the lives of deaf people.

The fact that educators in Spain so honored Bob for his contributions to deaf education when he had never been employed outside of the United States is a telling indication of how encompassing and far-reaching his life's work has been.

Perhaps the words of Bob's son, Brian Davila, best summarize Bob's life and work and the influence he had on many young people:

> There are two things that my father always taught me that I am very grateful about because it has made me the person I am. I was never allowed to say, "I can't." Never. I mean my whole life. That was out of my vocabulary. Second, I was never to sell myself short or underestimate myself. It could be something as simple as the school play. I might say, "I can't do that; I can't get in front of the crowd." But I had to do it because I could do it. Other people can do it.
>
> I guess the reason why my father was like that was because he was able to overcome all these obstacles all his life, so it was just ingrained in him. You can do whatever you want to do—those were the values he tried to instill in me.[33]

ॐ ॐ ॐ

On May 17, 2003, Bob presented an address at a beautiful and colorful commencement at California State University, Fresno. Honored by the University for his "rich cultural and educational experiences," Bob thus joined the ranks of other outstanding Hispanics so recognized, such as the Honorable Cruz Bustamante, lieutenant governor of California, and actor Edward James Olmos.

At this ceremony, Bob explained that when he finished college, he was a bit naïve, not knowing what to expect from the real world. "I didn't know what kinds of ethnic and social challenges I might encounter. What I did know was that my...[Hispanic] heritage had armed me with courage, resiliency, a strong work ethic, and determination. I would need those qualities to overcome many obstacles, the steepest of which undoubtedly was my deafness," Bob stressed, affirming his heritage.[34]

He also recalled his early life in California and how it centered around the Spanish-speaking communities in which he lived, saying, "My memory of sound, even music, is almost exclusively Spanish." He stood before the large audience and, reflecting on his own experience, told the young graduates and their families, "It is a sign of progress and a prelude to a long-promised future that every graduate at this gathering can aspire to whatever he or she is willing to work and sacrifice to achieve. That, indeed, is the promise of America."[35]

Looking up from the podium, Bob could see up close the Hispanic graduates to whom he was speaking. He had been the first college graduate in his family, and the same could be said for a significant number of the young people with him that day. California State University at Fresno, located in the hub of the San Joaquin Valley, had such a large graduating class of Hispanics that a separate ceremony was held. There were so many people attending that the commencement was held in a football stadium. "Speaking in front of 16,000 Hispanic people in California was one of the most significant events in my life," he said. "As I stood there, I realized that I truly had gone full circle since my childhood."[36]

AFTERWORD

SINCE BOB DAVILA COMPLETED HIS ROLE as chief executive officer at the National Technical Institute for the Deaf at Rochester Institute of Technology in December 2003, it has become apparent to us that he just would not "retire" from pursuing his legacy. "I'm up to my gills," he wrote us in October 2004 when we asked him a few questions about "retirement." That comment is perhaps as accurate a representation of Bob's "work ethic" as we might find. He has been up to his gills in work since he left the barrio in 1944, more than 60 years ago.

But, Bob's legacy is interpreted in many different ways. Susan Murray, his friend and colleague in the Office of Special Education and Rehabilitation Services, saw Bob's legacy as the writing of the *Deaf Students Education Services Policy Guidance* while he served as assistant secretary in the U.S. Department of Education under President George H. W. Bush. President Albert J. Simone considered Bob's legacy his general excellence and achievement as a vice president at RIT. After President Simone asked us to write this book summarizing Bob's life and work, we grew to believe, as educators, that Bob's legacy may be in the inspiration he has provided to deaf students everywhere, especially to young Hispanic students.

Victor Medina, for example, who was raised, like Bob, in California, found much in common with Bob. As a young Hispanic student at NTID, Victor used to stop by Bob's office to talk, and always found the door open. Victor recalls,

> He'd ask how I was doing in school and how my family back home was. We talked about how much we missed our homemade Mexican foods. I'd tell him what was going on with my life, good and bad. No matter what, he always

185

understood me because we were both deaf Hispanic men and had grown up in San Diego. He knew all the barriers I had faced.[1]

While Bob had no Hispanic deaf role models in deaf education when he was young, he did have deaf role models. As he has mused, "The very fact that I acquired the highest academic degrees and that I can honestly say I received an excellent education is due largely to the fact that other deaf persons reached those goals before I was motivated by their example."[2] This strengthened his resolve to *become* a deaf Hispanic role model. It was resilience that he demonstrated when he encountered his own teachers who had low expectations of Hispanic students. As he later reflected, "It is important to appreciate your background, to feel good about yourself. [Hispanics] have to be at the forefront, fighting for their rights, asserting themselves."[3] As a result, there is a long list of leaders in deaf education who were in turn inspired by Bob.

Since Bob's childhood, not nearly enough has changed regarding how poorly most Hispanic deaf children perform in school, how they are underrepresented in post-secondary education, how they generally live in depressed areas, how they are still often deprived access to high level jobs and health care, and how they score poorly on other social indicators of prosperity and hope. In this sense, Bob has *not* achieved one of his goals—there are still far too few Hispanics, especially those who are deaf, in leadership positions in the field of deaf education. Many people, both inside and outside of deaf education, believe that deafness precludes ethnic and/or racial "minority" group membership or status. It doesn't necessarily. The dearth of deaf members in the National Council of La Raza, the National Urban League or the National Association for the Advancement of Colored People, for example, suggests that the chasm between those organizations and deaf people of color is due to the perception that deafness overshadows race and ethnicity.

And this situation is not much better within the deaf community itself—with the exception of Bob and one or two others, there has been virtually no significant Hispanic or African-American Deaf participation and leadership in the National Association of the Deaf, Gallaudet University, NTID, or the program at California State University at Northridge. Many deaf professionals, even some who themselves are members of culturally diverse groups—have made the same argument that being deaf takes precedence over any other cultural identity. Both these perspectives shortchange most deaf people of color by doubly denying them their ethnic and racial heritage, first by their ethnic and racial kin and then by their deaf brothers and sisters.

In April 2004, Bob met with his friends Gilbert Delgado (left), Ramón Rodriguez (far right), and New Mexico's Governor Bill Richardson to discuss the education of deaf Hispanic children.

Bob's legacy is viewed by some as being a leader. No other deaf person has been elected to the top post of all three major professional organizations for educators serving deaf students—the Conference of Educational Administrators Serving the Deaf, the Convention of American Instructors of the Deaf, and the Council on Education of the Deaf. Bob held the position of vice president at Gallaudet University, and the top post at NTID. He also served as headmaster at the New York School for the Deaf at White Plains. Certainly, Bob's failure to become president of Gallaudet University in 1988 was one of the biggest disappointments of his life. No matter what he may say about having no regrets, his not being selected remained puzzling for many of his friends and supporters. He had substantially more administrative experience, especially in the postsecondary environment, than the other two deaf candidates, and as much or more support in terms of recommendations from the interviewing groups, but he did not make it into the final pool of three candidates. He did, however, rebound in an impressive manner. While having been excluded from being a finalist at Gallaudet, he nevertheless received a nomination from the president of the United States for the highest-level government post ever filled by a deaf person, obtaining the support of the United States Senate for that position after a rigorous vetting process.

Booker T. Washington once said, "Success is to be measured—not so much by the position that we have reached in life—as by the obstacles that we have overcome while trying to succeed." This book has described how Bob Davila found ways to go over and around obstacles to become a leader in the education of students who are disadvantaged by disability, ethnicity, and poverty. And this continued in his "retirement" from NTID. In 2003 Bob was appointed by President George W. Bush to serve on a 15-member National

Council on Disability, which advises the President and Congress on matters affecting the education, rehabilitation, and employment of 52 million Americans with disabilities. He was back in the thick of disability politics. He was also named by National University in La Jolla, California as a 2003 recipient of the Dr. Jerry C. Lee Endowed Chair for Technology and the Adult Learner. The Chair is dedicated to technological innovations in the classroom. He was back in the thick of educational issues. Then, in July 2004, Bob was appointed as senior vice president of the new National Programs division of Communications Services for the Deaf in Sioux Falls, South Dakota. Bob had oversight of the marketing and human service operations, involving field offices and telephone relay centers to address such issues as domestic violence and drug and alcohol counseling for deaf people across the United States. Additionally, under the leadership of Benjamin Soukoup, Communications Services for the Deaf has established extensive video relay and video interpreting services for deaf people around the country. The new division added a new video dimension to human services. With Bob's love for technology and lifelong commitment to bettering the lives of deaf people, it is not surprising that he accepted this new challenge. He was back in the thick of technology and access issues.

As he had done throughout his career, in retirement Bob remained ready to help a capable colleague obtain a position at a school for the deaf, in the government, or wherever he was currently an administrator. Loyalty and commitment were very important to him—he was intensely loyal to his friends and he expected them to act accordingly. For example, when his long-time friend Ramón Rodriguez encountered serious legal problems in 2006, Bob did not abandon him, even though he did not condone in any way what Ramón had done. "Guidance from the past is very important," he said two decades ago. "We learn from our mistakes, but if our present-day situation is not satisfactory we need to change it so that we can benefit by meeting the future."

If Bob knew you were truly committed to the education of deaf students, you had his support; if not, he could be dismissive. His loyalty and commitment to his chosen field of deaf education and to his own school background was never more evident than in his successful fight to have OSERS issue the landmark policy guidance statement that recognized the validity and importance of the continuum of alternative placements, including special schools for children with disabilities. It is not a coincidence that the highest honor accorded to a member of the Conference of Educational Administrators of Schools for the Deaf at its annual meeting is the Robert R. Davila Award.

As a professional and a leader, Bob faced many crises—we call them "moments of truth" in this book—with his family, personally, and in his professional life. As John F. Kennedy once said, "When written in Chinese, the word 'crisis' is composed of two characters—one represents danger and one represents opportunity." Bob made the most by learning from crises.

As this book was in production, in the fall of 2006, Bob found one more crisis that seemed to beckon him to serve the field once again. After a long and bitter dispute with Gallaudet students over the presidential search process to select a successor to I. King Jordan and the subsequent appointment of Dr. Jane K. Fernandes as the new president, the Board of Trustees of Gallaudet University rescinded her appointment. The board had been inundated with letters from many distinguished deaf and hearing leaders who saw the prolonged battle as damaging the university's reputation. The protests had paralyzed the university and included student arrests, a tent city, a march to Capitol Hill, removal of protesters at a gate using heavy construction equipment, and lockdowns of campus buildings.

Bob had joined other leaders in the "Unity for Gallaudet Movement." He wrote in an open letter to the Gallaudet Board of Trustees as an alumnus and a former tenured professor and senior officer with 17 years of service to Gallaudet University:

> Not even DPN consumed so much of the national and world deaf communities' time and attention as this present crisis has. Although we can partially thank developments in communication technologies since DPN for expanding the breadth of participation in this current issue, in the larger sense, the increase derives from the lessons learned from DPN which empowered deaf people for all time. This empowerment is now classically on display on Florida Avenue and throughout every community where deaf people make their homes. It cannot be ignored any more than it can be denied.[4]

Indeed, the situation at Gallaudet continued to unravel over the next month. The board of trustees acting chair, Brenda Brueggemann, resigned, as did one of the Congressional board members, Senator John McCain from Arizona. To have such a noted Senator resign from the board was indeed an ominous sign. In addition to these developments, while the protesters' tents came down, red flags about the status of the university were raised in various newspapers. On November 13, Gallaudet announced that nominations were being accepted for the position of interim president of the university and also that the timeline would be tight, resulting in the selection of the interim president by December 11. The Interim President Selection Advisory Committee was established with the charge of recommending to the Board three to five candidates by November 15, 2006.

In October, after the *Washington Post* mentioned that Bob Davila was a possible candidate for Gallaudet University's interim president, the blogs and networks were busy discussing his qualities as if he had himself applied for a long-term presidency. He had proven he could be a fix-it executive as a director and then vice president associated with the Pre-College Programs there for 16 years, but as Bob himself acknowledged to friends, to straighten out the situation at Gallaudet would take one "tough hombre," the description RIT President Albert J. Simone had used to characterize Bob himself. The very fact that he was considered by some as the right person to help heal the university is an indication of how highly regarded he is by some people.

Bob himself had not been approached by anyone from the board. He remarked wryly to a few of his colleagues that even if he were interested, "this mention in the [*Washington*] *Post* is a kiss of death."[5]

Bob's name was placed in nomination, and once more he was faced with a moment of truth. Despite his assignments with Communications Services for the Deaf and the National Council on Disability, Bob, now 74, was retired. He and Donna had just moved to a new home in Maryland. However, after lengthy discussions with his family and personal reflection, Bob decided to accept the nomination. Twenty-six individuals were nominated, 13 of whom accepted and submitted credential packages. In a letter to the advisory committee, Bob wrote: "I have had a very satisfying professional career and remain a person with abundant energy and drive and view the position of interim president of Gallaudet University as an opportunity to once again serve my alma mater to the best of my ability."[6]

The Advisory Committee soon narrowed down the selection to three finalists, who were interviewed on December 9. Bob was interviewed on the morning of December 9, a day which was also tinged with sadness for him, as he had learned that his long time friend and colleague, Winfield McChord, a former superintendent of the Kentucky School for the Deaf and American School for the Deaf, had died the evening before of a massive stroke. Despite the pressure of the interview and Bob's focus on the process, he found time that afternoon to email several of his friends the news of Win's death.

At 1:00 p.m. on December 10, a press conference was held at Gallaudet University. In her statement announcing the selection of Dr. Davila as the interim president, board chair Pamela Holmes noted, "Gallaudet is extremely fortunate to have Dr. Robert Davila as its interim president....He brings a wealth of experience and knowledge to Gallaudet at a time when the university faces many opportunities, as well as many challenges."[7] Roberto Refugio Davila, the son of Mexican migrant farmworkers, thus became the ninth president of Gallaudet University.

Dr. Robert R. Davila, President of
Gallaudet University, February 2007.
Courtesy of Gallaudet University.

In accepting his appointment, Bob spoke eloquently of his love of the university and he presented ideas for the future, emphasizing the importance of unity. "If we cannot do it together, it will not happen." He explained that Gallaudet values diversity, embracing many diverse groups with different thoughts and opinions. But, he emphasized, there is no better place than the academy to debate issues, and to continue that discourse it would be necessary to have trust, healthy communication, and support for each other. "We must accept that we can agree to disagree with each other without being angry," he signed. "That is the kind of environment I want to put into place."[8]

At his installation as the 9th President of Gallaudet University, Bob reflected on how much times had changed for deaf people, and how deaf people now were able to become professionals and leaders in so many fields; "It reminds me that when I was a little boy and [when] I was ready to leave college that people didn't have opportunities like that in those days... So I thank God that I'm still young enough to have benefited from the opportunities, and now old enough to appreciate what was and what will be for others."[9]

Bob had invited then-RIT president Albert J. Simone to give the commencement address at Gallaudet University two days after the installation. On May 11, 2007, President Simone signed a message to the Gallaudet graduates, "Bob Davila is with you now. The future remains bright for Gallaudet with everyone working together: you as new alumni, other alumni, your president and his team, the faculty and staff, continuing students, your colleagues at RIT/NTID, and all of your friends."[10]

We began this book with the Spanish proverb, "One cannot conquer the ocean without being brave enough to lose sight of the beach." ("*No conquistarás el océano si no tienes el valor para perder de vista la playa.*") In a sense, Bob's biography is a "moment of truth" for us all. In reading about the many obstacles he faced growing up poor and attempting to reach great heights as a leader, what opportunities may we, like Bob, seize to shape our own lives and work and, in turn, enrich the lives of others? In particular, how may we help deaf children today learn from Bob's "moments of truth?" How may we provide opportunities to help them develop courage in being able to lose sight of the beach to conquer the ocean?

Robert Davila:
Selected Honors and Awards

1979 Distinguished Foreign Lecturer, Annual Conference of Australian Teachers of the Deaf, Melbourne, Victoria, Australia.

1982 Man of the Year Award, Delta Epsilon Sorority, Gallaudet College.

1985 Member of Honor (first foreigner and first deaf person ever inducted), La Asociacion Espanola de Educadores de Sordos (A.E.E.S., Spanish Association of Educators of the Deaf), Spain.

Ang Puso Award, Southeast Asian Institute for the Deaf, Philippine Islands, for long-time service to programs for the deaf in the Philippines.

1986 Alumnus of the Year, School of Education, Syracuse University, Syracuse, New York.

1987 Inducted to the National Hall of Fame for Persons with Disabilities, Columbus, Ohio.

1988 Inducted to the Alumni Hall of Fame, Hunter College.

Daniel T. Cloud Education Leadership Award, California State University, Northridge.

1989 The George W. Nevil Award of Merit, The Pennsylvania School for the Deaf, June 1989.

1990 President's Award, National Association of Private Schools for Exceptional Children, January 1990.

Award of Merit, Conference of Educational Administrators Serving the Deaf, Rochester, New York.

Mary E. Switzer Award for Leadership in the Field of Rehabilitation, Assumption College, Worcester, MA.

Humanitarian of the Year Award, New Jersey Association of Schools and Agencies for the Handicapped, November 1990.

Doctor of Humane Letters, honoris causa, Hunter College, New York, New York.

1991 Doctor of Humane Letters, honoris causa, Rochester Institute of Technology, Rochester, New York.

Doctor of Humanities, honoris causa, Stonehill College, North Easton, Massachusetts.

1992 Triumph of the Spirit Award, National Council of La Raza, July 1992.

Leadership Award, Alexander Graham Bell Association, July 1992.

Distinguished Service Award, American Speech-Language and Hearing Association, November 1992.

Distinguished Service Award, American Society for Deaf Children, November 1992.

Shining Star Award, National Hispanic Council of the Deaf and Hard of Hearing, November 1992.

Distinguished Service Award, National Association of the Deaf, December 1992.

1993   Honorary Lifetime Membership, Empire State Association of the Deaf.

Thomas R. Fox Award for Outstanding Achievement, Fanwood Alumni Association.

Award for Exceptional Service, Affiliated Leadership League of and for the Blind of America, March 1993.

Georgiana Elliott Award for Contributions Toward Equality, Opportunity and Accessibility for Deaf and Hard of Hearing Persons, Texas Association of the Deaf, March 1993.

1994   Distinguished Service Award in the Area of Government, 25th Anniversary Edition, *Silent News.*

1996   Doctor of Laws, honoris causa, Gallaudet University, Washington, D.C.

1997   Annual Award for Exceptional Service to the Education of the Deaf established by the Conference of Educational Administrators of the Deaf.

1998   Lyon Founder's Award for exceptional professional contributions to the education of persons who are deaf, Rochester School for the Deaf, October 15, 1998.

1999   Communication Award, National Council on Communicative Disorders, September 7, 1999.

2000   Tripod Friend's Award, May 12, 2000.

2001   Award for Distinguished Service to the Deaf Community, The Learning Center for Deaf Children, Framingham, MA, October 25, 2001.

Communicator of the Year Award, St. Mary's School for the Deaf, September 27, 2001.

2002   APANSCE Award, Associació de Pares de Nens Sords de Catalunya (Association of Parents of Deaf Children of Catalonia)

2003 I. Lee Brody Lifetime Achievement Award, Telecommunications for the Deaf, Inc.

Willie Ross School for the Deaf Advocacy Award. October 9, 2003.

2005 Robert R. Davila Angel Award for Significant Contributions to ALDA established by the Association of Late Deafened Adults.

NOTES

CHAPTER I

1   Robert R. Davila, e-mail message to Harry G. Lang, April 23, 2004.
2   Davila to Lang, January 31, 2004.
3   Ibid.
4   Ibid.
5   Ibid.

CHAPTER 2

1   Robert R. Davila, e-mail message to Harry G. Lang, January 31, 2004.
2   Davila to Lang, January 13, 2004.
3   Davila to Lang, April 23, 2004.
4   Ibid.
5   Davila, in discussion with Lang, April 1, 2004.
6   Davila to Lang, November 1, 2004.
7   Ibid.
8   Davila to Lang, April 23, 2004.
9   Phil Garcia, "Robert Davila Is Quietly Opening Doors," *The New Mexico Progress* 79 (1986): 1.
10 Davila to Lang, January 31, 2004.
11 Ibid.
12 Davila, "Bob's Bulletin: Preparing the Next Generation of Leaders," *NTID Focus*, Spring/Summer 2003, 2.
13 Davila to Lang, April 23, 2004.

CHAPTER 3

1   Kenneth W. Norton, *The Eagle Soars to Enlightenment: An Illustrated History of the California School for the Deaf* (Fremont, CA: The Donald Parodi Memorial Charitable Trust, 2000).

2   Robert R. Davila, e-mail message to Harry G. Lang, November 1, 2004.

3   Phil Garcia, "Davila Recognized as Nation's Leading Deaf Educator," *The Forum* (San Diego, CA), November 1986, 15.

4   Davila to Lang, January 31, 2004.

5   Davila, "Blessed and Tormented," *The Hispanic Link Weekly Report*, October 20, 1986.

6   Davila to Lang, April 23, 2004.

7   Davila to Lang, January 31, 2004.

8   Davila, in discussion with the author, April 1, 2004.

9   Edward Sifuentes, "From Migrant to Presidential Advisor," *North County Times* (Escondido, CA), April 12, 2004, http://www.nctimes.com/articles/2004/04/12/news/coastal/4_11_0421_03_12.txt.

10   Davila to Lang, April 23, 2004.

11   Sifuentes, "From Migrant."

12   Ibid.

13   Davila to Lang, January 31, 2004.

14   Ibid.

15   Davila, interview with Kathleen Sullivan Smith, April 1, 2004.

16   Ibid.

17   California School for the Deaf (Berkeley) Yearbook, 1947–48.

18   Davila to Lang, April 20, 2004.

19   Yearbook.

20   Ibid.

CHAPTER 4

1   "Pathways to a Better Life: Robert Davila Works to Improve Deaf Education at the Nation's Model Schools," *Education Exchange*, Syracuse University School of Education, Winter 1986, 3.

2   Robert R. Davila, e-mail message to Harry G. Lang, September 24, 2006.

3   Davila to Lang, December 20, 2003.

4   Davila to Lang, January 31, 2004.

5   Bernard Bragg to Lang, n.d.

6   See Bernard Bragg and Eugene Bergman, *Lessons in Laughter* (Washington, D.C.: Gallaudet University Press, 1989).

7   Bragg to Lang, n.d.

8   Ramón Rodriguez to authors, n.d.

9   Ibid.

10   Ibid.

11   Davila to business manager, Gallaudet College, March 21, 1950.

12   Davila to Lang, September 24, 2006.

13   Rodriguez to authors, n.d.

14   Rodriguez, interview with Lang, March 29, 2004.

15   "And Davila Dashes Home...," *Buff and Blue*, Gallaudet College LX, 9 (May 26, 1951): 7.

16   Ibid.

17   Robert Lennan, e-mail message to Lang, October 12, 2003.

18   Davila to Lang, November 1, 2004.

19   Elwood A. Stevenson to Davila, March 17, 1953.

CHAPTER 5

1   Donna Davila, interview with Patricia DeCaro, August 15, 2003.

2   Robert R. Davila, e-mail message to Harry G. Lang, November 1, 2004.

3   Ibid.

4   Dean Irving S. Fusfeld to R. Davila, July 7, 1952.

5   R. Davila to Lang, November 1, 2004.

6   Robert R. Davila, *Buff and Blue*, Gallaudet College, April 1953, 3.

7   Ibid.

CHAPTER 6

1   Taras Denis, interview with Harry G. Lang, March 29, 2004.

2   Ramón Rodriguez, interview with Lang, March 29, 2004.

3   Robert Lennan, e-mail message to Lang, October 12, 2003.

4   Ibid.

5   Robert R. Davila, e-mail message to Lang, January 13, 2004.

6   Davila to Lang, April 20, 2004.

7   Davila to Lang, September 7, 2006.

8   Denis, interview with Lang.

9   Davila to Lang, December 20, 2003.

10   Davila to Lang, June 8, 2005.

11   Brent and Brian Davila, interview with Patricia DeCaro, March 17, 2005.

12   Ibid.

13   Ibid.

14   Ibid.

15   Ibid.

16   Ibid.

17   Ibid.

18   Ibid.

19   Ibid.

20   R. Davila to Jeffrey C. Martin, General Counsel, May 26, 1992.

21   "Robert R. Davila, JNAD's Source Materials Specialist," *Deaf American* 23 (December 1969): 18.

22   R. Davila to Lang, December 20, 2003.

23   R. Davila, Latino Commencement Remarks, California State University, Fresno, May 17, 2003.

24   R. Davila to Lang, September 24, 2006.

25   Ibid.

CHAPTER 7

1   Robert R. Davila, e-mail message to Harry G. Lang, May 4, 2004.

2   George Propp, e-mail message to Lang, November 2003.

3   Ibid.

4   Davila to Lang, November 12, 2004.

5   Brent and Brian Davila, interview with Patricia DeCaro, March 17, 2005.

6   Ibid.

7   Democrat and Chronicle (Rochester, NY), "A Diplomat for the Deaf: Davila Brings Verve, True Grit to NTID," November 24, 1996, 1A, 12A.

8   Ibid.

9   R. Davila to Lang, December 2004.

CHAPTER 8

1   U.S. Department of Health, Education and Welfare, Education of the Deaf: A Report to the Secretary of Health, Education, and Welfare by his Advisory Committee on the Education of the Deaf (Washington, D.C: U.S. Department of Health, Education, and Welfare, Office of the Secretary, 1965).

2   David Denton, "The Philosophy of Total Communication," supplement to *British Deaf News* (Carlisle, UK: British Deaf Association), August 1976.

3   Brent and Brian Davila, interview with Patricia DeCaro, March 17, 2005.

4   Ibid.

5   Ibid.

6   Ibid.

7   Ibid.

8   Fina Perez, interview with Patricia DeCaro, February 8, 2005.

9   Robert R. Davila, Position Paper, Internal Report, Kendall Demonstration Elementary School, November 13, 1974, 7.

10   Ibid.

11   R. Davila, in discussion with Harry G. Lang, March 14, 2005.

12   R. Davila, e-mail message to Lang, March 8, 2004.

13   Angel Ramos, *Triumph of the Spirit: The DPN Chronicle* (Apache Junction, AZ: R&R Publishers, 2006), 15.

14   R. Davila to Lang, September 27, 2006.

CHAPTER 9

1   Brent and Brian Davila, interview with Patricia DeCaro, March 17, 2005.

2   Robert R. Davila, in discussion with Harry G. Lang, March 14, 2005.

3   George Propp, e-mail message to Lang, November 2003.

4   Now called the Conference of Educational Administrators of Schools and Programs for the Deaf.

5   R. Davila, "Blessed and Tormented," *The Hispanic Link Weekly Report,* October 6, 1986.

6   Ibid.

7   Ibid.

8   "Focus on Hispanic Americans," *Vista* (Bakersfield, CA), March 7, 1987, 25.

9   Ibid.

10   Ibid.

11   Phil Garcia, "Davila Recognized as Nation's Leading Deaf Educator," *The Forum* (San Diego, CA), November 1986, 16.

12   R. Davila, "Blessed and Tormented."

13   Susan Murray to authors, August 9, 2005.

14   Ibid.

15   Ibid.

CHAPTER 10

1   Robert R. Davila, interview with Pat Johanson, July 11, 1988.

2   Ibid.

3   Ibid.

4   Davila, e-mail message to Harry G. Lang, March 12, 2004.

5   Davila, interview with Johanson.

6   Ibid.

7   Ibid.

8   Ibid.

9   Davila to Lang, March 12, 2004.

10 Ibid.

11 Ibid.

12 Ibid.

13 Davila, interview with Johanson.

14 Ibid.

15 Ibid.

16 Ibid.

17 Ibid.

18 Angel Ramos, *Triumph of the Spirit: The DPN Chronicle* (Apache Junction, AZ: R&R Publishers, 2006), 171.

CHAPTER 11

1 Cited in L. Siegel, "The Educational and Communication Needs of Deaf and Hard of Hearing Children: A Statement of Principle Regarding Fundamental Systemic Educational Changes," *American Annals of the Deaf* 145 (2001): 64–67.

2 William P. Johnson to Robert R. Davila, June 27, 1988.

3 Davila to George H. W. Bush, April 14, 1988.

4 George H. W. Bush to Davila, June 30, 1988.

5 Robert R. Davila, e-mail message to Harry G. Lang, March 30, 2004.

6 Fran Parrotta, e-mail message to Lang, January 26, 2004.

7 Ibid.

8 Davila to The Honorable Chase Untermeyer, January 30, 1989.

9 Davila to Lang, March 30, 2004.

10 Jeanne Glidden Prickett to Joseph Fischgrund, November 2, 2006.

11 Ibid.

12 Ibid.

13 Ibid.

14 Ibid.

15 Ibid.

16 I. King Jordan, memo to Gallaudet community, April 25, 1989.

17 Davila, personal data statement submitted as part of the nomination process for assistant secretary of the Office of Special Education and Rehabilitative Services, April 5, 1989.

18 Ibid.

19 Robert Lennan, e-mail message to Lang, October 12, 2003.

20 Taras Denis, e-mail message to Lang, July 27, 2005.

21 Parrotta to Lang, January 26, 2004.

22 Susan Murray to Oscar Cohen, January 25, 2004.

23   Davila to Lang, February 11, 2005.

CHAPTER 12

1   Robert R. Davila, e-mail message to Harry G. Lang, February 11, 2005.
2   Brent and Brian Davila, interview with Patricia DeCaro, March 17, 2005.
3   Kenneth J. Cooper, "Deaf Official Moves from Advocate to Insider: Assistant Education Secretary Hopes to Secure More Funding, Attention for Disabled," *The Washington Post*, February 20, 1990, A19.
4   *World Federation of the Deaf News* 3, December 1989, 23.
5   *Progress Report*, Gallaudet University, Spring 1989, 1.
6   Ibid.
7   Ibid.
8   "Commencements," *New York Times*, May 30, 1990, B4.
9   Paul Leung, "Dr. Robert Davila: The Man and His Mission," *Journal of Rehabilitation*, October/November/December 1989, 15.
10   Roger B. Porter to R. Davila, August 18, 1989.
11   Cooper, "Deaf Official."
12   "Robert Davila: Assistant Secretary, Special Education and Rehabilitative Services," *OSERS News in Print* 2 (Supplementary 1989): 3.
13   R. Davila, "Goals for Improving Services to Minority Individuals with Disabilities," *OSERS News in Print* 3 (Spring 1991): 2–5.
14   R. Davila, "Looking at the Past and the Future," Letter to Parents, April 1990.
15   R. Davila, "Goals for Improving."
16   Ibid.
17   Ibid.
18   Ibid.
19   R. Davila, presentation at the 15th Annual California Fiesta Educativa Conference ("Family, Culture, and Solidarity"), Los Angeles, CA, May 23, 1992.
20   Ibid.
21   R. Davila, e-mail message to Lang, June 26, 2004.
22   R. Davila to Lang, December 6, 2004.
23   R. Davila to Lauro Cavazos, December 12, 1990.
24   R. Davila, in discussion with Lang, May 23, 2005.
25   R. Davila to Lang, March 31, 2004.
26   Ibid.
27   Ibid.
28   Ibid.

CHAPTER 13

1   Robert R. Davila, "A Message from the Assistant Secretary," *OSERS News in Print* (Spring 1992): 2.

2   Davila, keynote address, National Association of the Deaf (NAD) convention, Denver, CO, July 1992, *NAD Broadcaster* 14, no. 9 (September 1992): 1, 6.

3   President George H. W Bush to Robert R. Davila, September 22, 1992.

4   Davila, email message to Harry G. Lang, June 8, 2004.

5   Federal Register Doc. 92-26319 Filed 10-29-92; 8:45 am.

6   Susan Murray, interview with Patricia DeCaro, June 22, 2004.

7   Ibid.

8   Davila, in "United States Mission to the United Nations, USUN Press Release #96-(92)," October 13, 1992, 3–4.

9   Davila, "New Leadership for a New Era," in *Disability and Diversity: New Leadership for a New Era,* ed. Sylvia Walker and others (Washington, D.C.: President's Committee on Employment of People With Disabilities and Howard University Research and Training Center, January 1995), http://www.dinf.ne.jp/doc/english/Us_Eu/ada_e/pres_com/pres-dd/davila.htm.

10   Davila to President George H. W. Bush, January 7, 1992.

11   Davila to Gil Delgado, January 1993.

12   Kenneth J. Cooper, "Deaf Official Moves from Advocate to Insider: Assistant Education Secretary Hopes to Secure More Funding, Attention for Disabled," *Washington Post*, February 20, 1990, A19.

13   Ibid.

14   Senator Paul Simon to Robert R. Davila, March 5, 1993.

15   Stuart Low, *Democrat and Chronicle* (Rochester, NY), "A Diplomat for the Deaf: Davila Brings Verve, True Grit to NTID," November 24, 1996, 1A, 12A.

CHAPTER 14

1   Robert R. Davila, e-mail message to Harry G. Lang, December 2004.

2   Brent and Brian Davila, interview with Patricia DeCaro, March 17, 2005.

3   Ibid.

4   Ibid.

5   Ibid.

6   R. Davila to Tom Grayson, Champaign, Illinois, February 16 1993

7   Phillip G. Vargas, "In the Shadow of the Mainstream: Without English, My Hispanic Countrymen Are Doomed to Fail in America," *Washington Post,* Sunday March 31, 1991.

8   Ibid.

9   Ibid.

10   Fran Parrotta, e-mail message to authors, June 11, 2004.

11   R. Davila to Lang, December 2004.

12   Robert Davila was co-chairman of the Federal Interagency Committee on
      Employment of People with Disabilities from July 1989 to January 1993;
      co-chairman of the Federal Interagency Committee on Developmental
      Disabilities from July 1989 to January 1993; chairman of the Federal
      Interagency Coordinating Council on Services for Infants and Toddlers
      from July 1989 to January 1993; a member of the President's Committee
      on Mental Retardation from July 1989 to January 1993; and a member of
      the Architectural and Transportation Barriers Compliance Board from July
      1989 to January 1993. His record of effective management and development
      of institutional resources included managing a $27 million annual budget
      while serving as a member of the Central Administration of Gallaudet
      University. As a senior officer of the U.S. Department of Education from
      1989 to 1993, Davila managed a $5.4 billion annual budget and supervised
      over 400 employees, mostly professional/technical staff. He also spoke at
      many conferences during these years, including the National Symposium on
      Educational Applications of Technology for Deaf Students, "Educational
      Technology: Opportunity for the Future," NTID, Rochester, NY, May
      1992; the 13th National Institute on Legal Issues on Educating Individuals
      with Disabilities, San Antonio, TX, May 1992; the National Association of
      the Deaf; and The Black Deaf Experience: Empowerment and Excellence,
      Decatur, GA, March 1992.

13   R. Davila, Presentation at the 15th Annual California Fiesta Educativa
      Conference ("Family, Culture and Solidarity"), Los Angeles, May 23, 1992.

14   R. Davila, "Black and Hispanic Deaf Children: Meeting Our
      Responsibilities," Paper presented at a meeting sponsored by The Conference
      of Educational Administrators of Schools and Programs for the Deaf,
      (Washington, D.C.: Gallaudet University, 1989), 1.

15   Ibid.,2.

16   Ibid., 3.

17   Ibid.

18   Ibid., 13.

19   Ibid., 7.

20   Davila, keynote address, National Black Deaf Advocates Convention,
      Atlanta, Georgia, March 14, 1992.

21   Ibid.

22   Gil Delgado to R. Davila, April 11, 1993.

23   Raúl Yzaguirre to R. Davila, January 6, 1994.

24   R. Davila, "Creating Pathways to Achieving Full Potential for Minority Deaf Persons" (keynote address, Second National Multicultural Deaf Conference, Lamar University, Beaumont, TX, November 1997).

CHAPTER 15

1   Robert R. Davila, e-mail message to Harry G. Lang, August 11, 2004.

2   Ibid.

3   Arlene Rice, interview with Oscar Cohen, April 5, 2005.

4   Ibid.

5   Ibid.

6   Ibid.

7   Ibid.

8   Susan Murray, e-mail message to Lang, January 25, 2004.

9   Ibid.

10   R. Davila, e-mail message to Lang, April 23, 2004.

11   Murray to Lang, January 25, 2004.

12   R. Davila to Pat O'Rourke, June 13, 1996.

13   R. Davila, commencement address, Lamar University, Beaumont, TX, August 1993.

14   Ibid.

15   Brent and Brian Davila, interview with Patricia DeCaro, March 17, 2005.

16   Ibid.

17   *NTID Focus* (Winter/Spring 1993): 23.

18   Ibid.

19   R. Davila, e-mail message to Fran Parrotta, April 26, 1996.

20   Ibid.

21   Albert J. Simone to R. Davila, May 9, 1996.

22   R. Davila to Albert J. Simone, May 13, 1996.

23   Gil Delgado to Davila, June 1996.

24   R. Davila to Delgado, June 14, 1996.

25   Ibid.

CHAPTER 16

1   Harry G. Lang and Karen K. Conner, *From Dream to Reality: A History of the National Technical Institute for the Deaf at Rochester Institute of Technology* (Rochester, NY: National Technical Institute for the Deaf, 2002), 23.

2   Gary Stern, "Deaf Educator Scores Another 1st," *Reporter Dispatch* (White Plains, NY), May 16, 1996.

3   Kathleen Sullivan Smith, "Robert R. Davila: A Story of Passion, Determination, and Success," *NTID Focus,* Spring/Summer 2003, 7.

4   Albert J. Simone, interview with Smith, April 6, 2004.

5   Ibid.

6   Wendell (Gus) Thompson, interview with Smith, February 23, 2004.

7   Ibid.

8   Ibid.

9   Robert R. Davila, statement on Fiscal Year 1998 Budget for the National Technical Institute for the Deaf, March 13, 1997.

10   Lori Leal to R. Davila, May 14, 1996.

11   R. Davila to Leal, May 15, 1996.

12   Cheri McKee, interview with Smith, February 27, 2004.

13   Ibid.

14   R. Davila, e-mail message to Harry G. Lang, December 12, 2004.

15   Simone, interview with Smith, April 6, 2004.

16   *Democrat & Chronicle* (Rochester, NY), "A Diplomat for the Deaf: Davila Brings Verve, True Grit to NTID," November 24, 1996, 1A, 12A.

17   Ibid.

18   R. Davila to Lang, September 27, 2005.

19   D. Robert Frisina, e-mail message to Lang, September 28, 2005.

20   R. Davila, "Reviewing the Past, Assessing the Present, and Projecting the Future," keynote address at the International Congress on Education of the Deaf, Sydney, Australia, July 9, 2000, 3.

21   Ibid.

22   R. Davila to Lang, January 4, 2005.

23   "Dyers' Commitment to NTID Grows," *NTID Foundation News* 7, no. 4 (Winter 1999), 2.

24   "Dyer Pledges $1.5M to NTID," NTID News Release, May 10, 2001.

25   Greg Livadas, "Deaf College's Chief Will Retire," *Democrat & Chronicle* (Rochester, NY), May 24, 2003.

26   Ibid.

27   R. Davila, "Bob's Bulletin: Preparing the Next Generation of Leaders," *NTID Focus*, Spring/Summer 2003, 2.

28   Ibid, 3.

29   Smith, "Robert R. Davila," 5.

30   Ibid., 6.

31   Videotape, R. Davila with Hispanic students from the Illinois School for the Deaf at the National Technical Institute for the Deaf, Rochester Institute of Technology, March 24, 2004.

32   Edward Sifuentes, "From Migrant to Presidential Advisor," *North County Times* (Escondido, CA), April 12, 2004.

33   Brent and Brian Davila, interview with Patricia DeCaro, March 17, 2005.

34   R. Davila, commencement address at California State University at Fresno, May 17, 2003.

35   Ibid.

36   R. Davila to Lang, October 9, 2006.

AFTERWORD

1   Kathleen Sullivan Smith, "Robert R. Davila: A Story of Passion, Determination, and Success," *NTID Focus,* Spring/Summer 2003, 6.

2   Robert Davila, "Education of the Deaf: A Candid Perspective from a Deaf Educator," presentation at the Second Latin American Conference on deafness and Communication, Buenos Aires, Argentina, November 1985.

3   Phil Garcia, "Davila Recognized as Nation's Leading Deaf Educator," *The Forum* (San Diego, CA), November 1986, 16.

4   R. Davila, "Open Letter from Dr. Davila," *Hearing Loss Web,* October 2006, http://www.hearinglossweb.com/Issues/Identity/gal06/davila.

5   Davila to Harry G. Lang, November 1, 2006.

6   Davila to Jane Dillehay, letter of intent for the Gallaudet University presidential candidacy, November 21, 2006, http://pr.gallaudet.edu/presidentialsearch/?ID=9905.

7   "Gallaudet University Names Robert Davila Interim President," Gallaudet University FFSA Coalition, December 11, 2006, http://bibliomarket.wordpress.com/2006/12/10/its-official-davila-takes-presidency/.

8   "Transcript: Dr. Davila's Acceptance Speech," Speech transcript by Brian Riley, December 10, 2006, http://bibliomarket.wordpress.com/2006/12/12/transcript-dr-davilas-acceptance-speech/.

9   Robert R. Davila, Installation speech as 9th president, Gallaudet University, Washington, D.C., May 9, 2007.

10   Albert J. Simone, Commencement address, Gallaudet University, Washington, D.C., May 11, 2007.

SELECTED BIBLIOGRAPHY

California News (California School for the Deaf) 104 (22), "Former Grad Nominated to Top Federal Post!" April 28, 1989.

Christiansen, John B. and Barnartt, Sharon N. *Deaf President Now! The 1988 Revolution at Gallaudet University.* Washington, D.C.: Gallaudet University Press, 1995.

Cooper, Kenneth J. "Deaf Official Moves From Advocate to Insider: Assistant Education Secretary Hopes to Secure More Funding, Attention for Diabled." *Washington Post,* February 20, 1990, sec. A.

Davila, Robert R. "The Black Deaf Experience: Empowerment and Excellence." In *A Deaf American Monograph: Viewpoints on Deafness,* edited by Mervin D. Garretson, 42: 49–51. Silver Spring, MD: National Association of the Deaf, 1992.

———. "Blessed and Tormented." *Hispanic Link Weekly Report,* October 20, 1986.

———. "Bob's Bulletin: Preparing the Next Generation of Leaders." *NTID Focus.* Spring/Summer 2003.

———. "Current Issues Facing Education of the Deaf." In *Deafness: Life and Culture II,* edited by M. D. Garretson. Silver Spring, MD: National Association of the Deaf, 1995.

———. "Deaf People in Society: Education and Access." In *Proceedings of the Franco-American Colloquium.* Paris: Foundation Franco-Americaine; New York: French-American Foundation, October 1991.

———. "Early Intervention—Present and Future." *Estudios A.E.E.S.* Revista, Madrid, Spain, 1986.

———. "Education of the Deaf: A Candid Perspective from a Deaf Educator." In *Proceedings of the Second Latin American Conference on Deafness and Communication,* November 1985.

———. "Effect of Changes in Visual Information Patterns on Student Achievement Using a Captioned Film and Specially Adapted Still Pictures." Doctoral dissertation, Syracuse University, 1972.

———. "Freedom of Choice: From Limited Options to Unlimited Opportunities." In *Perspectives on Deafness: a Deaf American Monograph,* edited by Mervin D. Garretson, 41: 43. Silver Spring, MD: National Association of the Deaf, 1991.

———. "Goals for Improving Services to Minority Individuals with Disabilities." *OSERS News in Print* 3, Spring 1991.

———. "Hispanics with Disabilities: An Ongoing Challenge." *National Hispanic Reporter,* September 1992.

———. "The Impact of Inclusion on Traditional Services for Deaf Children in the United States." In *Proceedings of the 18th International Congress on Education of the Deaf,* Tel Aviv, Israel, July 16–20, 1995. Edited by A. Weisel. Israel: Ramot Publications, Tel Aviv University, 1998.

———. Introduction. In "Special Issue on Culture and Chronic Illness," *Journal of Pediatrics,* July 1993.

———. "Mainstreaming: Programmatic Considerations." In *Proceedings of the International Congress on Education of the Deaf.* University of Manchester, England, August 1985. Edited by I. G. Taylor. Kent, England: Croom Helm Publishers, 1987.

———. "A Message from the Assistant Secretary." *OSERS News in Print,* Spring 1992.

———. "New Leadership for a New Era." *In Disability and Diversity: New Leadership for a New Era,* edited by Silvia Walker, Kimberley A. Turner, Meselech Haile-Michael, Ada Vincent, and Marilyn D. Miles. Washington, D.C.: President's Committee on Employment of People with Disabilities and Howard University Research and Training Center, January 1995.

———. "Promoting Effective Transition Practices." Keynote address, Conference of Educational Administrators of School and Programs for the Deaf (CEASD), April 27, 2002. Reprinted in *CSD Spectrum,* Fall 2002, 27–28, 30–32.

———. "Reviewing the Past, Assessing the Present, and Projecting the Future." Keynote address at the International Congress on Education of the Deaf (ICED), Sydney, Australia, July 9, 2000.

———. "Self-Reliance and Empowerment." In *Proceedings of the XI World Congress.* Tokyo, Japan: World Federation of the Deaf, July 1991.

———. "Trends in Postsecondary Education for the Hearing Impaired: A View from Kendall Green." In *Proceedings of the Special Seminar on Deafness.* Austin, TX: Texas Commission for the Deaf, 1982.

Davila, Robert R. and Tweedle, David R., eds. *Report of the Proceedings of the 47th Biennial Meeting of the Convention of American Instructors of the Deaf,* Greensboro, NC. Washington, D.C.: Superintendent of Documents, U.S. Government Printing Office, 1975.

Deaf American. "Dr. Robert R. Davila Elected President of Council On Education of the Deaf." February 1978.

———. "Robert R. Davila, JNAD's Source Materials Specialist." December 1969.

Denton, David. "The Philosophy of Total Communication." Supplement to *British Deaf News* (Carlisle, UK: British Deaf Association), August 1976.

Education Exchange. "Pathway to a Better Life: Robert Davila Works to Improve Deaf Education at the Nation's Model Schools." Syracuse University, Winter 1986.

Gallaudet Alumni Newsletter 12 (11). "Gallaudet Sets New Goals, Stresses Deaf Leadership." April 1, 1978.

Gallaudet Alumni Newsletter 23 (6). "President Bush Appoints Robert Davila to Head OSERS." July/August 1989.

Gallaudet Alumni Newsletter 28 (1). "Davila to Lead New York School for the Deaf." September 1993.

Gallaudet College News Release. "Alumnus is New Faculty Member for Department of Education at Gallaudet." July 31, 1972.

Gallaudet University Press Release. "President Bush Announces His Intention to Nominate Robert R. Davila, Ph.D. Assistant Secretary for Special Education and Rehabilitative Services, Department of Education." April 25, 1989.

Garcia, Phil. "Davila Recognized as Nation's Leading Deaf Educator." *The Forum* (San Diego, CA), November 1986.

———. "Robert Davila Is Quietly Opening Doors." *New Mexico Progress* 79 (1986).

Lang, Harry G. and Karen K. Conner. *From Dream to Reality: A History of the National Technical Institute for the Deaf at Rochester Institute of Technology.* Rochester, NY: Rochester Institute of Technology, 2002.

Leung, Paul. "Dr. Robert Davila: The Man and His Mission." *Journal of Rehabilitation,* October/November/December 1989.

Livadas, Greg. "Deaf College's Chief Will Retire." *Democrat & Chronicle* (Rochester, NY), May 24, 2003.

Low, Stuart. "A Diplomat for the Deaf: Davila Brings Verve, True Grit to NTID." *Democrat & Chronicle* (Rochester, NY), November 24, 1996, sec. A.

Low, Stuart. "NTID Welcomes Deaf Leader." *Democrat & Chronicle* (Rochester, NY), November 9, 1996, 1A, 4A.

National University Press Release. "National University Names Leading Deaf Educator to $2.2 Million Endowed Chair." September 29, 2003.

Norton, Kenneth W. *The Eagle Soars to Enlightenment: An Illustrated History of the California School for the Deaf.* Fremont, CA: The Donald Parodi Memorial Charitable Trust, 2000.

On the Green 16 (42). "Educators Bestow 2 Honors on New CEASD President." Gallaudet University, September 2, 1986.

OSERS News in Print 2. "OSERS Welcomes New Leadership." 1989.

Ramos, Angel. *Triumph of the Spirit: The DPN Chronicle.* Apache Junction, AZ: R&R Publishers, 2006.

Sifuentes, Edward. "From Migrant to Presidential Advisor." *North County Times* (Escondido, CA), April 12, 2004, http://www.nctimes.com/articles/2004/04/12/news/coastal/4_11_0421_03_12.txt

Silent News. "Davila Challenges Grads at Lamar University." October 1993.

Silent News. "Gallaudet Univ. to Award Honorary Doctorates to Three." December 1995.

Silver, Ann. "President Bush to Nominate Dr. Davila to Top Federal Post." *Silent News,* June 1989.

Smith, Kathleen S. "Robert R. Davila: A Story of Passion, Determination, and Success." *NTID Focus,* Spring/Summer 2003.

Statement by The Honorable Robert R. Davila, Assistant Secretary of Education for Special Education and Rehabilitative Services, and United States Advisor to the 47th Session of the United Nations General Assembly, in Plenary, on Item #93-(a), Conclusion of the United Nations Decade of Disabled Persons, October 12, 1992.

Stern, Gary. "Headmaster of School for Deaf Leaving for RIT." *Tarrytown* (NY) *Daily News,* May 16, 1996.

U.S. Department of Health, Education and Welfare. *Education of the Deaf: A Report to the Secretary of Health, Education and Welfare by his Advisory Committee on the Education of the Deaf.* Washington, D.C.: U.S. Department of Health, Education and Welfare, Office of the Secretary, 1965.

Vargas, Philip G. "In the Shadow of the Mainstream: Without English, My Hispanic Countrymen Are Doomed to Fail in America." *Washington Post,* Sunday, March 31, 1991.

World Around You. "Life of Striving Leads To Life of Success." Washington, D.C.: Gallaudet University Laurent Clerc National Deaf Education Center, February 1989.

About the Authors

HARRY G. LANG

Dr. Harry G. Lang is a professor in the Department of Research and Teacher Education at the National Technical Institute for the Deaf (NTID) at Rochester Institute of Technology. A member of the NTID faculty since 1970, he has also held a distinguished visiting professorship at the University of Leeds, England, and a joint faculty appointment with the University of Rochester. He holds a doctorate in education from University of Rochester.

Dr. Lang is an active researcher and exponent of deaf studies and minority education, serving on numerous educational and advisory groups such as those at the Western Pennsylvania School for the Deaf, the Gallaudet University Press Editorial Board, and the National Science Teachers Association. A prolific author, he has published eight books and numerous articles including such biographical works as: *Teaching From the Heart and Soul: The Robert F. Panara Story* (2007), *Edmund Booth, Deaf Pioneer* (2004), and *Deaf Persons in the Arts and Sciences: A Biographical Dictionary* (1995), co-authored with his wife, Bonnie Meath-Lang. He also served as the senior advisor on the production team for the 2007 PBS documentary "Through Deaf Eyes."

OSCAR P. COHEN

Dr. Oscar Cohen has spent over thirty-six years educating deaf children at Lexington School for the Deaf and Lexington Center for the Deaf. While at Lexington, he served as President of National Conference of Educational Administrators of Schools and Programs for the Deaf (CEASD), and as Chairman of the New York State 4201 Schools Association. Dr. Cohen holds an Ed.D. degree from Teachers College of Columbia University and an honorary Doctor of Laws degree from Gallaudet University.

215

In 2002, Dr. Cohen was appointed as the Executive Director of the Ralph Lauren Foundation, a corporate foundation that supports programs for cancer care and prevention, education, and community building.

JOSEPH E. FISCHGRUND

Mr. Joseph E. Fischgrund has worked nearly thirty years in the field of the education of deaf children. His academic background is in theoretical linguistics, specializing in the history of English language and English grammar. He holds a BA in English Literature from Franklin and Marshall College, an MA in English Linguistics from Ohio University, and a MA in Linguistics from Brown University.

He has served in various teaching and administrative positions at Rhode Island School for the Deaf, Governor Baxter School for the Deaf in Portland, Maine, and Lexington School for the Deaf in New York. He is currently the Headmaster of the Pennsylvania School for the Deaf in Philadelphia, a position he has held for the past twenty years. Mr. Fischgrund has published widely, concentrating on the subject of deaf students from racial, linguistic and ethnic minority backgrounds. He is a current editorial board member of *The Journal of Deaf Studies and Deaf Education.*

Index

Note: Page numbers with an *f* indicate figures.

ILLUSTRATION CREDITS

Pages 8, 10, 24, 33, 39, 45, 46, 53, 63, 97, 122, 161, 163
Courtesy of Robert R. Davila

Page 86
Courtesy of Gallaudet University Archives

Page 169
Courtesy of A. Sue Weisler, RIT University News Services

Pages 174, 175
Courtesy of NTID

Page 187
Courtesy of Gilbert Delgado

Page 191
Courtesy of John T. Consoli/Gallaudet University

Colophon

Typeset in Adobe Garamond Premier Pro.

Printed on Nature's Natural 50% post-consumer recycled paper.

Printed by Thomson-Shore, a member of the Green Press Initiative.

RIT Press is committed to preserving ancient forests and natural resources. We elected to print *Moments Of Truth* on 50% post consumer recycled paper, processed chlorine free. As a result, for this printing, we have saved:

 7 Trees (40' tall and 6-8" diameter)
 2,992 Gallons of Wastewater
 1,203 Kilowatt Hours of Electricity
 330 Pounds of Solid Waste
 648 Pounds of Greenhouse Gases

RIT Press made this paper choice because our printer, Thomson-Shore, Inc., is a member of Green Press Initiative, a nonprofit program dedicated to supporting authors, publishers, and suppliers in their efforts to reduce their use of fiber obtained from endangered forests.

For more information, visit www.greenpressinitiative.org